THE VICTORIA HISTORY OF HEREFORDSHIRE

CRADLEY

Anastasia Stylianou and Fergus Eskola-Oakes
with contributions from Jonathan Comber, Duncan James and Keith Ray

VICTORIA COUNTY HISTORY

First published 2025

A Victoria County History publication

ISBN 978-1-908590-88-6

Typeset in Minion pro
Published by the University of London Press
Senate House, Malet Street, London WC1E 7HU
https://london.ac.uk/press

Cover image: Print of Old Boys' School/Village Hall, *c.*1990, by Christopher Guy Willmott.

CONTENTS

List of Illustrations v
Foreword vii
Acknowledgements ix
Donors xi
Introduction 1
Cradley Parish 3
- Boundaries and Parish Origins 3
- Landscape 4
- Communications 5
- Population 9
- Settlement 12
- The Built Character 20

Landownership 28
- Patterns of Landownership 28
- Manors and Principal Estates 29
- Other Estates 45

Economic History 50
- Agriculture 50
- Woodland and Forest 63
- Mills, Crafts and Industry 67
- Markets and Fairs 79

Social History 80
- Social Character 80
- Communal Life 85
- Education 91
- Social Welfare 97
- Medical Services 100

Religious History 101
- Church Origins and Parochial Organisation 101
- Advowson and Church Endowment 102
- Clergy Houses 104
- Religious Life 106

Church Architecture	117
Protestant Nonconformity	128
Roman Catholicism	130
Local Government	131
Manorial Government	131
Parish Government	134
Post-1894 Arrangements	137
Appendices	139
Abbreviations	149
Glossary	153
Notes on Sources	157
Index	161

LIST OF ILLUSTRATIONS

Figures

1.	Chart of baptisms and burials in Cradley 1560–1960. (Produced by Anastasia Stylianou)	11
2.	Cradley and surrounding area as shown on Isaac Taylor's *New Map of the County of Hereford* (1754). (HAS AP25/2)	17
3.	Women filling buckets from the brook near Cradley Stores, *c.*1900. (CHC)	19
4.	Bullshead Cottage, rear (formerly front) view. Later 20th century. (CHC)	20
5.	a. Hawkhurst Cottage, *c.*1930. (CHC)	21
	b. Hawkhurst Cottage after restoration, *c.*1970. (CHC)	21
6.	Seed Farm from the air *c.*2000. (Photo from the Millennium Air Survey, © Chris Musson and the Woolhope Naturalists' Field Club)	25
7.	Pixiefields, a 1970s development, in 2023. (Photo by Charles Watkins)	27
8.	*Credeley*. Start of the rental of Cradley manor *c.*1288. (HAS, AA59/A/1, p. 148)	29
9.	Upper Vinesend house after its restoration viewed from the west, *c.*1960s. (CHC)	47
10.	Harvest and hopkilns 'near Cradley', 1930s or 1940s. (Photo by Miss Marjorie Wight, HAS, K80/205)	57
11.	Cutting hay at Seed farm, early 20th century. (CHC)	61
12.	Hop pickers at Seed farm, *c.*1900. (CHC)	63
13.	a. Photo of the probable seal impression of Thomas Hill, 1458. An equestrian figure turned face towards the viewer, a bird of prey in the left hand, a hunting horn held in the right. (HAS, CF54/1/25)	64
	b. Sketch of the probable seal impression of Thomas Hill. (Fergus Eskola-Oakes)	65
14.	Sawing at Seed farm, *c.*1905, with Mr Preston's engine. (CHC)	66
15.	Beanhouse Mill, mid 20th century. (CHC)	68
16.	Cradley Stores *c.*1897. (CHC)	77
17.	Cradley's victorious quoits team in 1907. (CHC)	87
18.	Oddfellows at the rectory of Cradley St James, *c.*1920s. (CHC)	88
19.	The Seven Stars, Stifford's Bridge, *c.*1916. (CHC)	90
20.	Teaching in Cradley Boys' School, *c.*1900. (CHC)	93
21.	The open-air school, West Malvern, *c.*1915. (*Malvern Gazette*, 13 June 2014)	96

22. Drawing of Cradley St James's church 1717 viewed from the south. (HAS, CF50/116, p. 417) 103
23. The Old Rectory, mid 20th century. (CHC) 105
24. Engraving of Thomas Bisse, rector 1713–31. (HCA, B.03.65/1 © Hereford cathedral) 112
25. Edward Renn Hampden, rector 1854–91 (HCA, B.04.102/2 © Hereford cathedral) 114
26. Cradley St James; elaborately decorated Anglo-Saxon stone frieze or panel, built into the north face of the tower. (Photo by Keith Ray, 2022) 118
27. Cradley St James; the tower south doorway with the probably reused Anglo-Saxon solid rounded arch. (Photo by Keith Ray, 2022) 119
28. Cradley St James; the medieval plank chest inside church. (Photo by Barry Sharples, 2023) 122
29. George Gilbert Scott's plan for proposed work on the chancel of Cradley St James. (HAS, HD10/29a) 124
30. Storridge, St John the Evangelist, 2020. (Photo by David Whitehead) 127
31. Cradley chapel, 2023. (Photo by Charles Watkins) 129

Maps

Maps were drawn by Cath D'Alton based on drafts by the authors © University of London.

1. Parish of Cradley (modern parish boundaries). 3
2. Parish of Cradley *c.*1839 (historical parish boundaries). 7
3. Cradley historical settlement to *c.*1800 (historical parish boundaries). 13
4. The manors of Cradley parish (historical parish boundaries). 35
5. Land use in 1839 (historical parish boundaries). 51

Tables

1. Wills identifying the testator's social status, 1550–1700. 82
2. Known rectors of Cradley and known dates in office. 106

FOREWORD

This history of Cradley is one of a series of parish histories published by the Victoria County History (VCH), which was founded in 1899 as a national project to write the history of every English county. The aim of the parish histories is to publish excellent local research and to inspire and encourage readers to become involved with VCH in other areas too. The Herefordshire VCH Trust has published histories of Eastnor (2013), Bosbury (2016) and Colwall (2020). Histories of Donnington (2023), Coddington (2023) and Mathon (2024) have also been completed and are available online.

Cradley is one of the largest parishes in Herefordshire, yet it is sparsely populated. Agriculture, both arable and pastoral, has always been at the centre of the parish economy, and from the 17th century onwards the production of hops and fruit became important. The parish is well wooded, especially to the east of Cradley brook. Evidence of medieval hunting is provided by the seal on a charter of 1458 belonging to landowner Thomas Hill which displays a rider bearing a bird of prey on his wrist. Like many Herefordshire parishes, Cradley has a rich variety of vernacular architecture, including many timber-framed cottages and farmhouses. The fine medieval church of St James, which retains several rare survivals of pre-Conquest decorative stonework, was rebuilt in the 12th century and restored in the 19th century. The chancel was designed in 1868 to plans by Sir George Gilbert Scott. The parish also includes the village of Storridge, whose Gothic revival church was designed by Frederick Preedy.

The writing of this parish history, like most such histories, has been very much a collaborative effort. Special thanks must be given to Anastasia Stylianou and Fergus Eskola-Oakes for their exceptionally thorough scholarship and editorial work, and to the many volunteers and other contributors to the volume who are listed in the acknowledgements.

Professor Charles Watkins
Chair of the Herefordshire Victoria County History Trust

Published with the generous support of a grant
from the Geoffrey Walter Smith Fund of
the Woolhope Naturalists' Field Club

With thanks to the Andrew Harris Trust and the
Margaret Mumford Trust

ACKNOWLEDGEMENTS

CRADLEY IS THE FOURTH PARISH history to be published under the auspices of the Herefordshire VCH Trust. It continues the work on the Ledbury area which commenced during the England's Past for Everyone project, sponsored by the VCH and the Heritage Lottery Fund. Like the histories of Eastnor, Bosbury and Colwall published in 2013, 2016 and 2020 respectively, it will eventually form part of a VCH red book on Ledbury and the neighbouring Malvern Hills parishes.

The work of VCH Herefordshire has been supported by many generous donors, to all of whom we are very grateful. We should particularly like to thank our benefactors and subscribers, who are listed on the donors page.

Cradley, like its predecessors, has been a team effort. We are especially grateful for everyone's collaboration in finding successful ways to navigate the challenges of the Covid-19 pandemic. The research, writing and editing of the volume was divided chronologically between the co-editors. Dr Anastasia Stylianou was responsible for the history of Cradley after *c.*1560 (the time at which Cradley manor passed from episcopal hands) and Dr Fergus Eskola-Oakes for the period preceding it. We are grateful to Dr John Chandler for kindly contributing to the editorial work in the final stages, and to Jonathan Comber for his tireless efforts both during archival research and in handling the publication and editorial process from a Herefordshire perspective.

As usual, the research here is the product of many hands. In particular, Professor Keith Ray contributed the sections on early settlement and the early history of Cradley church and Duncan James wrote the sections on the built character and parts of Cradley church.

David Whitehead researched Cradley's church of St James and its rectors from the 18th to the early 20th century, as well as searching for Cradley in the *Hereford Journal*. Jeffrey White provided valuable information from a local perspective, and material for the sections on Boundaries and Parish Origins and Landscape. Celia Kellett helped with research on the sections on Communications, Mills, Crafts and Industry and Education. Ian Dampney transcribed censuses and, together with a team of volunteers including Janita Goodwin, Catherine Best and Ann Strangwood, transcribed the wills held at HARC. Valerie Goodbury provided material on gloves, manors and quarries. Dr Edward Peters provided the results of his research into farm buildings and nonconformity. Margaret Humfrey helped research the chapter on Landownership, while George Demidowicz contributed material on Malvern Chase.

Special thanks are owed to Dr Janet Cooper and Professor Charles Watkins for their generous advice and allowing us to draw on their very wide-ranging experience. We are also extremely grateful to Dr Cooper for researching and selecting the final set of illustrations used in this volume.

Additional thanks are owed to Professor Chris Dyer for his feedback on the economic and social history chapters, Dr Elizabeth New for providing her expertise on medieval seals, Dr Claire Morton for her additional photography at the TNA, Professor Philippa Hoskin for a consultation on medieval clerical marriage, Dr Eryn White for her expertise on Welsh names and 16th-century palaeography, Dr Hollie Morgan for her Old English translation and Steven Forster for lending his mathematical knowledge.

Dr Eskola-Oakes researched and produced the initial drafts of the maps. We are grateful to our map-maker Cath D'Alton for producing the final versions.

We would like to thank the staff of HARC, Cradley Heritage Group, Hereford Cathedral Library, Worcester Cathedral Library, and Worcestershire Archive and Archaeology Service, who have been extremely helpful, as well as the staff of the other archives, record offices and libraries that have been consulted.

We also owe grateful thanks to Dr Adam Chapman and Dr Ruth Slatter of VCH Central Office at the Institute of Historical Research, University of London, for their work on the final editing of the book and seeing it through the press.

Finally, we also thank our respective families for their support, particularly Harold and Patsy for their love of Herefordshire's history, and Livia Eskola-Oakes for napping conveniently at crucial points in the volume's writing!

DONORS

Benefactors
Martin Colman
The Andrew Harris Trust
Mumford Memorial Trust

Subscribers
Roger Allsopp
The late Lawrence Banks
Janet Cooper
The late Tom Davies
Edward Peters
Robina Rand
Hilary Rosankiewicz
The late Mrs Alison Smith
Charles Watkins

INTRODUCTION

CRADLEY LIES WITHIN EAST HEREFORDSHIRE, situated beside the border with Worcestershire. It is about three miles from Great Malvern,[1] eight from Bromyard and nine from Ledbury.[2] The parish's history is thus closely linked to that of two counties. The parish borders Worcestershire to the north, and Herefordshire to the west. The eastern edge of the parish today nestles in the foothills of the Malvern hills, but, until 1897, stretched to North Hill. The southern boundary with Mathon follows an ancient bank, perhaps Bronze Age in date. The main settlement in Cradley has, since the medieval period, been near that border, on either side of the Cradley brook. Other villages and hamlets have long existed in the parish. The most important of these is the village of Storridge, an independent ecclesiastical parish since 1857.

The main landowners in the parish were the bishops of Hereford, until Cradley manor passed to the Crown in 1562; it then passed through the hands of a series of families, including the Barkeleys, Hoptons, Cottons, Yapps and Walls. Other, smaller manors also existed in the medieval and early modern periods at Barrow, Behennes, Hyde, Hanley and Cowleigh. While these smaller manors ceased to function by the 18th century, Cradley manor continued to play an important role in both landownership and local government until the later 19th century. Cradley was a wealthy ecclesiastical benefice, and its rectory was also a manor, with a manorial court, in the 19th century. Many of the parish's rectors were churchmen of high status, and Cradley's Old Rectory remains one of the finest houses in the parish.

Cradley's economy was always primarily agrarian, and it remained substantially agricultural in 2023. In the 19th century, the parish also had diverse crafts and service economies; however, over the course of the 20th century most aspects of these economies shrank drastically. From the medieval into the modern periods, Cradley was relatively wealthy for an agrarian parish. It was also a particularly large parish in comparison with its neighbours, in terms both of size and population, until the late 19th century. The parish successfully opposed the laying of a railway, and proposals to mine coal proved fruitless; this preserved Cradley's idyllic, rural feel, but meant that its economic and population growth slowed, in contrast to nearby Colwall and other parishes along the railway lines. Although there were major building projects in the second half of the 20th century, Cradley still boasts a high density of historic houses and cottages, many of them timber-framed, as well as much historic agrarian architecture, such as 18th-century barns and 19th-century hopkilns.

1 https://www.google.co.uk/maps (accessed 25 June 2021).
2 https://www.google.co.uk/maps (accessed 25 June 2021).

CRADLEY PARISH

Boundaries and Parish Origins

CRADLEY (2,339 HA.), WHICH BORDERS Worcestershire to the east, north (in part) and formerly also to the south,[1] is one of the largest parishes in Herefordshire.[2] The parish boundaries do not follow any major natural features or roads and instead mainly follow field boundaries. The northern boundary runs north-east past Hidelow Farm to Acton Mill Farm, then south past Upper Barrow Farm, east to Bearswood Farm, north-east past Birchwood Common and south-east to Coppice End House. From the corner of Norrest wood, the eastern boundary follows a minor road connecting Coppice End House with

PARISH OF CRADLEY (MODERN PARISH BOUNDARIES): displaying topography; current and historical boundaries; the modern road network, surviving woodlands and commons.

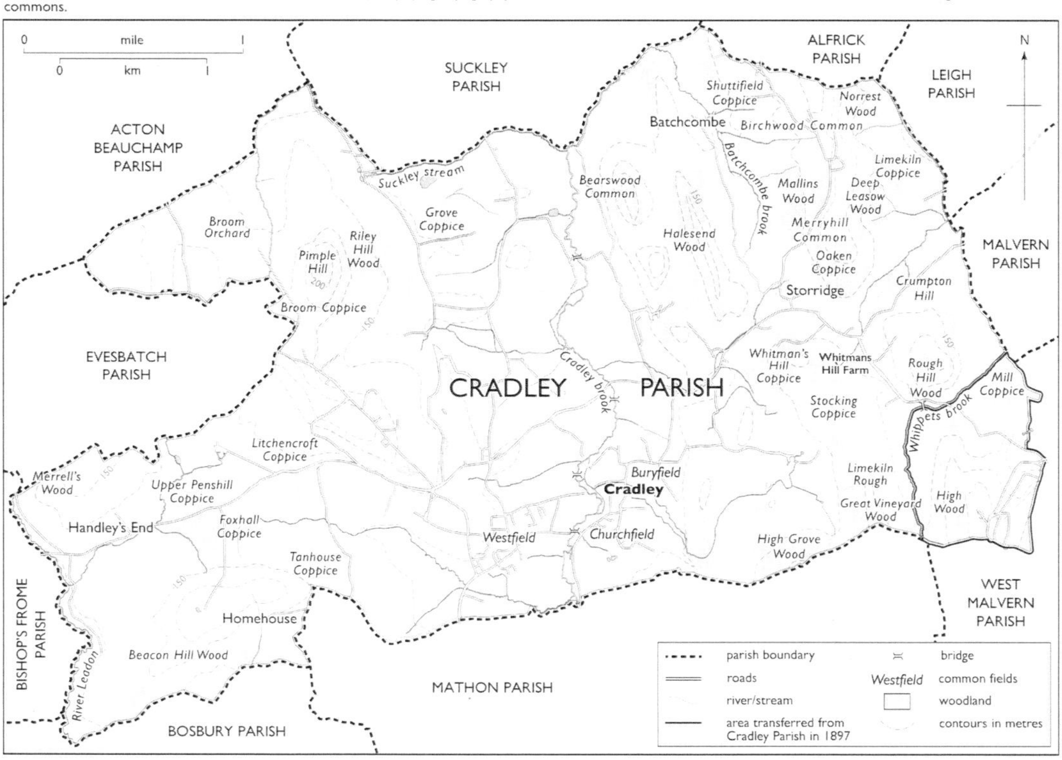

Map 1 *Parish of Cradley (modern parish boundaries).*

1 Mathon, its neighbour, lay in Worcs. until transferred to Herefs. in 1897: *VCH Worcs.* IV, 139.
2 Census, 2011.

the A4103, which it then cuts across, running down to Mill coppice and along Whippets brook (through Mill coppice and around High wood). The southern boundary cuts through High Grove wood, then across the Cradley brook, and follows Tanhouse Lane but diverges up to Tanhouse coppice, and then down, past Homehouse and across Beacon Hill wood, until it reaches the river Leadon, which the western boundary follows to Morrell's wood.[3]

In 1838, the parish was 5,756 acres.[4] In 1897, a diamond-shaped parcel of land (*c.*280 a.)[5] was transferred to Mathon Urban (renamed West Malvern),[6] thus altering the parish and county boundaries. Until this change they followed the continuation of the Bronze Age earthwork known as the Shire Ditch, which ran halfway along the middle part of the hills. The altered boundary followed Whippets brook past Mill coppice into Rough Hill wood, and then followed the road past Cowleigh Park Farm.[7] In 1897, a very small part of Cradley (comprising two houses and six people) was transferred to Leigh (Worcs.).[8]

The parish in 2021 had 1,674 residents and was relatively sparsely populated.[9] Cradley village developed in two parts, divided by the Cradley brook – the parish's main water source. Storridge, a smaller settlement, developed at the junction of roads to Malvern, Hereford and Worcester, and extended northwards on either side of a valley. Several distinct hamlets probably existed within the medieval parish, and in the early modern period hamlets to the east of Cradley village were noted by map-makers, presumably to mark the county boundary. Cowleigh (*alias* Cowley) is marked on maps of 1577 and 1784,[10] Crumpal or Grumpal, of 1754 and 1787,[11] and Storridge, of 1754.[12] By the early modern period, bridges, such as Stifford's Bridge, acted as foci of settlement.[13]

Landscape

Cradley has a strongly undulating topography. Much of the parish lies between 90 and 120m. above mean sea level, rising to 245m. in High Grove wood.[14] The east of the parish (especially that part transferred to West Malvern in 1897) is characterised by ridges of the Malvern hills, rising from the flood plains of the Teme valley.[15]

Cradley's superficial geology includes alluvium along the Cradley brook and numerous pockets of Mathon Sand and Gravel Formation, and Head (clay, silt, sand and gravel). Its solid geology has created two different landscapes. A large area in the

3 https://www.herefordshire.gov.uk/elections-1/administrative-map (accessed 17 Nov. 2022).
4 HCA, 6437/II/1.
5 OS Map 1:10560, Worcs. XXXIX.8 (1888 edn) and Worcs. XXXIX.12 (1895 edn).
6 59 & 60 Vic., c. 72 (Malvern Link (Extension and Water Act) 1896); *VCH Worcs.* IV, 139.
7 WAAS, r209.2 442.
8 *VCH Worcs.* IV, 101; Census Rep. Worcs., 1901, 26.
9 Census, 2021. See https://citypopulation.de/en/uk/westmidlands/admin/county_of_herefordshire/E04000732_cradley_and_storridge (accessed 3 Jan. 2024).
10 B. Smith, *Herefordshire Maps* (Almeley, 2004), plates 2 and 18.
11 Smith, *Herefs. Maps*, plates 22 and 8.
12 Smith, *Herefs. Maps*, plate 8 (featuring the 2nd edn 1793).
13 HAS, AH73/25–73; below, Communications.
14 OS Map 1:25000, Explorer Sheet 190 (2015 edn).
15 *VCH Herefs. Colwall*, 3–6; local inf.

west of the parish is composed entirely of St Maughan's Formation (argillaceous rocks and sandstone). The east side of the parish has a more varied geology, including a wide strip of Much Wenlock Limestone Formation, and another wide strip of Coalbrookdale Formation (silty mudstone). The north-east of the parish extends into geology characteristic of Worcestershire, including an area of Sidmouth Mudstone Formation, as well as possessing the distinctive Cowleigh Park Foundation (sandstone and conglomerate).[16]

In 2023, as in 1086, Cradley consisted of mixed arable, pasture, meadow and woodland. The '-ley' of Cradley probably derives from Old English *léah*, grassland or meadow, which previously meant woodland glade or clearing.[17] The Domesday manor also contained substantial open-field arable and wood pasture.[18] There is documentary evidence of continuing woodland clearance from *c.*1200, with the assarts rented out by the bishop. Evidence of assarting declines in the 14th century, probably because of economic changes caused by the Black Death.[19] Enclosure of common land, evident before *c.*1300, escalated rapidly in the late 16th century,[20] and by the early 19th century much of Cradley's commons had disappeared, and further erosion was ongoing;[21] in some places, such as Cradley's 'two thirds' of Malvern Chase, this was caused by illegal erection of dwellings.[22] Dense, long-established woodland remained in 2023 on ridges to the east of the parish, with fringes of rough grassland and scrub; elsewhere most land was pasture, with water meadows alongside the Cradley brook. In the south-west this brook, in a deep meandering channel lined with mature trees, flows through characteristic Herefordshire scenery with only scattered settlements, offering valuable wildlife corridors. To the west the landscape is more open, with mixed pasture and arable, and on the Leadon valley slopes the underlying red sandstone colours the soil.[23]

Communications

Roads

The Hereford–Worcester road (Bransford Road, A4103) bisects the parish, running west–east from Bishop's Frome, across Cradley brook at Stifford's Bridge, then north-east past Storridge towards Worcester through a gap in the hills. First mentioned in 1393 as the *regalem viam* (king's highway) leading to Worcester,[24] it is probably the same as

16 British Geological Survey, *Geology of Britain*, https://geologyviewer.bgs.ac.uk/, search term: Cradley, Herefordshire (accessed 22 Jan. 2025).
17 B. Coplestone-Crow, *Herefordshire Place-names* (Little Logaston, 2009), 72; M. Gelling, *Place-Names in the Landscape* (Stamford, 1993), 198–207, 237ff.; *Domesday*, 502.
18 Below, Settlement; Agriculture: The agricultural landscape.
19 Below, Population; Woodland and Forest.
20 Below, Agriculture: The agricultural landscape.
21 See complaints discussed in the *HJ* 26 Feb. 1806, and the coverage of the related 9 Aug. 1820 crown court hearing in the same.
22 Below, Agriculture: The agricultural landscape.
23 Inf. from local resident.
24 'Usque ad regalem viam que ducit v[er]s[.] Wigor', HAS, C96/1.

the 'common way' from Cradley to Worcester described in 1581,[25] and the 'Queensway' near Storridge in the period 1577–81.[26] In 1730, the section from Fromes Hill through to Cradley was the first in the parish to be turnpiked.[27] Before 1815 a meandering section of the turnpike road was replaced by a straighter alignment slightly north of the original.[28] In the 1840s a new section, from Storridge towards Leigh Sinton, replaced the old road further north (from Storridge Farm to Holywell Cottages),[29] and by 1842 many connecting roads had been turnpiked.[30] In 1828, tollhouses (now lost) existed at Mill Bank on Stifford's Bridge and at Brook;[31] Teazel Cottage, Holywell, survived in 2023, though the road was a dead end.[32] By 1834, there was also a tollhouse on Pontic bridge which is still extant as a dwelling.[33]

Ridgeway (*Ruggeweye*), recorded 1297–8, climbs Greenhill from the Hereford–Worcester road at Ridgeway Cross, and thence leads north-west along the high ground towards Bromyard.[34] In 1754 the Ridgeway Oak was a landmark.[35] Between 1816[36] and 1828 this section of the Ledbury–Bromyard road was turnpiked by the Bromyard trust,[37] which expired in 1875.[38]

From the junction at Ridgeway Cross, Chockbury Lane runs southwards; a medieval holloway, it was probably once the principal route linking Cradley to Ridgeway and the royal road. It heads south and then eastwards through Westfield towards King's Bridge into the village of Cradley.[39]

East of Ridgeway Cross, the Ledbury road meets the Hereford–Worcester road at Stony Cross, first depicted in 1754,[40] and passes south through Westfield. The road was turnpiked by the Ledbury trust in 1838 as far as the Stony Cross junction,[41] and a

25 HAS, AA59/A/2, f 55v.
26 HAS, AA59/A/2, ff. 9v–10.
27 3 Geo. II, c. 18; HAS, BJ2/1; WAAS, S705:27 BA385/1(vii).
28 M. Tonkin, 'Herefordshire toll-houses then and now', *TWNFC* 48 (1994–6), 406.
29 Not shown on the 1839 tithe map, but on William Jones's map of 1855: HAS, AK19/20.
30 Tonkin, 'Herefordshire toll-houses', 406.
31 http://www.turnpikes.org.uk/Tollhouses%20of%20Herefordshire.htm (accessed 17 Nov. 2022); OS Map 1:25000, Herefs. XXIX.5 (1904 edn); Geoff Gwatkin, Cradley Tithe Map 1839, privately published (Ross-on-Wye, 2003) [hereafter Tithe Map (1839)]; OS Map 1:25000, Herefs. XXIX.5 (1904 edn); http://www.turnpikes.org.uk/Tollhouses%20of%20Herefordshire.htm (accessed 17 Nov. 2022).
32 http://www.turnpikes.org.uk/Tollhouses%20of%20Herefordshire.htm (accessed 17 Nov. 2022); OS Map 1:25000, Worcs. XXXIX.4 (1887 edn).
33 HAS, K68/16; OS Map 1:25000, Herefs. XXIX.9 (1904 edn); local info.
34 In 2022 this road is the B4220: HAS, R13/10528. NB: On modern maps Ridgeway Cross is marked slightly to the west of its location in 1839, so that it is no longer actually on the crossroads that gave it its name.
35 Isaac Taylor, *New Map of the County of Hereford* (1754), HAS, AP25/2. A field named 'Yokefield' in the same location is recorded on the Tithe Map (1839).
36 WAAS, S705:27 BA385/1(vii).
37 HAS, AK19/21.
38 HAS, M64/2 24 May 1875; http://www.turnpikes.org.uk/English%20turnpike%20table.htm (accessed 1 Aug. 2023).
39 *Cradley Conservation Area Appraisal Draft* (2007), 10, 17, https://councillors.herefordshire.gov.uk/documents/s11645/9%20Cradley%20CA%20RL2.pdf (accessed 17 Nov. 2022); Hunt, *Cradley*, 82.
40 Taylor, *New Map*.
41 *VCH Herefs. Bosbury*, 4.

tollhouse (Stirt turnpike) was erected at the Mathon border but had gone by 1855.[42] The Ledbury trust expired in 1871.[43]

A king's highway to Bromyard crossed Barrow manor *c.*1275 at the northern parish edge.[44] This is probably the Suckley road that heads straight north from Stony Cross, passing through Grittlesend.

East of Cradley brook, the Mathon road passes northwards through Cradley village and joins the Hereford–Worcester road east of Stifford's Bridge. First recorded as Ome Way, a king's highway, in 1393,[45] by 1536 it was Ome Lane and ran past Buryfield.[46] South of King's Bridge the road is described as the Mathon–Cradley highway in 1589,[47] so it is unclear whether Ome Way/Ome Lane referred to the entire road or just the section north of Cradley village. At Storridge the Cowleigh road (first recorded 1754)[48] branches southwards from the Hereford–Worcester road down a valley, crossing Whippets brook.

PARISH OF CRADLEY c.1839 (HISTORICAL PARISH BOUNDARIES): including mentioned roads and first recorded dates, streams, bridges and mills.

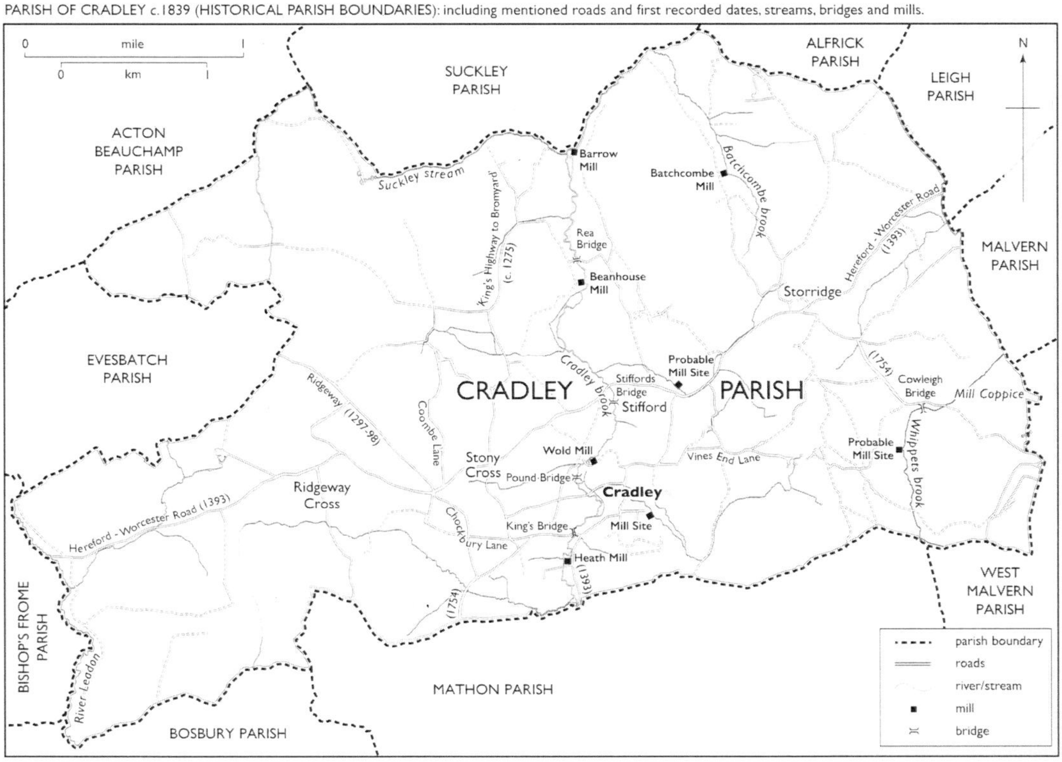

Map 2 *Parish of Cradley c.1839 (historical parish boundaries).*

42 HAS, CO81, AK19/20.
43 http://www.turnpikes.org.uk/English%20turnpike%20table.htm (accessed 17 Nov. 2022).
44 WCM, B236.
45 HAS, C96/1.
46 TNA, SC 6/HENVIII/1511 8d.
47 HAS, HD2/1/30.
48 Taylor, *New Map*.

Medieval minor routes include a road to Barrow Mill *c.*1275 and a path to Suckley.[49] A wain way existed near Churchfield in 1589.[50] Several holloways survive, including part of Cradley's main street, part of the lane to Vinesend and Chockbury Lane, which connects to Ridgeway.[51] By 1820 there were many public carriage roads,[52] and before 1900 private roads connected them to the large farms and houses.[53]

Bridges

Bridges crossing Cradley brook are (from north to south) Reabridge, Stifford's bridge, Pound bridge and King's bridge (recorded *c.*1307).[54] Stifford (so-called in 1306) presumably served as a common crossing point of Cradley brook before the bridge was erected.[55] Cowleigh bridge crosses Whippets brook. King's bridge, Pound bridge and Stifford's bridge were all subject to frequent flooding.[56] In 1886, after Pound bridge was washed away by floods, Bromyard Highway Board agreed to re-erect it.[57] After 1700, King's Bridge, Pound bridge and Stifford's Bridge all referred to areas of the parish, encompassing the settlements surrounding the bridges.[58]

Post

There was a post office at Ridgeway Cross by 1858,[59] which existed until 1942 or later.[60] By 1871, there was also a post office at Stifford's Bridge,[61] which continued until 1913 or later.[62] Additionally, there was a post office in Cradley village from at least 1851; by 1871, it was located in the shop later called the Stores, where it remained to 2013. In 2014, this was replaced by a sub-post office in the village hall which opened on two half-days a week and was still operating in 2023.[63] In 1923, the parish council supported a petition for a post office in Storridge.[64] By 1949, when it changed premises, it had become a sub-post office;[65] it was based at Rose Garth by 1980, and closed in 1985.[66] There was also a post office in the area of West Malvern, formerly part of Cradley.[67]

49 WCM, B231, B236.
50 HAS, HD2/1/30.
51 *Cradley Conservation Area Appraisal Draft* (2007), 10, 17 (accessed 17 Nov. 2022); Hunt, *Cradley*, 82.
52 HAS, AH73/69, pp. 51–9.
53 HAS, AH73/69, pp. 51–9.
54 HAS, P66/5.
55 HAS, P66/2; R13/10531.
56 Edwards, *Cradley*, 20.
57 HAS, M64/4, p. 6.
58 HAS, AH73/25–73.
59 *Cassey's Dir.* (1858).
60 *Kelly's Dir.* (1942).
61 Census, 1871.
62 *Kelly's Dir.* (1913).
63 *Kelly's Dir.* (1926); *Pigot's Dir.* (1850); Census, 1871; https://sites.google.com/site/ukpostofficesbycounty (accessed 24 Sept. 2023).
64 HAS, BL20/1, p. 242.
65 HAS, BL20/2, p. 326.
66 CHC, Parish Council Minutes, II, 20 Jan. 1981; 15 Sept. 1985.
67 The building is extant: inf. from local resident.

The nearest telegraph office was at Malvern until 1895 when an office opened at Cradley village post office.[68] The telephone arrived in Cradley in 1924.[69] Internet access was available from early 2005.[70]

Carriers and Buses

Five carriers are recorded between 1879 and 1913. In 1902, there were three Saturday carriers to Worcester,[71] and two to Malvern.[72] In 1917, two carried to Worcester on Saturdays, and one to Malvern on Tuesdays and Fridays.[73]

In 1920, a private motor bus service to Cradley was proposed.[74] By 1926, Midland Red[75] buses went to Worcester twice a week, and George Drew's bus went to Worcester on three days and to Ledbury, Bromyard and Malvern once a week respectively, on market days. After 1945, a school bus took Cradley children to secondary schools in Ledbury,[76] and in 1957 there was also a school bus to Malvern Chase.[77] In 1970, buses ran from Cradley to Bromyard, Ledbury, Great Malvern, Mathon and Worcester.[78] In 2023, First Worcestershire ran one return bus service between Cradley and Hereford (via Bromyard) on Wednesdays, and four return services daily (except Sundays) between Worcester, Cradley and Ledbury.[79] The nearest railway station in 2023 was at Malvern Link.[80]

Population

In 1086, there were 23 villeins, three bordars (smallholders) and six boors (low-status peasants) on the bishop's manor, as well as five slaves. There were also a priest, a reeve, two knights and a *radman* (riding man), with an unspecified number of bordars holding from them.[81] This suggests a total population of between 150 and 250, depending

68 *Kelly's Dir.* (1895); HAS, AH73/37 12 June 1895; HAS, N37/35 2 Apr. 1895.
69 Hunt, *Cradley*, 90; *Kelly's Dir.* (1926).
70 https://availability.samknows.com/broadband/exchange/WMRID (accessed 4 Jan. 2024).
71 The days on which the carriers operated seem to have been market days: *VCH Worcs.* IV, 376–90.
72 *Jakeman & Carver's Dir.* (1902).
73 *Kelly's Dir.* (1917).
74 HAS, BL20/1, p. 227.
75 Trading name of the Birmingham & Midland Motor Omnibus Co. Ltd.
76 HAS, BK13/1/15.
77 CHC, Parish Council Minutes, I, 63.
78 HAS, BW15/1/11, p. 154.
79 https://bustimes.org (accessed 1 Aug. 2023).
80 OS Map 1:25000 Explorer Sheet 190 (2015 edn).
81 *Domesday*, 502; for Boors, see *Domesday*, 1431. For the reeve, see Social Character below. For Radmen, see F.C. Suppe, *Military Institutions of the Welsh Marches: Shropshire* AD *1066–1300* (Woodbridge, 1994), 74, 86–7; and Mary A. Atkin, 'A study of "Radman villages" recorded in Domesday Book in Western Shropshire', *Shrops. Arch. And Hist. Soc. Transactions* 89 (2015), 15–26.

on household size and whether slaves were heads of households.[82] Hanley, the only other Cradley manor in the Domesday Book, had four bordars, a slave and a burgess, suggesting a population in the range of 20–30. The likely total parish population was therefore between 170 and 280.[83] By *c.*1288, 90 tenants held land from the bishop in the manor, including at least ten women, suggesting a population between 350 and 450, reflecting wider population trends.[84] Storridge (in Bosbury manor), had perhaps nine or more tenants, adding 35–45 to the total.[85] A little later, The Hyde had at least four or five tenants,[86] and the manors of The Barrow and Hanley were probably similar. Thus, the total parish population *c.*1300 probably exceeded 500.[87]

The Black Death's impact on Cradley's population is seen in a sharp decline in annual rents in 1349 on St Katherine's Hospital's manor of The Hyde.[88] In 1377, 186 parishioners over the age of 14 paid the poll tax, suggesting that the population fell to the low 300s.[89] The comparatively larger size of the customary tenancies recorded in 1496–7 implies that the population had not returned to the *c.*1300 level.[90] A lay subsidy paid in 1546 records 64 named taxpayers (54 men and 10 women) who possessed 20*s.* or more in goods or lands, equating to a total population of perhaps *c.*400.[91]

Baptism and burial records[92] suggest net population growth in the parish during the period 1560–1620, as births outpace deaths in each decade.[93] Mortality spikes, probably created by epidemics, can be seen in 1587[94] and 1614–15. After 1610, population growth apparently slowed, as numbers of both baptisms and burials declined; by the 1630s and

82 *Domesday*, 502, 514. These calculations follow the principles outlined in N. Goose and A Hinde, 'Sources and Methods: Estimating local population sizes at fixed points in time: part I – General Principles', *Local Population Studies*, 77 (Abingdon, 2006), 66–74; N. Goose and A. Hinde, 'Sources and Methods: Estimating local population sizes at fixed points in time: part II – Specific Sources', Local Population Studies, 78 (Abingdon, 2007), 74–88, 75–6; Smith estimates 225: Smith, *Malvern*, 21.

83 *Domesday*, 514.

84 Assuming households of between *c.*4 and *c.*5, HAS, AA59/A/1, pp. 148–53; C. Dyer, *Making a Living in the Middle Ages* (New Haven, 2002), 155–6.

85 HAS, AA59/A/1, pp. 153, 157–8.

86 Below, Manors and Principal Estates: Hyde manor, St Katherine's Hospital, Ledbury.

87 These figures presume all landholders were resident and that the women were widows with families. They assume average family sizes of 4.0 and 5.0 respectively. This yields a minimum of 450 and a maximum of 570.

88 Below, Agriculture; Hillaby, *St Katherine's*, 98; HCA, 7018/2, ff. 77–82. An antiquarian account cites from a dubious source that in 'A.D. 1349, Anno 23, Edward III., there died in Bosbury, Colwall, Coddington, and Cradley, 158 Tenants': F.T. Havergal, *Fasti Herefordenses and other Antiquarian Memorials of Hereford* (1869), 203.

89 The lower and upper estimates are *c.*290 and 380; see 'Local Population Studies, 78, 78–9'; *Poll Taxes of 1377–81*, ed. Fenwick, 358, 366.

90 Below, Social Character; HAS, AM33/13; TNA, SC 6/HENVIII/1511; BL, Add. Roll 27311.

91 This assumes a 30 per cent evasion rate, as discussed in *Local Population Studies*, 77, 69; *Local Population Studies*, 78, 79–80; *Herefordshire Taxes in the Reign of Henry VIII*, ed. M.A. Faraday (Hereford, 2005), 312.

92 Note that any Nonconformists and recusants may not be represented, and the figures may also include some residents of other parishes baptised or buried in Cradley; furthermore, this data cannot capture the full picture of migration to or from the parish.

93 Very few baptisms are listed prior to 1560, but are listed for all years thereafter except 1585–6.

94 Leominster suffered a plague epidemic in 1587: C. Creighton, *A History of Epidemics in Britain* (Cambridge, 1891), I, 349.

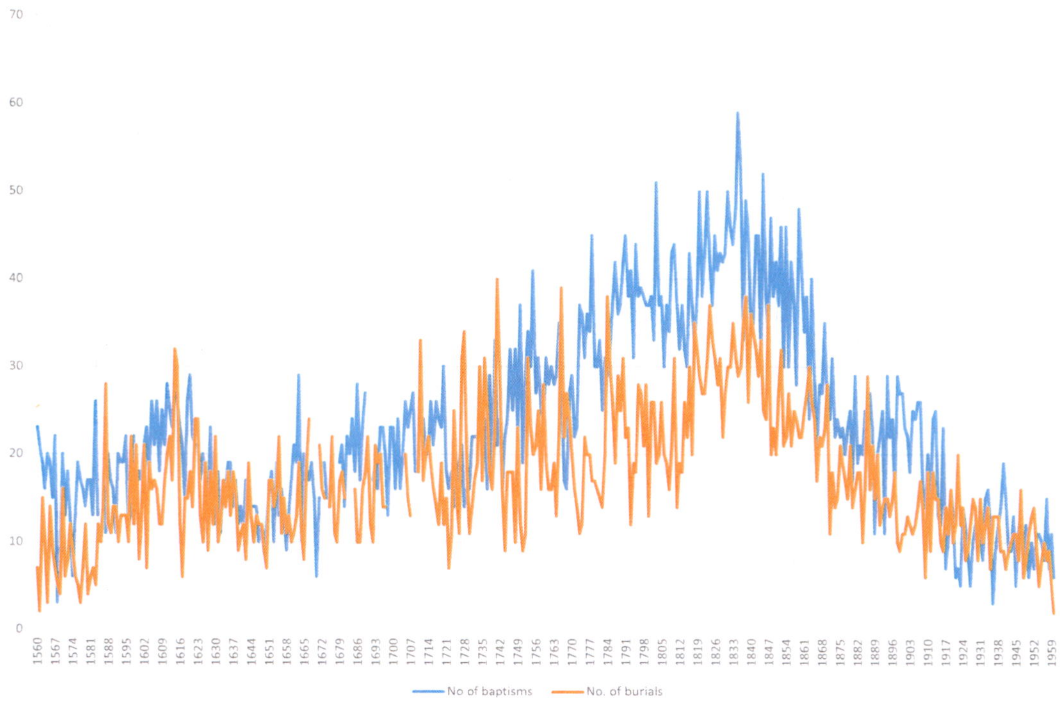

Figure 1 *Chart of baptisms and burials in Cradley 1560–1960.* (Produced by Anastasia Stylianou)

1640s only one more birth than death annually was recorded on average, and in the 1650s the numbers were equal.[95] In 1676, Cradley reportedly had 300 (adult) conformists and no Nonconformists. Although this was presumably an estimate (compared with precise figures returned by neighbouring parishes), by comparison with its neighbours, Cradley was one of the most populous parishes in the area.[96]

Baptisms and burials trended upward from *c.*1660, eventually peaking in 1835, and baptisms outstripped burials every year between 1725 and 1886. Outstanding peaks in mortality occurred in 1711, 1741, 1766, 1784 and 1886.

In 1841, there were 1,243 inhabitants in 366 households.[97] The population was fairly stable during the 19th century, peaking at 1,422 in 1871 and declining a little to 1,220 in 1911.[98] Baptisms and burials began to decline from *c.*1860, perhaps reflecting emigration from Herefordshire's rural parishes.

95 HAS, AH73/1.

96 A. Whiteman (ed.), *The Compton Census of 1676: A critical edition* (1986).

97 Census, 1841.

98 Censuses, 1871, 1911.

New housing projects since the 1950s, and Cradley's popularity with Worcester commuters and retirees, have driven growth in its population, from 1,162 in 1961[99] to 1,674 in 2021.[100] Storridge in 1905 had a population of 317;[101] in 1966 it was 264.[102]

Settlement

Before 1000[103]

Several assemblages of worked flints, which represent at least seasonal activity and are the first evidence of early human activity, are found around the upper Cradley brook valley.[104] Two major concentrations of worked flints have been found in the fields west of Upper Barrow Farm, indicating dispersed Mesolithic and more concentrated Neolithic settlement.[105] Directly north of Upper Barrow Farm, a possible round barrow partially survives as a circular mound.[106] More worked flints to the south of Upper Barrow Farm indicate settlement activity from the late 3rd to at least the mid 2nd millennium BC. An early Bronze Age flint scraper was found at Little Halesend.

Ancient linear earthworks are located along the crests of high north–south ridges in Halesend wood and near Whitman's hill. They probably date from the middle to late Bronze Age (if contemporary with the Shire Ditch on the crest of the Malvern Hills)[107] and represent some of the earliest territorial boundaries in this area. A simple narrow bank at Whitman's hill is another example of early boundaries and extends for *c.*1.3km. from the quarry at the northern end of the ridge (and may have extended further north) along the crest of the ridge to Bank wood in Mathon.[108] Another linear bank (in places a north-facing lynchet up to 4m. high) forms the boundary between Cradley and Mathon for over 2.5km.[109]

Early field systems survive as a series of small rectilinear enclosures. Examples are at Whitman's hill and Halesend wood, where lynchets form part of the boundaries and in a large field between Grittlesend and Nupend.[110] Elsewhere in Cradley, these enclosures were often isolated, suggestive of small embanked late prehistoric

99 HAS, BW15/1/9, p. 1047.

100 Census, 2021. See https://citypopulation.de/en/uk/westmidlands/admin/county_of_herefordshire/E04000732_cradley_and_storridge (accessed 3 Jan. 2024).

101 *Kelly's Dir.* (1905).

102 CHC, Parish Council Minutes, 283.

103 Keith Ray is the primary author of this section.

104 HER 51988, 51989, 52248, 52274, et seq.; see also K. Ray, 'Settlement to AD600', in S. Pinches, *Ledbury: People and Parish before the Reformation* (Chichester, 2010), for similar finds north of Ledbury. Although finds have not been found elsewhere in Cradley, this may not indicate a lack of human activity.

105 In 2000, Keith Ray was shown a polished stone axe-head found close to Ridgeway Farm in Evesbatch parish.

106 HER 53244. It is recorded on Tithe Map (1839) as Barrow Meadow. Below, Manors and Principal Estates, for more on The Barrow.

107 For Shire Ditch, see M. Bowden, *The Malvern Hills: An ancient landscape* (Swindon, 2005), 16–17.

108 HER 52190.

109 HER 31808.

110 HER 53550.

CRADLEY HISTORICAL SETTLEMENT TO c.1800 (HISTORICAL PARISH BOUNDARIES): including common fields and locations of evidence of pre-1000 settlement.

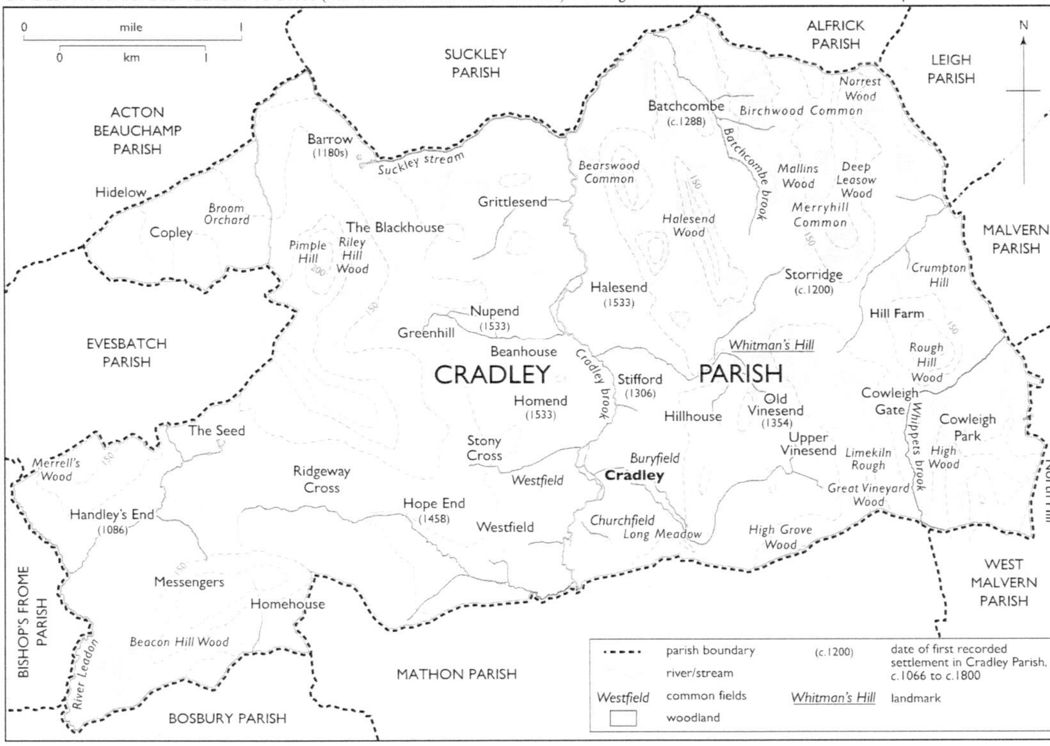

Map 3 *Cradley historical settlement to c.1800 (historical parish boundaries).*

farmsteads. Two possible hut sites of a late prehistoric farmstead were found at Ridgeway, with the middle to later Iron Age pottery found there indicating a transition from an enclosed domestic farmstead to an open site where metalworking was undertaken.[111] Another probable farmstead is visible on aerial photographs 150m. north-east of Copley Farm.[112] Another 'enclosure' near Grittlesend has numerous ditch lines, none of which appear to relate to the 1839 tithe map boundaries, indicating a complex site which probably changed over time. The site has ditches that cross (at different depths) and multiple pits.

Although there is no evidence of settlements in the Romano-British period, sherds of a Roman jar and a 2nd-century coin have been found.[113] In Storridge, kiln debris and wasters, mainly to the east and south of Hill Farm,[114] probably represent kiln sites or the associated settlements, part of the 'Severn Valley Ware' industry which extended from the Malvern hills to the environs of Worcester.

111 HER 10470; T. Hoverd, *Herefs. Archaeol. Report* 30 (2001).

112 HER 53131.

113 HER 49587, 49931.

114 HER 5462, 6717, 10649, 12161. A total of 181 sherds of mostly 1st to 2nd century AD Severn Valley ware were found at 10649.

Apart from surviving pre-Conquest fabric in the church, there is little evidence for the early medieval period.[115] Cradley church may have stood within a circular or oval enclosure, possibly 200m. in diameter, seen on an aerial photograph linking it with an earthwork north-east of the church. Some of the many medieval strip lynchets extending up hillsides from the settlement may originally date from the late Saxon period. The only early medieval artefact is an Anglo-Saxon coin found by a detectorist near Stony Cross, Westfield.[116]

Medieval and Early Modern Settlement

Cradley's settlement pattern, like other Herefordshire parishes, was primarily of scattered farmsteads and hamlets rather than nucleated villages, and this may be reflected by the five sub-tenancies recorded in 1086.[117] There was a particular focus of settlement in the south of the parish around the Cradley brook, indicated by the Anglo-Saxon fabric in the church and the presence of a Domesday mill.[118] At least three medieval common fields were located here: two, Churchfield and Buryfield, lay east of the brook, near the church, while Westfield was west of the brook.[119] Further north, common fields are also recorded in the valley of Suckley stream near Winthill and Barrow, as well as in the Hyde area.[120] Additional settlement was concentrated in the south-west corner of the parish, where Hanley and three smaller manors that preceded it were located.[121]

Surname evidence from *c.*1288 references a number of small settlements and homesteads, many surviving in 2023 as cottages or farmsteads, which suggests a high degree of continuity. The surname 'of Home', probably deriving from *hamm* (meadow), first appears in 1221–2. Three men named 'of Home' each held half a yardland *c.*1288. In 1345–6, 'Hommelond' was described as a tenement, and by 1533 as a messuage and yardland of customary land. Separately, 'Homeyend' in 1533 is similarly described.[122] There were at least three men called 'of Batchcombe' *c.*1288, which in 1496–7 contained at least one messuage and one yardland of land.[123] Hales and Halesend are first recorded in 1533 as two separate messuages, although 'of Hales' appears in the early 13th century; *c.*1288, three tenants called 'of Hales', held three yardlands between them.[124] In 1784, Halesend was described as a village.[125] A family named 'of the Hethe' held land in socage

115 Below, Church Architecture: The pre-Conquest Church; HER 31074.
116 HER 4820.
117 Above, Population.
118 Below, Church Architecture: The pre-Conquest Church.
119 Below, Agriculture: The agricultural landscape.
120 Below, Agriculture: The agricultural landscape.
121 Below, Patterns of Landownership: Hanley/Handley's End/Little Hanley.
122 Osbert, son of Reginald of Hame, held a yardland in Cradley *c.*1221; HAS, AA59/A/1, p. 150; TNA, C 146/3218; HAS, R13/10537. D.M. Stenton (ed.), *Rolls of the Justices in Eyre: Being the rolls of pleas and assizes for Gloucestershire, Warwickshire and Staffordshire, 1221–1222* (1940), 639.
123 They held between them at least one and a half yardlands: HAS, AA59/A/1, p. 152; AM33/13, rot. 21d.
124 J. Barrow (ed.), *English Episcopal Acta 7: Hereford 1079–1234* (1993), no. 363; HAS, AA59/A/1, p. 151; HAS, R13/10537.
125 For the Halesend Estate, see below, Landownership: Halesend; HAS, BJ2/1.

from the bishop in the early 13th century.[126] Five tenants were named 'of Hethe' *c.*1288.[127] A 'Le Hetheplace', recorded in 1458 and 1533, was described as including a messuage and a customary yardland.[128] Hope is recorded in 1267.[129] The surname 'of Hope', however, is first mentioned in the early 13th century, and two customary tenants with that name appear *c.*1288.[130] 'Hopend' was described as a messuage in 1458 and 1533.[131] 'Vinesend' and 'Vineslond' are both recorded in 1533,[132] but the surname Vyneges appears in the 1220s.[133] Four tenants were named 'fyneges' *c.*1288, holding between them 2½ yardlands, of which 1½ were freehold.[134] 'Vyneghus', recorded in 1354, is probably Old Vinesend Farm, parts of which date from the 14th century.[135] Three farms named Vinesend, Old, Upper and Lower, existed close together by the 17th century.[136]

Storridge, first recorded in John's reign,[137] apparently referred to both the settlement and that part of Bosbury manor lying in Cradley parish. Of eight tenants surnamed 'of Storridge' *c.*1288, two were from Cradley manor, and six from Bosbury.[138] In 1754, Storridge and Crumpal were depicted on a map as hamlets.[139]

Although a mill is mentioned at Stifford in the 1330s and a messuage *c.*1402, no other evidence suggests that it was a hamlet in this period.[140] In Hanley, The Hyde and The Barrow, the settlement pattern was probably similar.

Toponyms *c.*1288 recording places now lost include 'of Calcoumbe' (three tenants, one holding a customary half-yardland), and at or of 'Lideyard' (four tenants, one also holding a customary half-yardland).[141]

In 1682, Cradley manor comprised six divisions for rental purposes, apparently corresponding with foci of settlement. Vinesend, Halesend and Nupend yielded higher total rents than Stifford's End, Hopend and 'Buriend'.[142] In 1671, 110 houses with 198 hearths were charged hearth tax; a further 56 houses were exempt, making a total of 166 houses in the parish.[143]

126 *Cur. Reg.* 16, 1767.
127 Two tenants held half-yardlands, one of which was freehold; the rest held customary land of between 12 and 16 a., supplemented in some cases by forlet land; HAS, AA59/A/1, p. 152.
128 HAS, AA59/A/1, pp. 148–50; CF 54/1/25.
129 Robert of Furches held a half-yardland from the bp there, and probably still held it *c.*1288: *Reg. Swinfield* I, 138. HAS, AA59/A/1, p. 149.
130 Ernaldo of Hope: *English Episcopal Acta: Hereford 1079–1234*, no. 363. The other two tenants held half a yardland and 12 a. of customary land: HAS, AA59/A/1, pp. 148–50.
131 HAS, CF 54/1/25.
132 HAS, R13/10537; for the possible significance of the name, see also below, Agriculture: Vineyards.
133 *English Episcopal Acta: Hereford 1079–1234*, no. 363.
134 HAS, AA59/A/1, pp. 148–53.
135 *Cal. Pat.* 1354–8, 56; WAAS, 705:1087 BA12989 (xxxiv).
136 Below, Other Estates.
137 *Cal. Inq. Misc.* I, 146; below, Manors and Principal Estates: Storridge, manor of Bosbury.
138 HAS, AA59/A/1, pp. 149, 153.
139 Smith, *Herefs. Maps*, plate 22.
140 HAS, R13/10531.
141 HAS, AA59/A/1, p. 152.
142 HAS, E21/1. This roll omits the manors of Overbarrow, the Hyde, Bosbury, Hanley and Cowleigh.
143 M.A. Faraday, 'The hearth tax in Herefordshire', *TWNFC* 41 (1973–5), 83.

Cradley village was certainly a nucleated settlement before the 18th century, since 16th- and 17th-century timber-framed houses are grouped around the church,[144] which overlooks the main street. This is a deeply cut 'narrow sinuous' holloway lined with the uncrowded cottages, and its character may have changed little since the Middle Ages.[145] The church, the nearby brook (capable of powering a number of mills) and available stream water (flowing beside the former post office building) together explain why this cluster of dwellings arose. But Cradley's location, bounded north and south by the Buryfield and Churchfield common fields, on the west by brook, meadow and Westfield, and to the east by the heavily wooded Lumbridge hill, gave it limited scope to expand.

Settlement from the 18th to the 21st Centuries

Cradley's population grew and settlement expanded during the 18th and 19th century,[146] especially in the south-east. This was the most densely populated area of the parish in 1841 and included North Hill, with 463 inhabitants; the least densely populated was the north-east, with 289, while the north-west had 387 and the south-west 365.

Westfield appears to have emerged in part because of Cradley village's constriction. Scattered 17th-century buildings in the vicinity indicate a dispersed pattern, but by 1754 a small settlement had become established around a cluster of faintly sketched minor roads south of Stony Cross and Chockbury Lane, and by 1840 Westfield was described as a village.[147]

The area of North Hill then within Cradley was sparsely populated before 1800, with only one farm (Birches). The population grew steadily thereafter, with *c.*30 properties by 1839,[148] and continued to grow until it was transferred to West Malvern.[149]

The mid to late 20th century saw settlement in the parish reorientated, with Cradley and Westfield villages in the south-east both expanding significantly, while many smaller rural settlements shrank. Until the 1940s, building projects were isolated or small-scale, normally adding no more than a few houses a year. Large council housing developments took place in the following decades,[150] and private developers built *c.*40 houses.[151] In 1960, Bromyard Rural District Council (RDC) encouraged private developers to build more dwellings in Cradley,[152] and noted in 1961 that the housing density there was now the highest in their district, highlighting the scale of modern building projects in the parish.[153] Cradley village's constricted position, however, limited its potential for expansion, and caused Westfield rapidly to overtake it, so that, unlike the old common fields of Buryfield[154] and Churchfield, Westfield was largely built over. In 1964, Cradley village had *c.*57 dwellings, and Westfield

144 Above, Settlement.
145 *Cradley Conservation Area Appraisal Draft* (2007), 10 (accessed 1 Aug. 2023).
146 Above, Population.
147 HAS, BJ2/1.
148 V. Goodbury, *West Malvern: A history of the village* (West Malvern, 1994), 2; Tithe Map (1839).
149 Censuses, 1841–91.
150 Below, Social housing.
151 HAS, BK13/1/15.
152 HAS, BW15/1/9, p. 967.
153 HAS, BW15/2/6, p. 984.
154 In the 21st century, the area is often called Buryfields, while historical documents often call it Buryfield, e.g. Tithe Map (1839).

Figure 2 *Cradley and surrounding area as shown on Isaac Taylor's New Map of the County of Hereford (1754). (HAS AP25/2)*

(including Stony Cross) had *c.*100, but by 1972 this number had almost doubled. After the 1950s, the Buryfield and Westfield[155] areas saw the most development.[156] Housebuilding has continued, including some aimed at meeting affordable housing needs; an estate of 51 new homes, on a 6-a. site built in 2022 adjacent to Pixiefield, mostly offered shared ownership units or those with 'affordable' rent.[157]

Social Housing

Until the mid 20th century, most housing for the poor stood in the south-east of the parish, the most impoverished area in Cradley.[158] Already, by 1779, the parish owned houses for the poor, including some at the northern end of the Malvern hills.[159]

155 Especially the Pixiefields estate, constructed in the 1970s: HAS, BW 15/3/2, p. 258.
156 CHC, Parish Council Minutes, I, 21 Nov. 1972; HAS, BW15/3/2, p. 216.
157 https://www.livingspacehousing.co.uk/project/pixiefields (accessed 1 Feb. 2022).
158 Above, Settlement.
159 HAS, N37/33 17 Oct. 1779.

By 1844, there were multiple parish houses at Crumpsend hill and North Hill,[160] and in the early 19th century a workhouse on Barley hill.[161] The era of modern council housing in Cradley began in 1919 with the parish council's decision to build six additional cottages, responding to legislation enacted that year.[162] In 1943, Bromyard RDC noted a shortage of council housing in the parish, and began housebuilding on a large scale, introducing around 40 houses before 1960 and 70 thereafter,[163] mostly at Buryfield, on former meadow land adjoining the old common field.[164]

Public Services

Martley Rural Sanitary Authority proposed, in 1878, to lay a sewer to North Malvern, which would serve the North Hill area of Cradley.[165] After 1900, large properties sometimes had their own provisions for heating, light and sewage disposal, such as generators, boilers and cesspools;[166] cottages, by contrast, tended to rely upon earth closets, fireplaces and water from wells.[167] By the mid 20th century, mains services began to be provided for the parish. Electricity was supplied after proposals made under 1938 legislation to extend coverage to the area were approved by Malvern Council in 1945 and Bromyard RDC in 1947.[168] Further power lines were added to serve outlying parts over the next two decades.[169] In 1950, most houses received water via bores, rather than from a central water supply,[170] although, during the 1950s, a patchy supply began to be established.[171] Mains water arrived in the 1960s, although there were complaints that coverage was insufficient,[172] and in 1962 Bromyard RDC proposed a widespread network of piped water running through the parish, to be laid alongside or underneath many of the roads. These plans, in progress by 1964,[173] included a small reservoir by Ridgeway House.[174] In 1963 Bromyard RDC took out a loan for a sewerage and sewage disposal scheme for Cradley, which was completed in 1967.[175]

160 HAS, N37/35, passim.
161 Below, Social Welfare; Parish Government: Poor law administration.
162 HAS, BL20/1, p. 220. The 1919 Housing and Town Planning Act, known as the 'Addison Act'.
163 HAS, BW15/1/7, p. 262; BW15/2/3 26 July 1945; 18 July 1946; BW15/2/4, p. 72; pp. 75, 120; BW15/1/8, p. 352.
164 Tithe map (1839); e.g. HAS, BW15/1/8, p. 84; HAS, BW15/1/9, p. 1040; HAS, BW15/1/10, p. 1112; HAS, BW 15/2/3, p. 15, and 18 July 1946, p. 32. HAS, BW15/1/8–10.
165 HAS, N37/35 31 Jan. 1878.
166 HAS, M5/6A/1; HAS, J33/43; HAS, J33/12.
167 HAS, M5/6A/1; HAS, M5/6A/5; HAS, M5/6A/7; HAS, M5/6A/8; HAS, M5/6A/11.
168 HAS, BW15/1/8, p. 132; Hunt, *Cradley*, 112; WAAS, 493 BA9196/6(i). This was undertaken by the Shropshire, Worcs. & Staffs. Electric Power Co. following the Electric Power Consolidation Act (1938).
169 HAS, AH73/32.
170 HAS, BW15/1/8, pp. 325–6, 331.
171 HAS, BW15/1/9, p. 846.
172 HAS, BW15/1/9, p. 907; Hunt, *Cradley*, 112.
173 CHC, Parish Council Minutes, I.
174 HAS, BB32/23/3, 5, 6.
175 HAS, BW15/1/10 2 May 1963, p. 1115; also 1 Apr. 1975, p. 1194; 20 May 1965, p. 1202; 7 Dec. 1967, p. 1369.

Figure 3 *Women filling buckets from the brook near Cradley Stores, c.1900. (CHC)*

Figure 4 *Bullshead Cottage, rear (formerly front) view. Later 20th century. (CHC)*

The Built Character[176]

Like its neighbours, Cradley has many timber-framed, 'black-and-white' buildings, mostly built in the 16th and 17th century, suggesting a major rebuilding campaign *c.*1600.[177] Star-section brick chimney stacks are a feature of many of Cradley's historic buildings, suggesting that they were constructed within a common time frame. These buildings remained in use, many hardly altered at all (apart from a certain dilapidation), into the early 20th century, with few additions to the housing stock during three centuries.[178] In the 1950s this changed, as major building projects commenced.

The parish's historic houses fall into two categories: cottages and larger houses. The cottages are small, mostly one-and-a-half storeys originally (although many have since had their roofs raised), usually just two bays long, and many dating to the 17th century.

176 Duncan James is the primary author of this section, which draws upon his 'The Buildings of Cradley Herefordshire: A Report Concerning their Historic Significance, Prepared for the Victoria County History', May 2020, HAS, PAM1598.

177 This supports the contested Great Rebuilding theory: see W.G. Hoskins, 'The Rebuilding of Rural England, 1570–1640', *Past & Present* 4:1 (1953), 44–59, https://doi.org/10.1093/past/4.1.44 (accessed 3 Jan. 2024). In Cradley the campaign was not connected with population growth.

178 Maps of the parish carry this message very clearly.

Figure 5a *Hawkhurst Cottage, c.1930. (CHC)*

Figure 5b *Hawkhurst Cottage after restoration, c.1970. (CHC)*

Bullshead Cottage (late 17th century)[179] is typical. Appletree Cottage, Storridge, is a fine example of a two-bay, one-and-a-half-storey building. Here brick infill replaces wattle and daub panels. The roof has been raised, but only on the south side, probably in the 19th century. Before this was done, there would have been a pair of dormer windows in the roof. The blocked off-centre doorway once gave access into what was the service room, as indicated by the massive gable-end chimney stack.[180]

Hawkhurst Cottage (17th century)[181] is a good example of a grander cottage, with substantial timber framing and a magnificent brick chimney stack which it once possessed at the north end of the range.[182]

The larger and more significant houses, which are (or were) also mostly timber-framed and 16th- to 17th-century in date, typically consist of more than three bays, often with wings, and are two or three storeys high. Built from locally sourced oak, they were, for the most part, plain, robust structures, with little exterior decoration or interior embellishments. Many of them were, and some still are, the landholding farmhouses. A few farmhouses rose in status, this marked, as in the case of Lower Nupend, by refacing the timber-framed house in brick along with installing new fenestration in the 18th century.[183] More recently, some of these large houses have been sold off and divorced from farming activity to be restored and gentrified. Often, in addition to these changes, the farm buildings have been converted to domestic accommodation. Most of these larger houses are still extant, mainly because the parish did not experience any major changes in wealth until more recent times.

A number of Cradley's substantial houses clearly have a layout plan reminiscent of the medieval open hall. Many aspects of this earlier design, until *c.*1500 a standard template for the larger house, survived to influence the form of later houses; it can be seen, for instance, in Upper Vinesend and Barrow Mill.[184] All the larger, higher-status houses are situated on high ground and are prominent elements in the landscape, with visibility from the house of (and of the house from) the surrounding countryside.

There are three features that characterise historical houses, large and small, in the Cradley area, suggesting they were constructed within a common time frame. First, the small diagonal braces used at a lower level in the frame, which can lead to the mistaken observation that the roof has been raised – for example, at Lower Nupend, Cowleigh Gate Farm and Brookholm. Second, chimney stacks that have 'nibs' on the brick chimney shaft. This can be seen at Old Upper House Farm, Cowleigh Gate Farm, Stores Cottage, Hawkhurst Cottage, Lower Vinesend and Upper Vinesend. Third, square framing, either two panels high on each level, such as at Lower Nupend and Cowleigh Gate Farm, or three panels high, such as at Upper Vinesend and Crumpton Oaks Farm[185] (*alias* Hill Farm, Storridge). Close studding (as at Upper Vinesend) is rare and a high-status feature. Smaller houses and cottages have two panels to each storey. Where the front of a cottage

179 NHLE, no. 1177144, Bullshead Cott. (accessed 3 Jan. 2024).

180 NHLE, no. 1177319, Apple Tree Cott. (accessed 27 Feb. 2024).

181 NHLE, no. 1082306, Hawkhurst Cott. (accessed 3 Jan. 2024).

182 Photographed in 1931 but now reduced to a fragment of its former size.

183 At Lower Nupend, only the front of the house was refaced.

184 For Barrow Mill, see below, Manors and Principal Estates: Netherbarrow, Beanhouse and Barrow Mills; Mills, Crafts and Industry: Corn Mills.

185 NHLE, no. 1177322, Crumpton Oaks (accessed 1 Aug. 2023).

is three panels high, as at Bullshead Cottage, it is because it is one-and-a-half storeys high. Thinner framing timbers are typically used on 18th-century cottages, such as Appletree Cottage, giving the impression that the panels are larger.

Notable houses illustrative of the built character of the parish include: Lower Nupend, Cowleigh Gate, Crumpton Oaks; Lower Vinesend and Old Upper House Farm.[186]

Lower Nupend is a large timber-framed house of 16th- and 17th-century date,[187] remodelled in the 18th century with a brick south front and a brick staircase tower, reflecting the farm's rise in status in that period.[188] A significant component that indicates a 16th-century date is that of the coffered ceiling in the ground-floor front bay of the cross-wing, where the beams have wide chamfers and form a nine-panel layout. These panels have been filled with decorative plasterwork of 17th-century date. The beams may also have been plastered and a narrow decorative beading created along the edges.

Cowleigh Gate is a timber-framed, 17th-century house, situated on high ground facing the Cowleigh road. The main range is two storeys high and two-and-a-half bays long, laid out on an approximate north–south orientation. At the northern end is a two-bay, two-storey cross-wing. A large chimney stack occupies the half-bay where the main range meets the side of the cross-wing. The building stands on a high stone plinth that has a doorway giving access to a cellar beneath the southern end bay. The main brick chimney (since lost) had triangular nibs projecting from the faces of the two square shafts. A large 19th-century addition, with a higher ridge line, has been made to the back of the house.

Crumpton Oaks (called Hill Farm in 1839)[189] is 16th- to 17th-century in date, timber-framed and two storeys high. The main range (possibly two bays) is laid out on an east–west alignment with a two-bay cross-wing at the east end. Projecting from the south side of the west bay of the main range is a two-storey, two-bay, timber-framed wing of 17th-century date. Inside this part of the building there is a moulded beam, which is, according to the RCHME inspectors, 15th-century in date, although it could be a little later. The sketch in their report shows a typical late 15th- or early 16th-century profile, similar to that found on the bressumer of Cradley Village Hall of 1531. To the west of the farmhouse and yard there are signs of pottery and area burning, possible signs of a kiln.[190]

Lower Vinesend,[191] at first sight, seems to be relatively small, which makes it seem strange that it is surrounded by a wide range of barns indicating a wealthy and successful operation in the 18th and 19th century. However, the house, when visited in 1931, was larger than the present surviving structure but in a derelict condition, as can be seen in the RCHME inspectors' photograph. The house is 17th-century and timber-framed, laid

186 The information on architectural history of the houses, unless stated otherwise, is drawn from HAS, PAM1598. The information on the architectural history of the farm buildings is contributed by Dr J.E.C. Peters, based upon his evaluations of farm buildings in the parish.

187 The name Nupend (Nupyende) is first recorded in 1533 as a messuage and customary land inhabited by Richard Hales: HAS, R13/10537.

188 NHLE, no. 1177303, The Lower Nupend (accessed 1 Aug. 2023).

189 Tithe map (1839); RCHME – Notes, 10.

190 HSM, 12161.

191 This property has also been variously known as Whitbournes (e.g. HAS, R13/10537) and Whiterns (e.g. HAS, BJ2/1).

out on a north–south axis, with a two-storey bay attached to the east side of the south bay.[192] What is now missing is the two-storey cross-wing that was at the south end of the range in 1931.[193] The agricultural buildings include a 17th-century, four-bay barn. Some of the agricultural buildings have now been converted to domestic use, including two circular hopkilns now converted into a house.

Old Upper House Farmhouse is a significant example of one of Cradley's historic timber-framed houses.[194] First recorded in 1533 as Tailors, the house probably dates from the 15th century, given that it contains at least one pair of cruck blades.[195] This suggests that the core of the building was a single-storey hall, laid out on an approximate north–south axis. The hall is likely to have had a floor inserted later, probably in the late 16th or early 17th century, when a massive three-flue chimney stack was built at the upper end of the hall range. To the south of the house, there was a large pond, which suggests that the site could have been moated.

More unusual, architecturally interesting properties include the post office, Seed Farm and The Old White House.

The earliest part of the post office is the one-and-a-half-storey range that stands aligned east to west, gable end on the road.[196] It is of late 16th- or early 17th-century date and consists of three bays raised on a stone plinth. The sloping site has allowed a cellar to be made beneath the west bay, with direct access from the street. Within the east bay, there is a massive chimney stack serving back-to-back fireplaces and a bread oven. There appear to be four flues, with diagonally set brick shafts. Extending north from the site of the middle bay is a narrow, two-bay 17th-century range of similar height to the main range and slightly later in date. It is surrounded by single-storey extensions, which, in particular form shop premises along the west side at the front of the site. Of particular interest are the decorative features on the front of the building, which are rare on the exterior of Cradley's timber-framed buildings.[197] Most significantly, there is a 'token' jetty, with a decorative bressumer with double-ovolo moulding. Under both ends of the bressumer there are also token consoles carved from the flared or jowled tops of the corner posts. The faces of the consoles have incised decoration. This work shows some links with the decorative style of late 16th-century timber-framed buildings in Ledbury.[198] It seems probable that the building may have originally formed part of a mill.[199] It may not have been built as a single three-bay house, but could have formed an upper cross-wing to a hall range that stood on the site of the present (later) north range.

192 RCHME – Notes, 13; NHLE, no. 1349688, Lower Vinesend fm ho. (accessed 1 Aug. 2023).

193 Although this was not photographed by the RCHME, their ground plan and written description provide the evidence.

194 This is a significant building that has not, as yet, been recorded by the RCHME, although it has been Grade II listed since 1952 – NHLE, no. 1082285, Upper Ho. (accessed 1 Aug. 2023).

195 Taylors was described as containing a messuage and customary land in the hands of Richard Woodiatt, HAS, R13/10537. RCHME, *An Inventory of the Historical Monuments in Herefordshire*, II, East (1932), HMSO, 61; *Woolhope Transactions* (2015), 76.

196 Above, Communications, for the history of the post office.

197 Barrow Mill has a decorated storeyed porch and Upper Vinesend has large panels of unusual diagonal bracing.

198 D. James, 'An analysis of the Historic Fabric of Late 16th and Early 17th century buildings in Ledbury, Herefordshire', unpubl. report for VCH (2007).

199 Below, Mills, Crafts and Industry.

Figure 6 *Seed Farm from the air c.2000. (Photo from the Millennium Air Survey, copyright Chris Musson and the Woolhope Naturalists' Field Club)*

Seed Farm is a stone-built house, described by the RCHME as 16th-century, but may be, in parts, earlier. The name is first recorded in the late 13th century as 'La Sudde'.[200] The main range is laid out on an east–west alignment with a cross-wing at the west end. The cross-wing on the east end is timber-framed. It is possible that the rest of the house was built with timber framing but has been remodelled and the walls replaced with stone. An indication that this may be the case is that the two gables on the west wing have timber trusses that are offset from the outer edge of the wall, suggesting that the original framed walls have been encased in stone.[201] A building originally used as a granary and for cider making forms one wing of the house; since the 1960s, it has been converted for domestic use.[202] The spring-fed moat extends around three sides of the house.[203] Seed Farm possesses the earliest surviving cowhouse and stables in Cradley (they are timber-framed and date from the late 17th or early 18th century), and two Grade II listed barns.[204]

200 Below, Manors and Principal Estates: Hanley, Handley's End, Little Hanley.

201 NHLE, no. 1082256, Seed Fm Ho. (accessed 1 Aug. 2023).

202 J.E.C. Peters, unpubl. report on the architectural history of Cradley's agricultural buildings.

203 CHC, Seed Farm Sales Particulars 2012.

204 J.E.C. Peters, unpubl. report on the architectural history of Cradley's agricultural buildings; CHC, Seed House Farm Sales Particulars 2012.

Another interesting, unusual property is The Old White House.[205] It is a substantial, timber-framed fragment of a larger house; the range is laid out on a north–south axis on a sloping site. The building probably survived because it was used for storage. The site has been visited and analysed by RCHME in 1931 and by Jim Tonkin in 1969, but neither was able to explain fully the architectural history of the building.[206] What can be said is that it has been heavily restored, and that it is a two-bay, two-storey structure, raised on a rubble-stone plinth that forms a basement. The first floor has a shallow jetty on the east side, supported by three shaped consoles under a moulded bressumer with a double-ovolo moulding. There are two gables on the east side and one on the north. The present gable on the south side (which was not there in 1931) is a modern replacement. The south wall is of brick and there is a modern extension on the west side.[207]

Today much of the parish housing is modern (post-1950), and many houses have been built on small estates particularly in West Cradley. The properties are generally detached and mostly two storeys, although there are clusters of bungalows (many with loft conversions), as on Credenleigh Street, Pixiefields, Oaklands and Huntingdon. At Buryfields there are purpose-built, terraced, two-storey flats (constructed as council housing).[208] In the 21st century, building projects have somewhat diversified this picture. The 2022 development adjacent to Buryfield, a mixture of bungalows and family houses, is almost all semi-detached,[209] and at Stony Cross recent houses are in contemporary architectural style with eco-friendly features, including one deemed of 'exceptional quality'.[210]

The oldest extant farm building in Cradley is one pre-17th-century structure at Lower Nupend, but, since it was later much altered and extended, its original use is not clear. Most surviving farm buildings in the parish date from the 19th century, although a few examples from the 17th century and a number from the 18th have survived.[211] Cradley features numerous historical barns, in both timber and brick, including threshing barns from as early as the 17th or early 18th century. These are timber-framed, walls boarded, and of three to four bays. Hayward's Barn in Ridgeway is one of the few surviving Herefordshire examples of a field barn, built to serve a detached portion of the farm or an area with awkward access from the farmstead;[212] it was converted to a mission room in 1856.[213] Since *c.*1950, a steady stream of former farm buildings have been converted

205 NHLE, no. 1307538, White Ho. (accessed 1 Aug. 2023).

206 RCHME – Notes, 44; J.W. Tonkin, 'Reports of sectional recorders, buildings, 1969', *TWNFC* (1969), 39:3 (1969), 484.

207 The earliest likely reference to The Old White House is in the period 1577–81 when a Thomas Farley of the Whytehouse was recorded: HAS, AA59/A/2, ff. 9–10v.

208 'Pixiefields', 'Oaklands', 'Huntingdon', 'Buryfields' and 'Credenleigh' on https://streetcheck.co.uk (accessed 1 Aug. 2023).

209 https://www.livingspacehousing.co.uk/project/pixiefields (accessed 1 Aug. 2023).

210 https://www.newenglishliving.co.uk/wp-content/uploads/2018/06/Brochure-New-English-Living.pdf (accessed 1 Aug. 2023). This is a so-called Paragraph 55 house.

211 This para. contributed by Dr J.E.C. Peters, based upon his architectural evaluations of farm buildings in the parish.

212 J.E.C. Peters, 'The Barns of Eastern Herefordshire', in *Essays in Honour of Jim & Muriel Tonkin* (Hereford, 2011), 123; Hunt, *Cradley*, 70, 75.

213 Hunt, *Cradley*, 70.

Figure 7 *Pixiefields, a 1970s development, in 2023. (Photo by Charles Watkins)*

into houses, flats, offices and holiday properties.[214] Some historical farm buildings have also been demolished as they became redundant and derelict; the stone farm buildings at the Red Lion inn were considered unsafe by the then owner, Allied Breweries Ltd, and demolished in 1977.[215]

214 CHC, Parish Council Minutes, I–II, examples at 18 Jan. 1983; 21 Oct. 1986; 18 Oct. 1985. Below, Mills, Crafts and Industry: Tourism and hospitality.

215 CHC, Parish Council Minutes, II, 20 Sept. 1977.

LANDOWNERSHIP

Patterns of Landownership

THE PATTERN OF LANDOWNERSHIP IN medieval Cradley was complicated. The two manors recorded in 1066, Cradley (belonging to the bishop of Hereford) and Hanley, had increased by the 13th century to at least five. The Barrow and The Hyde in the north probably originated as freeholds of Cradley manor, though neither was then under the bishop's overlordship; the north-eastern corner of the parish, including Storridge, was apparently transferred to the bishop's manor of Bosbury. A sixth manor, Cowleigh, in the south-eastern corner, was a separate lordship that extended into Worcestershire; it may have existed by the 13th century, and certainly by the 15th. There were several sub-manors; that of the Hill family existed by the 15th century and perhaps earlier, while the rectory and Behennes/Beanhouse are both recorded as manors in the 16th century. Throughout the period, the wealthier parishioners appear to have held land scattered around the parish, and many held sub-tenancies from other tenants. Around 1288, the manor may have contained *c.*4,500 a. of customary land and over 600 a. of freehold.[1]

Under the 1559 Act of Exchange, the Cradley manor was taken from the bishop of Hereford by the Crown, which soon sold it, and it then passed to a number of gentry families. In the early modern period, most of the parish's other manors (The Hyde, Little Hanley and Overbarrow) belonged to, and were rented out by, religious institutions;[2] only the rectory manor, held by the rector, still functioned as a manor by the later 19th century.

Many houses and estates, which belonged to prosperous yeomen or minor gentlemen before 1700, grew in wealth and size over the following centuries, and smaller estates formed alongside them. Important estates emerged later, including that held by Madresfield (owned by the Lygon family) during the 18th and 19th century and the Duchy of Cornwall's current Cradley estate. In 1838, the 14 major landowners all owned more than 170 a., and between them held 4,461 a. (78 per cent of the parish). Their number decreased during the century, so that by 1889 only eight landowners held more than 170 a., and the total held between them had reduced to 2,697 a.[3]

1 This figure presumes 60-a. yardlands (for discussion see Medieval Landholdings); HAS, AM33/13, rot. 21d.; TNA, SC 6/HENVIII/1511, rott. 8d., 9; HAS, AA59/A/1, p. 149.

2 St Katherine's Hospital (Ledbury); vicars choral of Hereford cathedral; and dean and chapter of Worcester cathedral, respectively.

3 Hunt, *Cradley*, 153.

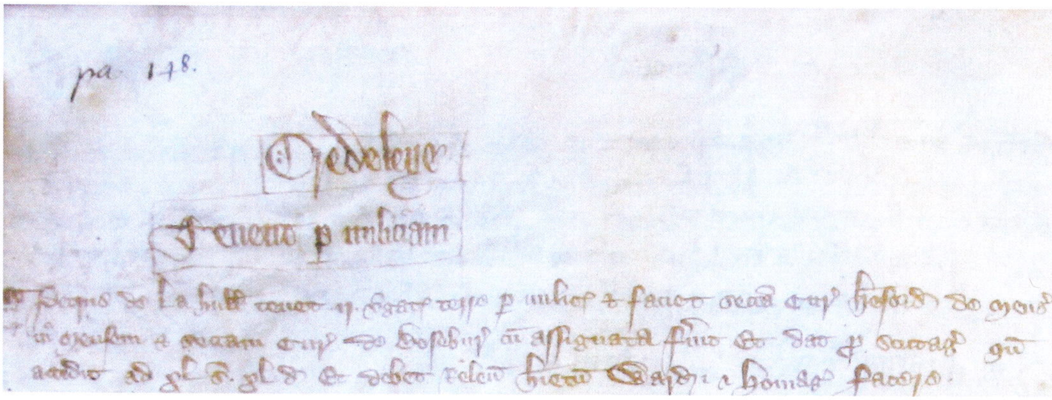

Figure 8 *Credeley. Start of the rental of Cradley manor c.1288. (HAS, AA59/A/1, p. 148)*

Manors and Principal Estates

Cradley Manor before 1562

In 1066, Cradley, valued at £10, was one of the bishop of Hereford's most valuable manors.[4] It remained in episcopal hands until 1559, when, during a vacancy, Elizabeth I used new legislation to make an unequal exchange of manors, bringing the manor into the Crown's ownership and so ending more than five centuries of episcopal control.[5] The new bishop, John Scory, did not receive compensation until 1562.[6]

Although the precise boundaries of the manor are unknown, by the late 12th century parts of the western, northern and eastern edges of the parish lay outside it. Surname evidence *c.*1288 suggests that it included Batchcombe in the north-east, and by the 16th century the Batchcombe brook formed the boundary with Storridge, part of the manor of Bosbury.[7] To the south-west, the manor was bounded by Hanley, and although the boundary between the two manors is unclear, by 1533 Cradley had expanded to include Seed Farm, formerly part of Hanley.[8] By 1533, a messuage of customary land called the Blackhouse marked part of the northern boundary with the manor of The Barrow.[9]

4 *Domesday*, 500–3. See below, Church Origins and Parochial Organisation, for reputed link to the cathedral. A 'Crydesleah' that features in an account of a Herefordshire lawsuit dating from between 1016 and 1035 recorded in the Hereford Gospels has been misidentified as Cradley by scholars including A.J. Robinson (ed.), *Anglo-Saxon Charters* (1939), H.P.R.Finberg, *Early Charters of the West Midlands* (Leicester, 1972), no. 421, and early editions of P.H. Sawyer, *Anglo-Saxon Charters* (1968) until Coplestone-Crow, *Herefordshire Place-names*, 55, identified it as a lost settlement in Brilley. The on-line edition of Sawyer (https://esawyer.lib.cam.ac.uk/about/index.html, accessed 21 Jan. 2025) has the new identification.

5 *Cal. Pat.* 1558–60, 440.

6 *Cal. Pat.* 1560–3, 285–9.

7 HAS, AA59/A/1, p. 149, TNA, C 146/3218.

8 See below, Manors and Principal Estates: Hanley/Handley's End/Little Hanley.

9 HAS, R13/10537. See Tithe Map (1839).

In 1086, the bishop held in demesne land sufficient for three ploughs, and a mill; of the five principal tenants, the priest's holding of 1½ yardlands, and the reeve's and *radman*'s of half a hide each, pre-dated 1066. The two knights held by military service one hide and 1½ yardlands respectively, but whether these were post-Conquest creations or pre-existing tenancies is unknown.[10] By the 13th century, the bishop's liberty in Cradley and Berton combined was listed as five hides.[11] In the 1260s, Cradley was one of the episcopal manors reportedly plundered by the opponents of the Savoyard Bishop Peter de Aigueblanche.[12] Around 1288, the bishop's demesne comprised *c.*96 a. arable, 5 a. pasture and 3 a. garden, but no mill is mentioned.[13] By 1404, he possessed little demesne in the manor, and an assessment during the vacancy following Bishop Trefnant's death stated that in Cradley, apart from rents and perquisites, the bishop had 'no other lands, tenements or yearly profits or issues',[14] and there is no evidence of a subsequent change.[15]

Of the five principal tenancies recorded in 1086, the priest remained a landholder throughout the medieval period, but those of the reeve and *radman* were no longer identified as such *c.*1288.[16] There is some mystery in tracing the lands held by military service. At this date, the only family clearly recorded as holding by military service was the Hills, though they are not recorded among the bishop's knight's fees in Edward I's reign.[17] A prominent local family took its name from the parish. Maurice of Cradley was a witness in the 1190s, and several bishop's knights during Edward I's reign were 'of Cradley'; Geoffrey of Cradley, among the largest landholders *c.*1288, with a yardland, mill and assarts, did not hold by military service, and his family's connection to the 13th-century knights 'of Cradley' is unclear.[18] In 1242, a claim, backed by the bishop's attorney, that the Heath family held their land by military service, was rejected, a jury declaring that it was held in socage.[19] It is possible that the hide held by a knight in 1086 was later separated from the bishop's manor and became The Hyde manor. In 1527, Bishop Booth sold to Rafe Sheldon the wardship and marriage of Walter Halcuit's heirs, including control of all the lands and tenements held of the bishop by knight service in Cradley and elsewhere.[20]

10 *Domesday*, 502.

11 It is unknown why Cradley was listed combined with Berton in this instance. It is the only recorded occasion: HAS, AA59/A/1, p. 243.

12 *Cal. Pat.* 1266–72, 373.

13 HAS, AA59/A/1, p. 152.

14 *Cal. Inq. Misc.* VII, 152. See below, Agriculture: Medieval landholdings.

15 Surviving court rolls exclude the demesne: HAS, AM33/13, rot. 21d.; a mill is possibly mentioned in 1536: TNA, SC 6/HENVIII/1511, rott. 8d., 9, 16d.

16 HAS, AA59/A/1, pp. 149–53; for the reeve, see below, Manorial Government.

17 See below, Manors and Principal Estates: The Hill estate.

18 In 1283, Roger de Cradley was described as a knight, while Robert and Walter were included on a list of the bp of Hereford's knight's fees: HAS, AA59/A/1, p. 148; W.W. Capes (ed.), *Charters and Records of Hereford Cathedral* (Hereford, 1908), 152–3; HAS, AL19/2, f. 22v.

19 *Cur. Reg.* 16, 1767.

20 Little else is known of Walter: *Reg. Bothe*, 193. A Walter of Halcuit is also recorded in the 1533 rental holding land in the manor from the heirs of Cowleigh, HAS, R13/10537.

The manor had been leased out by 1379, when John Hill was recorded as the farmer.[21] In the period 1538–44, John Myntrigge was described as holding the manor in farm.[22]

Cradley Manor after 1562

Surviving estreats between 1561 and 1596 name only the seneschals, not the manorial lords.[23] By 1606, and probably much earlier, the manor seems to have been divided into two.

One part descended from Robert Gower (d. 1599) to his son John (d. 1625), and John's wife Anne, on whom it had been settled in 1586–7. In 1629, it was settled on John's son Robert and Robert's intended wife Frances Skinner,[24] and later sequestrated, for Robert's recusancy only (apparently, he did not bear arms against Parliament). Although Abel Gower, lessee of half the manor, compounded, there is no record that Robert compounded for his share, and no further reference has been found to any Gowers as manorial lords.[25]

By 1605/6, Rowland Berkeley also held part of Cradley manor,[26] which, by 1619, had passed to William Berkeley.[27] William transferred (probably by sale) his holding in 1650 to Richard Hopton, warranting against any claim by relatives and descendants.[28] Later, in 1650, the property passed to James Hopton (perhaps related to the gentry family of Canon Frome),[29] who held it until at least 1658;[30] his widow was the owner in 1670, when she held a court,[31] and in 1672.[32]

By 1685, John Cotton (d. *c.*1690) was lord of the manor,[33] by then undivided, and in 1690 Alethea Cotton held manorial court, presumably as his widow, and that year also bore their son Robert.[34] Alethea and Robert held the manor jointly until Alethea's death *c.*1702; trustees then controlled the manor until Robert came of age in 1711. Robert remained lord until his death in 1761 or 1762,[35] whereupon the Revd Walter Cotton (d. *c.*1779) succeeded, and then Walter's brother Michael;[36] on his death it was divided between four sisters, a brother-in-law (Dr William Fell)[37] and a nephew, John Arden (d. 1803).[38]

21 *Poll Taxes of 1377–81*, ed. Fenwick, 370.
22 TNA, C 1/1031/53–5.
23 TNA, SC 2/176/54.
24 TNA, C 142/453/71. *VCH Worcs.* III, 179–91.
25 M.A.E. Green (ed.), *Calendar of the Proceeding for the Cttee for Compounding* (1891), 1781, 1809.
26 TNA, CP 25/2/300/2JAS.
27 HAS, W9/1.
28 TNA, CP 25/2/556/1650.
29 http://bromyardhistorysociety.org.uk/newsletter-five (accessed 17 Nov. 2022).
30 HAS, AH73/69. WAAS 889:749 BA8782/64:14.
31 HAS, R13/10576.
32 TNA, CP 25/2/662/24CHASII.
33 HAS, R13/10588; HAS, W9/1. The Cotton family may have purchased or inherited the Lordship in 1682: HAS, E2/1; see D. Stuart, *Manorial Records* (Chichester, 1992), 43.
34 *Alumni Oxon.*, I, 334; HAS, BJ2/1.
35 HAS, W9/1; HAS, W9/13; HAS, BJ2/1; TNA, PROB 11/883/230.
36 TNA, PROB 11/1151/74.
37 'William Fell' in https://venn.lib.cam.ac.uk (accessed 17 Nov. 2022).
38 HAS, BJ2/1; HAS, BJ43/29/2; TNA, PROB 11/883/230; TNA, PROB 11/1151/74; TNA, PROB 11/1389/318.

The manor was sold in 1806 to Thomas Price and William Handy of Worcester,[39] who sold it in 1807 to Samuel (d. *c.*1842) and William (d. 1844) Wall of Worcester.[40] Samuel's share passed to his son, also Samuel, and then his son, John Binns Wall (d. *c.*1845).[41] William's share was inherited by the Revd William Ellis Wall, and after John Binns Wall's death, trustees functioned as acting lords alongside Willam Ellis Wall.[42]

In 1861, the manor was sold to John Jones of Worcester,[43] and immediately resold to James Cuddon for £6,850.[44] In 1863, Cuddon sold it to Richard Yapp of Halesend,[45] with which property the lordship was thenceforth associated.[46] Richard Yapp (d. 1873) left the manor to two devisees in trust for his son George Yapp Bailey;[47] these thus became acting lords,[48] and continued until at least 1902.[49] In 1931, Samuel Herbert Enderby of Halesend was lord;[50] he died in 1956,[51] and in 1959 Bernard A. Higgins of Halesend held the lordship,[52] which presumably remained in his family until 2003, when the Halesend estate and attached lordship were sold.[53] Ronald Cottam purchased Halesend and probably also the lordship; he sold Halesend *c.*2010.[54]

There is no documentary evidence that the medieval bishops possessed a hall or other residence on the manor, presumably because their manor house at Bosbury was nearby. Visits to Cradley, however, are recorded.[55] The original Cradley Hall was a 'handsome' Elizabethan house.[56] Although nominally the manor house, from at least the 18th century the Cradley manorial lords rarely resided there.[57] In 1805, the year before the lordship was sold, the site of Cradley manor was put up for auction, comprising Cradley Hall and five farms (Seed, Batchcombe, Whitmonds, Whippiatts and Crumpal Hall).[58]

39 HAS, AH73/38.
40 HAS, AH73/38; HAS, AH73/69; HAS, W9/7; HAS, W9/31; HAS, W9/33; HAS, W9/1.
41 HAS, AH73/69; WAAS, 970.5:99 BA892 VI [Second Series I], 324–34.
42 HAS, AH73/69; WAAS, 970.5:99 BA892 VI [Second Series I], 324–34. HAS, S82/31; HAS, AC91/1; HAS, BJ43/29/28.
43 HAS, AH73/38; WAAS, 970.5:99 BA892 VI [Second Series I], 324–34.
44 HAS, AH73/69.
45 TNA, MAF 20/52/788; HAS, AH73/69; *Slater's Dir.* (1859), 34.
46 See below, Other Estates.
47 TNA, MAF 20/52/788.
48 HAS, BJ2/1.
49 *Jakeman & Carver's Dir.* (1902), 178.
50 HAS, BJ2/1.
51 *Kelly's Handbook* (1977 edn), 468.
52 HAS, BJ2/1.
53 https://www.worcesternews.co.uk/news/7657416.chance-to-be-lord-of-the-manor (accessed 17 Nov. 2022).
54 Inf. from local resident. The family is variously spelled Cottom and Cottam in documentary evidence.
55 Swinfield's household expenses included wine transported from Bosbury, and hay and oats provided by Cradley's rector for 35 horses which had conveyed Swinfield and his household. The roll also records clothes being washed there once: *Expenses of Swinfield*, 74, 142; John Trillek held a visitation of the parish in 1346: *Reg. Trillek* I, 30.
56 HAS, AH73/38.
57 HAS, AH73/25; HAS, Q/REL/6/9/1–45; WAAS, 009.1 BA2602/34.
58 HAS, BJ2/1.

In 1863, when Richard Yapp bought the lordship and effectively transferred the seat to Halesend,[59] Cradley Hall degenerated into a farmhouse,[60] and was demolished *c.*1889.[61] A replacement farmhouse had been built by 1909, when described as a homestead, and later as a Victorian house.[62] It remained as Cradley Hall house in 1991, at the heart of its 1,929-a. estate, but was then sold to the Mercantile and General Reinsurance Company and later passed to the Duchy of Cornwall.[63]

The Hill Estate

This appears to have originated as one of the tenancies by knight service held from the bishop in 1086.[64] Around 1288, Peter of the Hill of Cradley held two yardlands of freehold land through knight service from the bishop of Hereford,[65] and thenceforth the Hills seem to have remained the bishop's most significant tenants and prominent figures in Cradley society. Peter and his successor Adam regularly served as charter witnesses for the Barrow family.[66] Adam was succeeded by another Peter who in 1333 was granted by Edward III life exemption from service on juries, assizes or recognisances.[67] A John Hill, mentioned in 1354, was a sub-collector for the 1377 poll tax in Cradley, and was listed in 1379 as the farmer of the manor.[68] His son Thomas, and wife Alice, appear in 1393, but Thomas had apparently been succeeded by his son John by 1401.[69] The mention of a court belonging to the Hills in the early 15th century, possibly at Stifford, suggests manorial status by that date.[70] John's son Thomas was active in 1458 and by 1475 both John Hill and Thomas Hill held land in the parish, although their relationship to each other is unclear.[71] Another John Hill appears in the 1523 subsidy, assessed at £4 for goods. By 1534, Richard Hill was one of the richest men in the parish and was described as a gentleman in 1546.[72] The family still held by knight service in 1579.[73]

The core of the Hill family lands appears to have been centred on Stifford, stretching southwards towards Lumbridge hill and westwards to the border of Buryfield and Churchfield.[74] The eastward extent is unclear. Several medieval fishponds in the vicinity

59 TNA, MAF 20/52/788.
60 HAS, AH73/38.
61 HAS, AH73/38.
62 HAS, M5/6A/10; HAS, CO7/3.
63 HAS, CO7/3; below, Other Estates: Duchy of Cornwall.
64 Above, Cradley manor before 1562.
65 HAS, AA59/A/1, p. 148; also recorded in 1304, HAS, AL19/2 f. 145. Earlier a Ralph 'de Hulla' witnessed a charter of bp Giles de Braose to Little Malvern priory in the early 13th century: W. Dugdale, *Monasticon Anglicanum* 4 (1846), 449.
66 WCM, B230, B232, B231, B233, B234, B235A, B235B.
67 This was before the Scottish campaign resulting in the battle of Halidon Hill, and so Peter was probably a soldier: *Cal. Pat.* 1330–34, 428; WCM, B238A; TNA, C 146/3218.
68 *Poll Taxes of 1377–81*, ed. Fenwick, 358, 366, 370.
69 HAS, R13/10530, R13/10531.
70 HAS, R13/10531.
71 HAS, R13/10534, R13/10535.
72 *Herefs. Taxes*, 24R3, 36R19, 45bR6, 46R14, 45R26; HAS, 40/1/7, will of Richard Taylor, 1546.
73 HAS, AA59/A/2, f. 209v.
74 HAS, R13/10531; C96/1; HD2/1/30; P66/1–5.

of Stifford were probably part of the family's lands.[75] The family must have held or acquired other land in the parish besides their two yardlands and 6 a. of assart *c.*1288.[76] In 1346, William of Cowleigh held La Buriend from the gift and feoffment of Peter of the Hill,[77] and in 1393 the rector of Cradley was holding some land from Thomas Hill.[78] In 1411–12, Thomas's son John, and Alice his wife, granted for their lifetimes three messuages, a mill, 135 a. of land and 16 a. of meadow to William Wallewayn and his wife Ellen, to hold of the chief lords for ever for 40*s.* annual rent.[79] In 1475, more land was granted away by John Hill and his wife Joanna, and this passed to Thomas Hill and his wife Agnes.[80]

What was probably the family's principal residence was described in 1393 as including a hall (*aula*) with, between it and the kitchen (*coquina*), rooms (*camera*) and a chapel (*capella*).[81] By 1667, their primary residence was Hill House at Stifford's Bridge.[82] This building survives today, being a 17th-century, timber-framed house, with extensive 18th- and 19th-century additions (particularly to the north) which hide much of the earlier structure.[83] This appears to be in the same general vicinity as, and perhaps on the site of, the earlier medieval hall.[84]

Leonard Hill the elder lived at the Hill House in 1667.[85] The property passed down through the Hill family[86] until the death of Susannah Caldwell (née Hill) in 1808, whose heir was her son Tracey Caldwell.[87] It then passed down through the Caldwell family[88] until inherited in 1856 by Joseph Shapland and his wife Susannah (née Hales), daughter of Frances Hales (née Caldwell).[89] The property, 220 a. in 1909–10,[90] continued in the Shapland family until the Hill House estate was sold at auction by Mr B.C. Hood Shapland in 1929.[91]

In the 19th century, a two-storey extension with two gables was made to the north end of the range; this was demolished at some point after 1930. The southern range has also been reduced in length. There are extensive outbuildings, some of which were

75 HER 3862, SO 7387 4814. They are probably those described *c.*1330 as near Stifford mill, Adam de Hulle's meadow and including a floodgate: HAS, P66/5.

76 HAS, AA59/A/1, p. 149; for lands held outside Cradley, including at Colwall, see TNA, CP 25/1/83/53, 2; CP 25/1/83/48, 14; and HAS, P66/4.

77 TNA, C 146/9784.

78 HAS, C96/1.

79 TNA, CP 25/1/83/52, 43.

80 HAS, R13/10534; R13/10535. A Thomas died in 1480, but his widow was called Elizabeth: *Cal. of Probate and Administration*, 79/434.

81 Because of damage, this charter cannot certainly be identified with a Hill residence, though the context strongly suggests it: HAS, C96/1; R13/10537.

82 TNA, PROB 11/327/309.

83 NHLE, no. 1082282, Hill Ho. (accessed 1 Aug. 2023).

84 HAS, C96/1.

85 TNA, PROB 11/327/309.

86 HAS, AH73/64; HAS, AH73/25.

87 HAS, BJ2/1.

88 HAS, S82/12; HAS, BJ2/1.

89 HAS, BJ2/1.

90 HAS, AG9/5.

91 *Kelly's Dir.* (1905 edn); Edwards, *Cradley*, 54; HAS, M5/6A/3. No return was made for Hill House in the 1941 National Farm Survey.

THE MANORS OF CRADLEY PARISH (HISTORICAL PARISH BOUNDARIES): Historical manorial boundaries where known and other landmarks once recorded within the bounds of the manors of Cowleigh, The Barrow, Hanley/Little Hanley, The Hill family sub-manor, Behennes/Beanhouse, Vinesend and Madresfield, c.1066 to c.1800.

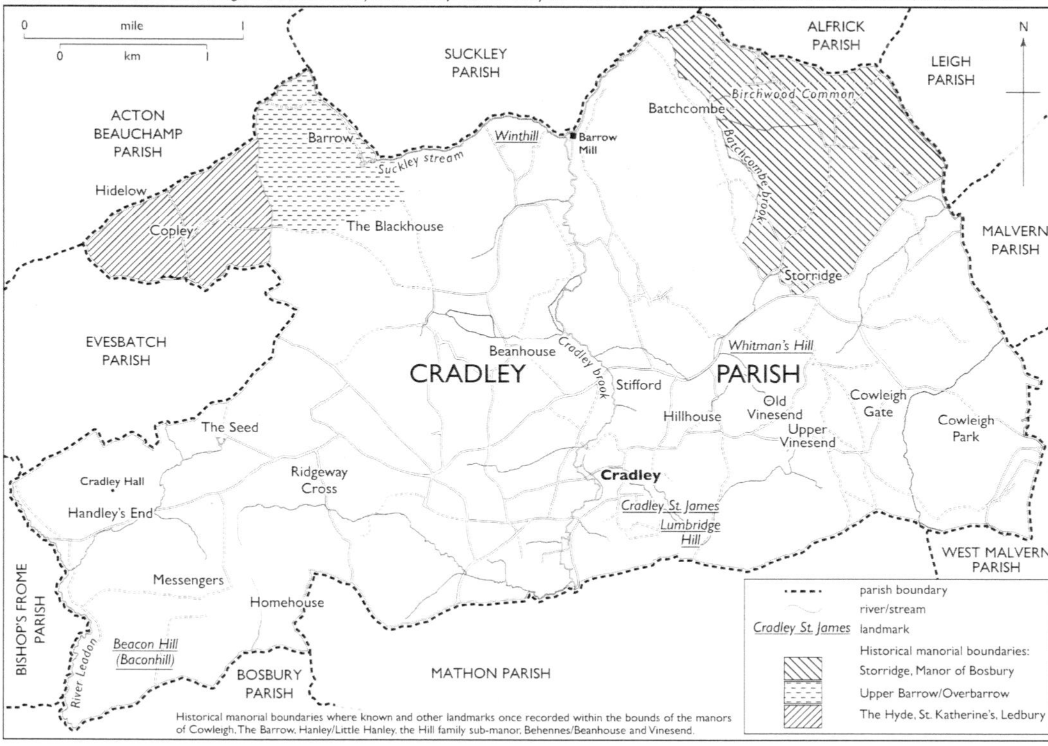

Map 4 *The manors of Cradley parish (historical parish boundaries).*

domestic accommodation for servants. In the 1930s, the framing was hidden behind stucco, but is now exposed. The size of the house and the extensive range of outbuildings demonstrate that this was a wealthy farm, while the reduction in the size of the house in the 20th century reflects national trends in terms of changes in wealth and status and the reduction in need for servant accommodation.[92]

Rectory Manor

Cradley rectory manor probably derived from the 1½ yardlands held by the priest in 1086.[93] The 1589 terrier mentions that the rector of Cradley had the right to hold courts baron. A dovecote attached to the rectory, also noted in 1589, also suggests that the rector then had the status of manorial lord, since until *c.*1600 this was a prerequisite for owning doves.[94] The rector Edmund Skinner held a court baron in September 1624.[95] The rectory continued to operate as a manor until at least 1868–9, since at this time it enfranchised some of its lands.[96]

92 Duncan James is the primary contributor to this paragraph. See HAS, PAM1598.

93 Above, Manors and Principal Estates: Cradley manor before 1562.

94 HAS, HD2/1/30; https://www.buildinghistory.org/buildings/dovecotes.shtml (accessed 1 Aug. 2023).

95 HAS, W9/1.

96 TNA, MAF 9/112/48–9; TNA, MAF 20/52.

Hyde Manor, St Katherine's Hospital, Ledbury

The Cradley landholdings of St Katherine's Hospital, Ledbury, equated essentially to the manor of The Hyde (*alias* The Hythe or Hidelow). The name suggests that it originated as a hide of land held from the bishop by a knight in 1086.[97] By the early 13th century, the vill of Hyde belonged to John of Stanford, who probably before 1231 granted the rents from it to Bishop Hugh Foliot 'or to whomsoever he assigns it' as a debt repayment. Foliot used this towards the foundation of St Katherine's Hospital, and John made a subsequent grant between 1237 and 1253 of a half-yardland, dirȩctly to the 'hospital of Ledbury' for the salvation of John and his wife's souls.[98]

Originally the rents were for £1 12*s.* 6*d.* from four main tenancies equating to approximately 160 a., and largely covered the area of the subsequent Hidelow and Copley farms.[99] In 1281, the manor court recorded The Hyde as including seven messuages, three yardlands and 13 a. of land as well as a barn.[100] In 1316, the hospital received £1 18*s.* 6*d.* in rents from The Hyde,[101] and by the 1330s it received rents from five tenants.[102] The area was sometimes referred to as Cradleyshyde.[103]

Hyde manor continued to be rented out after 1550, though after *c.*1700 Copley farm was sometimes excepted from the lordship rent and leased separately. In 1820, when St Katherine's mortgaged the property along with many of their other landholdings, Hidelow farm was 199 a. and Copley farm 55 a.[104] By 1862, the properties leased were being called Hidelow farm or estate, and Copley farm, rather than the lordship of Hyde. In the later 1880s, the former property had shrunk to 122¾ a., and the latter property was 56½ a.[105] In 1941, Hidelow belonged to W.J. Griffiths, and Copley to M. Matthews.[106]

The Barrow and Successors

The medieval manor of The Barrow was located along the northern edge of the parish, and may derive its name from a possible prehistoric barrow within its bounds.[107] The manor's origin is unclear; it is not recorded in 1086, but existed by the late 12th century or earlier.[108] Most of the manor occupied the valley of the Suckley stream which formed its northern boundary with the parish of Suckley (Worcs.). A 1339 inquisition post mortem classified the manor as Herefordshire but referred to it as Barrow by

97 Above, Manors and Principal Estates: Cradley manor before 1562.
98 HCA, 7018/1/3, ff. 156–7; Hillaby, *St Katherine's*, 32–3.
99 HCA, 7017/1/3, ff. 155–6; Hillaby, *St Katherine's*, 32.
100 HCA, 7018/2, f. 77.
101 Hillaby, *St Katherine's*, 37.
102 HCA, 7018/2, f. 82.
103 HCA, 3295; TNA, CP 25/1/82/33, 132.
104 HAS, AS12/3.
105 HCA, 6437/II/1.
106 TNA, MAF 32/6/15.
107 Above, Settlement before 1000; HER, 53244, SO 71456 49895; Coplestone-Crow suggests the OE word *bearu* (grove) as the origin, but does not appear to be aware of the existence of the barrow at the site: Coplestone-Crow, *Herefordshire Place-names*, 72.
108 *Cur. Reg.* 17, 697.

Worcestershire.[109] On the west it was bordered by The Hyde and stretched as far east as Winthill and probably Cradley brook. The less clearly defined southern boundary must have ended north of 'the Blackhouse' (shown on the 1839 tithe map), since that was in the bishop's manor in 1533.[110] By *c.*1300, the manor comprised an uncertain number of crofts and messuages, and at least one mill.[111]

The overlordship of the manor is first mentioned in 1329, when the Barrow family held the manor from Robert of Staunton (Worcs. later Glos.). Robert quitclaimed most of his rights to John of Stanford, including the render of the issues of the manor, 46*s.*[112] In 1338, Sir Giles de Badlesmere held half a knight's fee at 'Barrow by Worcester' held by John of Stanford. When the Badlesmere family first became connected with Barrow is unknown, but it was not among Giles's father's possessions when he was executed for treason in 1322. Nor is it clear whether the half knight's fee represents the entirety of the manor.[113] Giles died childless in 1338, and the half knight's fee, along with that of Upcote, became part of the dower of his wife, Elizabeth Montagu, daughter of the earl of Salisbury and later wife of Hugh le Despenser (d. 1349). When Elizabeth died in 1359, she had no recorded lands in Herefordshire,[114] suggesting that elements of the dower had expired or reverted on her remarriage. If so, the half knight's fee probably passed to one of Giles's sisters, though this is not recorded.[115] The overlordship thereafter becomes obscure, but by 1515–16 the manor, or a half-share of it, was in the hands of the prior and convent of Worcester.[116]

The Barrow family held the manor from 1198 or earlier.[117] By 1242 it had descended from Robert of the Barrow to another Robert of the Barrow, one of whose sons, John, succeeded to the lordship after *c.*1275. John son of John was lord of Barrow by 1329. Also lord of Stanford, he was referred to variously as John of the Barrow, lord Stanford and John of Stanford.[118] How he became lord of Stanford is unclear, though the neighbouring Stanford family held The Hyde before 1231.[119] Charters of the Barrows and Stanfords suggest that they maintained active links with other prominent Cradley families, since the Hills and the Cowleighs appeared regularly as witnesses.[120]

The Barrow seems to have been divided before 1388.

109 *Cal. Inq. p.m.* VIII, 149–50.
110 See Map 4 above; Tithe Map (1839); HAS, R13/10537.
111 WCM, B231, B238A, B239, B241, B242, B243B.
112 WCM, B237; 'Parishes: Staunton', *VCH Worcs.* IV, 197–202.
113 *Cal. Inq. p.m.* VIII, 149–50.
114 *Cal. Inq. p.m.* VIII, 149–50; *Cal. Inq. p.m.* X, 414–20. See also *Cal. Inq. p.m.* IX, 328–32.
115 Barrow is not subsequently mentioned in the possessions of any of the sisters.
116 Below, Manors and Principal Estates: Overbarrow.
117 *Cur. Reg.* 17, 697.
118 Which Stanford his title referred to, and whether acquired through marriage or inheritance, are unknown; WCM, B235A, B237, B238A, B238B, B239. HAS, P66/5 has been dated *c.*1330, but John of Stanford as a witness calls that into question.
119 Above, Manors and Principal Estates: Hyde manor, St Katherine's Hospital, Ledbury.
120 Below, Manors and Principal Estates: Cowleigh; WCM, B238A, also HAS, P66/5.

Overbarrow

A half-share, comprising the western part of the manor in Cradley, bounded to the east by The Hyde and including the manor house, was in 1388 held by Roger Parker, and then passed in turn to Roger's daughter and sole heir Agnes Werthur.[121] In 1425, Agnes confirmed a grant of the half-share to four clerks, probably as part of a settlement.[122] In 1434, her son Robert Werthur, gentleman, quitclaimed the half-share, as well as lands in Cradley, to Roger Blount, son and heir of James Blount.[123] In 1491, the manor was referred to as 'Baruwe Court' also called 'Overbarew',[124] and by 1515–16, when it belonged to the prior and convent of Worcester, it was Overbarrow. After the priory's dissolution in 1540, Henry VIII granted the manor to the new dean and chapter in 1542.[125] In 1649, Overbarrow, along with all dean and chapter lands, was sold,[126] but the buyer is unknown, and in 1660 it reverted to the cathedral.[127] It continued to be held by the dean and chapter of Worcester cathedral and rented out until at least 1845.[128]

John Pichard of Suckley held the manor in farm by 1515–16,[129] and in his will in 1521 assigned it to his eldest son, Richard, in return for Richard paying his younger brother John £6 13*s.* 4*d.* when his apprenticeship in London ended. Richard may have converted this money into land, as a manorial court in 1546 recorded on Richard's oath that John held a 9-a. freehold in Tickley in Cradley, land formerly their father's.[130]

From the 18th century, the house and land of Overbarrow were sometimes called Upper (or the) Barrow, Berrow or Burrow. Various occupants of the house and estate are recorded during the 19th century,[131] but until 1909–10, when it comprised 200 a. and was valued at £3,800,[132] its owners are unknown; it was then owned by S.A. Featherstone (of Leigh, Worcs.), but rented out. Further occupants are recorded during the first half of the 20th century, but whether tenants or owners is unclear.[133]

The existing early 17th-century house (now The Old White House) at The Barrow is of two storeys, with an attic and cellar, and is unusual in having no trace of an original stair. The building was probably once linked to the smaller house to the south-west (which is timber-framed, later encased in stone).[134] The large detached house seems to

121 WCM, B234A.
122 WCM, B244.
123 WCM, B241–2 and B234A.
124 WCM, B609.
125 WCM, E182, E101; Overbarrow was the only Herefordshire land included in the grant, B1605B; *L&P Hen. VIII*, 1542, 31.
126 T. Cave and R.A. Wilson (eds), *The Parliamentary Survey of the Lands and Possessions of the Dean and Chapter of Worcester Made in or about the Year 1649* (1924), 111–12.
127 H.J. Habakkuk, 'Landowners and the Civil War', *Econ. Hist. Rev.*, 18:1 (1965), 130–51, passim.
128 WAAS, 009.1 BA2602/34. Land tax and tithe documents appearing to show long-term tenants (e.g. the Ballards) as owning the property are almost certainly incorrect.
129 WCM, E182.
130 Probably the Tickley recorded in 1776 and on the 1839 tithe map; *The Picards or Pychards of Stradewy (now Tretower) Castle and Scethrog, Brecknockshire* (1878), 141; WCM, E182 and E101.
131 *Cassey's Dir.* (1858); *Slater's Dir.* (1859); HAS, N37/42.
132 HAS, AG9/5.
133 Edwards, *Cradley*, 34, 56. *Kelly's Dir.* (1917, 1922 edns). No return was made for Upper Barrow in the 1941 National Farm Survey.
134 Duncan James is the primary author of this section. HER, 35313; RCHME, 44.

have had a hall and parlour on the ground floor, and two chambers at both first-floor and attic levels.[135] Unusually, it had clasped purlins at collar and upper-collar levels (later partially altered), representing a late use of a type of roof rarely found in the county even in the late medieval period.[136] From at least the 12th to the 14th century, the manor possessed a chapel, though no trace has been found of it.[137]

Netherbarrow, Beanhouse and Barrow Mills

The eastern half of the divided Barrow manor is not recorded until 1521, when John Pichard of Suckley assigned the lease of the farm of Netherbarrow to his daughter Lucy.[138] Although she may have been the leaseholder, in his will the lands John held in the lordship of Cradley were rearranged to form 'the manor of the lordship of Behennes', which was to go to his heir, Richard Pichard. A fulling mill and a corn mill in Barrow, however, which stood within the new lordship, were made into an estate for another son, Thomas Pichard.[139] Whether Netherbarrow then included Barrow mills or belonged to another estate is unknown, but 'Nether Mill' depicted on Isaac Taylor's 1754 map suggests a connection. In any case, the eastern half of The Barrow manor seems, at least partially, to have been absorbed into the new manor of Behennes.[140] In 1533, the land was referred to as 'Bennyas' and held as freehold from the bishop by Richard Pichard for 20*s.* 6*d.*,[141] and in 1575 Richard Pichard made his will, naming his son William Pichard as his heir.[142]

The Revd Edmund Skinner (rector of Cradley) owned the property by 1671,[143] and his will describes it as only a messuage or tenement. His grandson Edmund Hurden inherited in 1678,[144] and the house perhaps then passed into the Hales family, as in 1736 Mr Hales was one of the two residents,[145] and in 1772 George Hales resided there.[146] Widow Hales owned the Beanhouse by 1798 and paid £4 3*s.* 6*d.* land tax, suggesting that it was a sizeable property.[147] It continued in the Hales family until 1856,[148] when Frances Caldwell Hales died intestate, and it passed to Frances Caldwell Pyne, her customary heiress.[149] Before 1871, the estate belonged to John Holmes, as in that year Charles Purser inherited Beanhouse from him and it became the centre of Purser's Beanhouse estate.[150] In the later

135 J.W. Tonkin, 'Buildings, 1969', *TWNFC* 39 (1967–9), 484.
136 HER, 35313.
137 Below, Religious History; J. Barrow (ed.), *English Episcopal Acta 35: Hereford 1234–1275*, Appendix 1, vi and xvi; WAM, B240.
138 *The Picards*, 141.
139 *The Picards*, 141.
140 Interchangeably spelled Beanhouse and Bean House in later documents.
141 HAS, R13/10537.
142 Richard had 11 children, of which 8 were boys: *Calendar of Probate and Administration Acts 1407–1550*, 577/10.
143 Below, Religious History.
144 Appendices, Sample 2, will 89.
145 HAS, AH73/25.
146 HAS, N37/33; HAS, S82/10; HAS, AH73/69.
147 CHC, Copy of Land Tax 1798.
148 For the descent through the Hales family: HAS, N37/33; HAS, S82/10; HAS, AH73/69; HAS, Q/REL/6/9/1–45; HAS, N37/29; HAS, BJ2/1, IV-96/9.
149 HAS, BJ2/1, IV-144/7, 157, 160/1.
150 HAS, M5/6A/4.

1880s, Beanhouse farm was 101¾ acres.[151] Purser died in 1917,[152] and part of Beanhouse and its estate was sold in 1917.[153] In 1929, Maxwell James lived at the Beanhouse,[154] but the estate, 222 a., was sold at auction in 1931.[155] In 1937, A.M. James was living there. By 1941, Beanhouse farm was greatly diminished, recorded with only 31 a. of agricultural land;[156] it then belonged to H.F. Gibbs.[157] In 1973, Col. R. Harrison owned the property.[158] Beanhouse farmhouse is an early 19th-century, painted-brick, three-storey building.[159]

If Beanhouse was one important part of Behennes manor, Barrow mills[160] (once part of Barrow manor) was possibly another. The mills remained in the Pichard family until at least the mid 1540s.[161] It seems then to have belonged to a branch[162] of the Long family between at least 1682 and 1736.[163] In 1798, £2 9*s.* land tax was charged on the property, suggesting it was quite a small estate.[164] By 1854, it belonged to Richard Yapp the elder, lord of Halesend manor;[165] after his death, the estate was divided, a portion being sold to repay the deceased's debts.[166] The remainder was sold at auction in 1919.[167] In 1941, there were two farms at Barrow mills (of 65½ a. and 40 a.), both belonging to R.W. Hickman.[168]

Barrow Mill farmhouse is a 17th-century Grade II* listed building.[169] Although relatively small, it retains decorative features and the number of chimney stacks indicates a house formerly of higher status. It is a three-bay, two-storey, timber-framed range, laid out on a north–south axis, with a two-bay cross-wing at the south end coeval with the main range, and an extension at the back of the bay at the north end. A storeyed porch, with shaped consoles under a moulded bressummer and with turned, mirror balusters in the sides, marks out the principal lobby-entry access. To the rear is a tower housing an open-well 17th-century staircase, with richly moulded and pierced balusters and a moulded handrail. The newel posts are square with strapwork designs on the sides and moulded finials and pendants. The house stands on a building platform cut into the hill at a higher level than the Cradley brook.[170]

151 HCA, 6437/II/1.
152 HAS, N37/23; HAS, N37/42; HAS, N37/13; HAS, AG9/5; Edwards, *Cradley*, 38.
153 HAS, M5/6A/4.
154 Edwards, *Cradley*, 56
155 HAS, M5/6A/4.
156 TNA, MAF 32/6/15.
157 TNA, MAF 32/6/15.
158 HAS, BW15/3/3.
159 NHLE, no. 1307498, Beanhouse fm ho. (accessed 1 Aug. 2023).
160 Also spelled Barrowmills in some documents.
161 After Thomas Pichard died *c.*1540, the mills passed to his son John the younger, who then sold it to his uncle John Pichard the elder, younger brother of Richard and Thomas: TNA, C 1/866/83.
162 R. Long's will of 1698 makes it clear that this was *not* the same person as Richard Long of Halesend, but rather a kinsman: HAS, 133/2/3, will of Richard Long of Barrowmill, 1700.
163 HAS, N37/60; HAS, BM81/1/19; HAS, AH73/25.
164 CHC, Copy of Land Tax 1798.
165 Below, Halesend; *Slater's Dir.* (1859).
166 Order of 28 Feb. 1876 in the cases Yapp v Williams and Lechmere v Williams: HAS, BJ43/29/43; HAS, AG9/5; HAS, N37/42.
167 HAS, M5/6A/5.
168 TNA, MAF 32/6/15.
169 Above, The Built Character. This paragraph was contributed by D. James.
170 NHLE, no. 1082296, Barrow Mill (accessed 1 Aug. 2023).

Storridge, Manor of Bosbury

For an unknown reason, Storridge, the north-east corner of Cradley parish, formed part of the bishop of Hereford's Bosbury manor.[171] It seems to have already had a distinct identity from Cradley *c.*1200, when both were mentioned in a description of Herefordshire borders,[172] and by *c.*1288, Storridge's tenants were included in the Bosbury manor rental.[173] By the late 16th century, Storridge referred to the Bosbury lands in Cradley. The Cradley to Worcester 'Common Way' formed the southern boundary of the manor, the west was marked by the Batchcombe brook, which ran to the northern edge of the parish, and the east and north by the parish boundaries of Leigh and Suckley.[174] Rentals suggest that approximately five yardlands belonged to Storridge, of which two yardlands and 12 a. were freehold and the rest customary.[175]

One freehold yardland was held of the bishop by knight service, in return for homage, wardship, heriot, relief and marriage. It was held *c.*1288 by Richard son of Mariot, and by Richard ap Powell (Rhisiart ap Hywel) and then his widow Alice in the late 16th century.[176]

In the 19th century, the manor of Bosbury, Colwall and Coddington held one customary messuage called Storridge, and many other parcels of pasture, orchard, arable land, hopyards, coppices and woods in or near Storridge; together these comprised the Storridge Estate. In 1815, the estate was 366 a., 25 a. of which were in Alfrick (Worcs.), and the rest in Cradley.[177] By 1833, it was rented to Mary Little; in 1856, the bishop enfranchised and sold it for £1,029 to her and her son Thomas Henry Little.[178]

Hanley/Handley's End/Little Hanley[179]

Hanley, in the south-western corner of the parish, was apparently defined by the Leadon on the west, while to the north it originally encompassed the Steens brook valley, with Evesbatch forming its northern border. Hanley embraced part of Beacon Hill, with Bosbury manor marking its southern border, but the eastward extent is unknown. In the 14th century, it encompassed Seed Farm to the north-east, and may have extended as far as Ridgeway.[180] Homeland, the later Home House, was part of Cradley manor by the 14th century and marked part of Hanley's south-eastern boundary.[181]

By 1066, Hanley comprised three separate manors, held by Leofing, Godwin and Alfward, who were described as able to 'go where they would'. By 1086, it had been combined into a single manor held by Adelelm from Drogo Fitzpons. It comprised

171 *VCH Herefs. Bosbury*, 1, 22–3; *Expenses of Swinfield*, 29.
172 *Cal. Inq. Misc.* I, 146.
173 *Cal. Inq. Misc.* I, 444.
174 HAS, AA59/A/2, f. 55v.
175 HAS, AA59/A/2, ff. 9v., 10, 21v., 25.
176 HAS, AA59/A/2, f. 21v.; AA59/A/1, p. 153.
177 WAAS, S705:27 BA385/1(vii).
178 HAS, C65/10; cf. HAS, BJ43/25/13; also HAS, AA63 (25 Oct. 1833).
179 Not to be confused with the messuage 'Hanleys' at Halesend.
180 TNA, C 146/9769; C 146/9686; C 1/831/62; Tithe Map (1839). Several field names just east of Seed Farm in 1839 include 'cannons' and may denote that they were once part of the manor when it was later in the ownership of the vicars choral of Hereford.
181 TNA, C 146/9769; C 146/9686, C 146/3218; C 1/831/62; Tithe Map (1839).

1 hide and 1½ yardlands paying tax and included a burgess, though the borough is not stated. The manor's value in 1086, 12*s.*, had reduced from 13*s.* in 1066.[182] Hanley is poorly documented thereafter. Around 1259, a Henry of 'Henlegh' gave half a mark for taking an assize of novel disseisin.[183] A Walter Boxe held a cottage and 8 a. in Cradley and Hanley in 1400.[184] By 1533, The Seed and its lands had passed to Cradley manor, and this loss probably led to the name Little Hanley, which was adopted after 1400.[185] By the 1530s, the Hall family of Mathon had become substantial landowners, as Sybill Hall then held 100 a. with appurtenances in 'Lytill Hanley' in Cradley parish.[186] In 1541, William Hall of Mathon, yeoman, agreed to sell Overbocke in Little Hanley to Henry Bridge, gentleman, of the Leye.[187]

The overlordship and lordship of the manor are unclear. Robert de Furches of The Seed (*La Sudde*) held a court for land in Hanley in the late 13th century, suggesting lordship of the manor or a sub-manor within it.[188] In 1330, The Seed was in the hands of Henry of Cowleigh, whose wife Margery was presumably a Furches heiress.[189] It is not clear if Henry held all of Hanley, though he did hold widely spread lands within its bounds, including Messengerland, around present-day Hill Farm.[190] If he did hold the manor, it was not in chief. His lands seem to have passed to William of Cowleigh, though some remained, perhaps as dower, to Henry's second wife, Juliana.[191] The transmission of the manor or sub-manor is unclear following William's death and prior to The Seed's incorporation in Cradley manor.[192] By 1533, The Seed was a possession of the 'heirs of Cowleigh'.[193] By 1631, Little Hanley belonged to the vicars choral of Hereford cathedral.[194] From then, until sold to the Revd William Ellis Wall in 1867, it was rented to tenants.[195] The house was still described as a 'manor house' in the 17th to early 19th century.[196]

182 *Domesday*, 514.
183 TNA, C 60/57, 44 HENRY III (1259–60), https://finerollshenry3.org.uk/content/calendar/roll_057.html#it033_011 (accessed 1 Aug. 2023).
184 *Cal. Close* 1405–9, 16.
185 HAS, R13/10537.
186 TNA, C 1/831/62.
187 HAS, F78/5/131; the Leye is near Weobley. For the Leye and the Bridge family, see *The Topographer for the Year 1790: Containing a variety of original articles illustrative of local history and antiquities of England,* vol. 2 (1790), 280. A Roland Bridge also held the unlocated 'Sytees' in the parish: HAS, F78/5/132.
188 TNA, C 146/9734. Below, Manorial Government.
189 TNA, C 146/9686; C 146/3218. In 1351, his heir William granted land in Cowleigh and Vinesend to Thomas the Clerk, vicar of Great Malvern: *A Descriptive Catalogue of Ancient Deeds,* II (1894), C.2491.
190 In 1345, Henry's widow, Juliana, quitclaimed Le Messengerland, also in Hanley, to Alan Charnes (also spelled Charles), her stepdaughter Isabella's husband: TNA, C 146/9769. William of Cowleigh subsequently renewed the grant: TNA C 146/3218.
191 TNA, C 146/9769.
192 See previous paragraph, and below, Manors and Principal Estates: Cowleigh.
193 HAS, R13/10537; below, Manors and Principal Estates: Cowleigh.
194 HCA, 3860/1.
195 HCA, 3860/1–22.
196 HCA, 3860/2, 8, 14. See above, The Built Character, for Seed Farm.

Cowleigh

The name first appears between 1225 and 1234, when an assart was granted by Bishop Hugh Foliot 'on *Calilleg Buron* around the dike'.[197] This probably refers to the ancient earthwork running along the ridge between Upper Vinesend and Cowleigh Gate Farm. As a manor, Cowleigh (also spelled Cowley or Couley) first occurs in 1384 as *Couley iuxta malverno*, when it had two parts in Herefordshire and a third in Worcestershire.[198]

The history and tenurial status of the Herefordshire portion is unclear.[199] Walter Corbet, esq., was described as Cowleigh's lord, 1414–15, followed by Thomas Corbet, 1455–6.[200] The family had an earlier connection with Cradley and Cowleigh when a Thomas Corbet in 1279 held five freehold yardlands from the bishop worth 39*s*., including the land of Henry of Cowleigh.[201] Whether or not this signifies that the Cradley part of Cowleigh was then part of Cradley manor is unclear, and Cowleigh is never mentioned as being on the bishop's manor. Before 1414, the only other Corbet recorded in the parish is Roger Corbet, assessed at 20*s*. (the highest in the parish) in the 1379 poll tax.[202] He was probably a member of the cadet branch who held Tytherington (Glos.).[203] It seems probable that the Corbets were Cowleigh's overlords during at least the late 13th and 14th century.

An 'of Cowleigh' family frequently witnessed Cradley charters in the late 13th and 14th century. In addition to Cowleigh, *c*.1288 the family held freehold a yardland from the bishop in Cradley manor.[204] In 1351, William of Cowleigh held lands and tenements in Cowleigh and Vinesend in Cradley.[205] In 1354, Bishop Trillek accused him of despoiling his manors of Cradley, Bosbury and Colwall, by felling trees, damaging crops and grass, driving away 20 horses and a mare worth £20, and assaulting and imprisoning some of the bishop's men and servants. So severe was William's extortion of the bishop's bondsmen and tenants that they dared not stay there and till the land, so that the bishop entirely lost his profit. Trillek forced William to make a recognisance for £100 to compensate himself and his tenants.[206]

197 *Duas acras terre de asarto super Calilleg Buron circa fossatas*: *English Episcopal Acta: Hereford 1079–1234*, no. 363.
198 While the family's name was often spelled Couley in the Middle Ages, for consistency's sake, Cowleigh will be used. TNA, CP 25/1/289/54, 106.
199 *VCH Worcs*. IV suggests that the half-hide of land in the manor of Mathon in 1086 held of Roger de Lacy by a tenant Odo, may have been Cowleigh. While possible, there is no further supporting evidence for this theory. *VCH Worcs*. IV, 139–40; *Domesday*, 509.
200 TNA, C 146/9657.
201 This is on an additional membrane stitched to a page of the Cradley rental, which may pre-date the compilation of the main rental: HAS, AA59/A/1, pp. 149–50.
202 *Poll Taxes of 1377–81*, ed. Fenwick, 370.
203 A Roger Corbet, esq., of Tytherington (Glos.) served in a variety of campaigns, 1372–83; TNA, E 101/31/37, m. 1; E 101/40/5, m. 1; C 76/66, m. 15; BL, Cotton, roll XIII.8, m. 1: see http://www.medievalsoldier.org/dbsearch (accessed 1 Aug. 2023). See also M. Julian-Jones, 'The land of the raven and the wolf: Family power and strategy in the Welsh March. 1199–*c*.1300, Corbets and Cantilupes' (Univ. of Cardiff PhD thesis, 2015), 189. Note that Tytherington (*Tyderynton*) is wrongly described as being in Worcestershire.
204 Frequently spelled Couley or Cowley: HAS, AA59/A/1, p. 149. Henry de Cowleigh WCM, B230, B232, B234, B235B, B236; William, B238A, B239 and TNA, C 146/3218. For more on William, see below, Social History.
205 'Vyneges', above, Settlement; *Ancient Deeds*, II, C.2491.
206 *Cal. Pat*. 1354–58, 56; *Reg. Trillek*, 107–10.

By 1383, the Cowleigh family apparently no longer held the manor. The clerk, Henry Cantilupe, granted two parts of the Herefordshire side to Richard Ruyhale and Elizabeth his wife, with additional lands in Cradley and Bromyard.[207] Elizabeth retained the manor for life after Richard's death, despite her remarriage to Richard Oldcastle, and still held it in 1409.[208] In 1427, Cowleigh included five messuages, 40 a. of land and 4 a. of meadow in Cradley,[209] and several Cradley manor properties, including The Seed and Buriend, seem to have belonged to Cowleigh's owners until the early 16th century.[210] By 1533, the owners were the unnamed 'heirs of Cowleigh', from whom Thomas Harewell held unspecified land in Cradley manor.[211] Thomas' father, Edmund, died in 1532 and was recorded as being seised of half the manor. In 1604, Sir Edmund Harewell sold Cowleigh manor's site to Rowland Berkeley. Berkeley's son, William, in turn sold it to Sir William Devereux of Leigh Court in 1624.[212]

In 1625, Sir Walter Devereux and Robert Berkeley of Spetchley had licence to enclose and make a park for deer and other game at Cowleigh, Cradley and Leigh;[213] this is probably the origin of the more modern name of the Cradley portion of the Cowleigh estate, Cowleigh Park.[214]

In 1634, Sir Walter Devereux of Leigh Court settled Cowleigh (alias Cowley House) – 'a manor of capital messuage'[215] – on his son Essex, when he married Anne Courteen.[216] Essex drowned childless in 1639, so presumably his widow inherited for life and then the estate reverted to Sir Walter's heirs.[217] The Devereux family sold the manor in 1646, most probably to the Lechmeres,[218] who certainly owned the property by 1674, when Edward Lechmere was lord of Cowleigh manor.[219] Anthony Lechmere owned Cowleigh Park in 1706;[220] Edward Lechmere lived at Cowley in 1824.[221]

By 1841, Cowley Park belonged to the Earl Beauchamp of Madresfield (Worcs.).[222] By 1919, when the earl sold the properties at auction, his Cowleigh estate had expanded to include not only Cowleigh Park Farm, but also Cowleigh Gate Farm, Croft and Birches Farm, and Hill Farm, more than 350 a. altogether.[223]

207 TNA, CP 25/1/289/54, 106.

208 *Cal. Close* 1405–09, 431–2. Richard Ruyhale was lord of Birtsmorton (Worcs.): *VCH Worcs.* IV, 29–33. The land was held by three fees in 1427: TNA, CP 25/1/292/66, 67.

209 TNA, CP 25/1/292/66, 67.

210 TNA, C 146/10351, C 146/9734, C 146/10337, C 146/10056. Others mentioned include TNA, C 146/9784, C 146/9767, C 146/9710, C 146/9719, C 146/9714, C 146/9708.

211 HAS, R13/10537.

212 *VCH. Worcs.* IV, 139–40.

213 *VCH. Worcs.* IV, 101–11.

214 First surviving usage 1706, see below.

215 Nothing more is known about this building.

216 WAAS, 892 9 BA870.5:99, 6, XI, 240.

217 *VCH Worcs.* IV, 103.

218 Seemingly a different branch of the family to that at Hanley Castle: *VCH. Worc.* IV, 89–101.

219 *VCH. Worcs.* IV, 139–40.

220 HAS, AH73/69.

221 HAS, Q/REL/6/9/1–45.

222 Below, Other Estates: Madresfield estate.

223 HAS, AH72/2.

Cowleigh Park farmhouse[224] dates from the 16th century, with later alterations. The building comprises two storeys and an attic, and is timber-framed and painted brick, with a historic tile roof. The projecting gabled wing to the right-hand side is 19th-century, while the one-storey extension and attics to the left are late 18th- or early 19th-century.[225] Some of the original agricultural buildings (such as the former sheds for yard cattle, likely 18th-century) have been converted to dwellings at an unknown date after 1972.[226]

Other Estates

Upper Vinesend

Vinesend is first recorded as a messuage and half a yardland of freehold land called 'Vyngeyend' in 1533 held by Richard Falke.[227] James Turner (d. 1667) lived at (Upper) Vinesend,[228] and left £20 annually to endow a free school, to be raised from the estate.[229] The property probably then passed to his nephew,[230] Edmund Skinner, rector of Cradley (d. 1678), who left the 'mansionhouse' to his grandson, William Norden.[231] The property then passed to Norden's daughter, Susannah Tolly,[232] and her daughter Elizabeth in 1742, when she married Robert Cliffe. William Cliffe became the owner, perhaps from 1771, when he married,[233] and after his death, by 1804, it probably passed to Allen, his only surviving child.[234] By 1834, it belonged to William Bateson Cliffe,[235] who lost it in 1849, having defaulted on his mortgage, when his banker sold it to John Allen.[236] In 1869, the property was sold to the Earl Beauchamp of Madresfield.[237] By 1886, it belonged to John Shapland and formed part of the Vinesend estate.[238] Upper Vinesend continued in the Shapland family for the next half-century;[239] although the estate was divided up and auctioned in 1920,[240] the family continued to own Upper Vinesend Farm until it too was sold in 1929.[241] In 1968, N.L. Harris had permission to alter and restore Upper Vinesend Farm.[242]

224 See below, Mills, Crafts and Industry: Tourism and hospitality.
225 NHLE, no. 1082801, Cowleigh Pk fm ho. (accessed 1 Aug. 2023).
226 J.E.C. Peters, unpubl. report on the architectural history of Cradley's agricultural buildings.
227 Also spelled Fallk: HAS, R13/10537; M.A. Faraday, *The Herefordshire Musters of 1539 and 1542* (2012), 68–9.
228 HAS, N37/60.
229 HAS, HD5/14/107. Below Social History: Cradley Boys' School (Old Boys School).
230 TNA, PROB 11/327/309.
231 HAS, C98/18.
232 HAS, C96/18.
233 HAS, C96/15, i; HAS, C96/18.
234 HAS, C96/15, i.
235 HAS, N37/27; HAS, N37/29; HAS, Q/REL/6/9/1–45.
236 WAAS, 892 BA970.5:99, VI [Second Series I], 324–34, 426–8.
237 WAAS, 892 BA970.5:99, VI [Second Series I], 324–34, 426–8.
238 HAS, N37/42.
239 HAS, M5/6A/2–3; HAS, AG9/5. Above, Manors and Principal Estates: The Hill estate.
240 HAS, M5/6A/2.
241 HAS, M5/6A/3.
242 HAS, BW15/3/1. No return was made for Upper Vinesend in the 1941 National Farm Survey.

The large, timber-framed two-storey house retains a 16th-century main range on a north-east to south-west alignment, and a large 17th-century, two-storey cross-wing at the south-west end.[243] On the front, the storeyed porch is possibly not on the site of the earlier entrance. At the back, a single-storey service extension with rubble-stone walls and a cat-slide roof was subsequently replaced or enlarged with a double-gabled block. The main range may have continued north-east by at least one extra bay, or there may have been another cross-wing at this end. An unusual decorative feature, on the main range and relating to the earlier part of the building, is the panels containing a central post with diagonal timbers converging downwards. Originally the full height of the range from wall plate to sill beam, they seem to have been associated with close studding in the adjacent panels. A very similar example of diagonal bracing is in Upper House, Colwall (Evendine Lane),[244] and another (though different) on Ledbury's market hall (1616); but it is usually employed within square panels in northern Herefordshire and through Shropshire and Cheshire. The extensive decoration and storeyed porch (probably a 17th-century addition), and the use of 'nibs' on the brick chimney stack and the elaborate cap (now lost), indicate that Upper Vinesend was a house of considerable status.[245] A large, 18th-century brick barn also survives.[246]

Madresfield Estate

By 1839,[247] the Earl Beauchamp of Madresfield owned the Cowleigh Park estate, which he rented out, and which he had presumably acquired from the Lechmere family at some point after 1824.[248] In 1866, he acquired further farms and lands in Cradley,[249] including the Upper Vinesend estate from 1869 until 1886 or earlier.[250] Storridge school was built on his land.[251] Earl Beauchamp's Cradley holdings in 1909–10 comprised coppicing; land at the Birches; Cowleigh Gate Farm; land at Cowleigh Gate; land at Whitman's hill; land near Storridge; land and buildings at the Hill farm; a cottage or garden at Whippits; and cottages at Crumpton hill.[252] Most of these properties were sold by auction in 1919.[253] But in 1960 the Madresfield estate still owned land at Whippets brook, and at and around Whitman's Hill Quarry, which it retained in 1986.[254]

243 Part of this paragraph was contributed by D. James. This description relies on the RCHME notes of 1931, made when the house was derelict. It has since been restored and enlarged: NHLE, no. 1082255, Upper Vinesend fm ho. (accessed 1 Aug. 2023).

244 D. James, 'Reports of sectional recorders, buildings, 2014', *TWNFC* 62 (2014), 176–8.

245 This paragraph contributed by D. James; see HAS, PAM1598.

246 J.E.C. Peters, unpubl. report on the architectural history of Cradley's agricultural buildings,

247 Tithe Map (1839). See also HAS, N37/29.

248 Above, Manors and Principal Estates: Cowleigh.

249 WAAS, 892 BA970.5:99, VI [Second Series I], 324–34.

250 WAAS, 892 BA970.5:99, VI [Second Series I], 324–34; HAS, N37/42.

251 Below, Education.

252 HAS, AG9/5.

253 HAS, AH72. For Storridge School, see below, Education.

254 CHC, Parish Council Minutes, II, 21 Feb. 1986.

Figure 9 *Upper Vinesend house after its restoration viewed from the west, c.1960s. (CHC)*

Halesend

First recorded in 1533 as 'Halesond' or 'Helysond', this was a messuage of customary land held by William Bullock in Cradley manor.[255] It belonged to the Long family in 1698, when Richard Long lived there,[256] and to Richard Long Racster in 1798 (through his mother Mary Racster, née Long),[257] when taxation records suggest that it was among the larger properties in the parish.[258] The Racster family[259] retained it until 1838, when Mary Racster sold it to Richard Yapp.[260] His son, also Richard, inherited in 1854,[261] and was lord of Cradley and owned large estates there.[262] He used Halesend as his chief residence,[263] which thus became the *de facto* seat of the lords of Cradley

255 HAS, R13/10537.

256 This was not the same person as Richard Long of Barrowmills, but rather a kinsman; HAS, 126/6/11, will of Joyce Fifield, 1698; HAS, 133/2/3, will of Richard Long of Barrowmill, 1700; HAS, SA2/3. For the property's descent through the Long family, see also: HAS, BJ2/1; HAS, AH73/25.

257 HAS, BJ2/1.

258 CHC, Copy of Land Tax, 1798.

259 HAS, BJ2/1; HAS, Q/REL/6/9/1–45.

260 HAS, BJ2/1.

261 HAS, BJ43/29/43. See also TNA, PROB 11/2194/9, will of Richard Yapp, 1854.

262 Most significantly, the Halesend, Little Halesend and Barrow Mills estates; see HAS, BJ43/29/43. See Manors and Principal Estates: Netherbarrow, Beanhouse, Barrow Mills.

263 HAS, AN98/17.

manor. George Bailey Yapp, Richard's son, inherited most of his father's property, including Halesend, in 1873, under the administration of trustees.[264]

In 1909–10, when still controlled by Yapp's executors,[265] the Halesend estate (162 a.) was valued at £7,257, and Halesend coppicing (108 a.) at £1,308.[266] It was sold by auction in 1919,[267] and by 1922 Samuel Enderby (d. 1956)[268] resided at Halesend as lord of the manor.[269] Bernard Arthur Higgins, lord of Cradley, was owner and lived there in 1959,[270] and still in 1979.[271] The property continued in the Higgins family until offered for sale with the lordship of Cradley manor in 2003.[272] Between 2003 and *c.*2010, it belonged to Ronald Cottam, who converted the farm buildings into dwellings (in 2021 marketed as Halesend Hamlet).[273] The owner from *c.*2011,[274] and in 2021, was Luke Johnson (entrepreneur and former owner of the bakery chain 'Patisserie Valerie' and other catering businesses).[275]

The house, of *c.*1830, may be a single-phase remodelling of an earlier building. It is of two storeys and stuccoed, square in plan with a wing projecting to the north. The front portico is positioned off-centre. On raised ground, it is highly visible but remote. The estate farm buildings are set carefully to the north, away from the gentry residence.[276]

Malvern Chase[277]

In 1584, the royal forest was adjudged to extend as far as Cowleigh Gate as its north-western limit,[278] although how far Malvern Chase intruded into the eastern edge of the parish is unclear. Henry III's grant of the chase to Gilbert de Clare, earl of Gloucester (d. 1295), was challenged in 1280 by the bishop, Thomas Cantilupe, who claimed that Clare's rights over bishopric lands, including in Cradley, conflicted with the bishop's 1241 charter of free warren. A royal inquiry affirmed the bishop's free warren, and this allowed Bishop Trefnant to defeat another legal challenge a century later.[279]

In 1628, the area of the chase within Cradley was only 60 a., and much of this was disputed between Cradley and Leigh.[280] When the chase was disafforested under Charles I, this became part of the royal enclosed area called the King's Third.

264 HAS, BJ43/29/43.
265 HAS, N37/42; HAS, AG9/5.
266 HAS, AG9/5.
267 HAS, M5/6A/5.
268 *Kelly's Handbook* (1977 edn). No return was made for Halesend in the 1941 National Farm Survey.
269 *Kelly's Dir.* (1922 edn).
270 HAS, BJ2/1.
271 *London Gaz.*, 16 Mar. 1979 (High Sheriffs appointed).
272 *Worc. News*, 4 Mar. 2003 (Lord of Cradley Manor); inf. from local resident.
273 Inf. from local resident, 25 June 2021.
274 https://www.herefordshire.gov.uk/info/200142/planning_services/planning_application_search/details?id=110350 (accessed 1 Aug. 2023).
275 Inf. from local resident, 25 June 2021; *Who's Who* (2023 edn).
276 This paragraph was contributed by D. James. NHLE, no. 1082275, Halesend (accessed 1 Aug. 2023).
277 *VCH Herefs. Colwall*, 6, 51–3, for further discussion of Malvern Chase and the Thirds.
278 Smith, *Malvern*, 25–7.
279 Below, Manorial Government; *Reg. Trefnant*, 164–5; Smith, *Malvern*, 21.
280 WAAS, 705:24 BA81/366; Soc. of Antiquaries, Sal/MS/520/I/23/ff. 168–90.

The Cradley King's Third was quickly sold by the Crown, and passed through the hands of several families,[281] until sold in 1920 to Malvern Urban District Council, and passing to the Malvern Hills Conservators in 1994.[282] Its northern boundary ditch and bank, constructed in the 1630s, form a distinctive earthwork, seen when descending from the northernmost rise on End Hill towards the former Lamb Inn.[283]

Duchy of Cornwall

The Mercantile and General Reinsurance Company owned properties in Cradley, from the 1960s to 1991, including Seed Farm by 1962[284] and Hill Farm by 1969.[285] In 1991, the Duchy of Cornwall purchased its Cradley holdings (750 ha.) which, in 2023, formed part of its Hereford estates. It is mainly Grade 3 land (good to moderate), with some woodland,[286] and extends over Cradley's border into Evesbatch, including Woodend Farm, Cradley Hall Farm, Hill Farm, Hollings Hill Farm and surroundings; it does not include the homesteads of Seed Farm and Homehouse Farm.

Other

In 1841, the churchwardens or trustees of the poor of St Nicholas parish, Worcester, owned and rented out Poors Land in Cradley.[287] It was owned in 1853 by the Bosbury Union guardians,[288] who sold it to the Revd William Ellis Wall.[289] In 1886, the Ecclesiastical Commissioners owned Homehouse and Pitlick farms.[290]

281 WAAS, b705:295 BA1751/8; WAAS, 705:1428 BA 12981/3/7.

282 Malvern Hills Trust deeds: conveyance, 6 Dec. 1994, Malvern DC to Malvern Hills Conservators.

283 The primary author of this paragraph was George Demidowicz.

284 HAS, BW15/2/6, p. 1074.

285 HAS, BW15/3/2, p. 165.

286 https://duchyofcornwall.org/hereford.html (accessed 17 Nov. 2022).

287 HAS, N37/29. This may have been 'Poors Meadow', beside Wold Mill, or Lower or Upper Poors Meadow near Baconhill Farm: Tithe Map (1839).

288 HAS, N37/29.

289 WAAS, 892 BA970.5:99, VIII (71A), 115–16.

290 HAS, N37/42.

ECONOMIC HISTORY

UNTIL THE LATER 20TH CENTURY, agriculture was at the centre of Cradley's economy: cultivation of grains and rearing of cattle and sheep were consistently fundamental, and, from the early modern period, hop and fruit production. Beer brewing and cider making were also important. Agriculture remained economically very significant in 2023, but employed proportionally far fewer parishioners than previously. Cradley's numerous mills stood mostly on the main branch of the Cradley brook; quarrying and forestry were also significant. After 1900, the diverse range of crafts and service economies shrank drastically, so that in 2023 the parish had only a few shops and one pub, although there were a few holiday properties and guesthouses. Increasingly, parishioners were either retired or commuted to work elsewhere, although home working following the Covid-19 pandemic restrictions in 2020–1 may have reversed this trend.

Agriculture

The Agricultural Landscape

Cradley's landscape has inevitably dictated its use. The west, as depicted in 1839, was predominately arable land, with meadow concentrated around the valley of Cradley brook and its tributaries. In the east, the Malvern hills are characteristically mixed woodland and hillside pasture, apart from clusters of arable land in the valleys, particularly in the south around Vinesend, and in the north between Storridge and Batchcombe.[1] Arable cultivation accounted for half (2,921 a. of 5,666 a.) Cradley's tithable land in 1838.[2]

Although some medieval common or open fields cannot be confidently located,[3] Westfield, Buryfield and Churchfield, in the central south of the parish, were the principal fields on the bishop's manor. Westfield is first mentioned *c.*1307, when a Walter le Webbe held 14 selions there from the Hill family at 'Riddeweiyn' (possibly Ridgeway) between 'Wokareswalle' and 'Opesboke'.[4] The plots or selions recorded there from 1496–7 are 'Arundell', 'Addeslond', 'Tyrell' and 'Lewesacre'.[5] Buryfield (variously spelled), first mentioned in 1393, lay directly north-east of St James's church, and in 1533 several episcopal tenants held selions of customary land there.[6] Buryfield common

1 See Map 5 below.
2 HCA, 6437/II/1. This can also be seen in the Tithe Map (1839).
3 For a general overview, see above, Settlement: Medieval and early modern settlement.
4 HAS, P66/2.
5 HAS, AM33/13 rot. 21d.; CF 54/1/16; CF 54/1/25; R13/10537; TNA, SC 6/HENVIII/1511 rot. 8d.
6 HAS, C96/1; R13/10537.

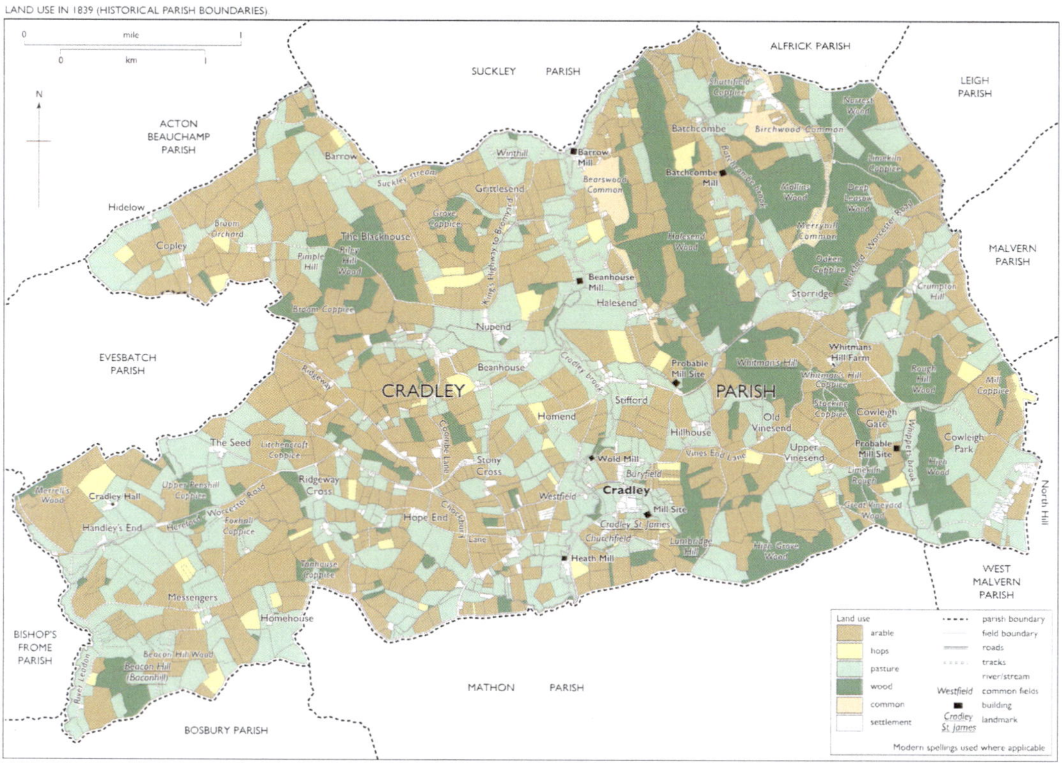

Map 5 *Land use in 1839 (historical parish boundaries).*

field remained in 1877, where individuals owned 'rudges' or selions.[7] Churchfield, south of St James's church, was a common field in 1589.[8] Selions are recorded in an unidentified 'Stonyforlong' in 1533.[9] Barrow manor possessed several common or open fields before 1300, and a Barrow field is mentioned in 1327;[10] tenants held selions in 'Sullithurne', 'Morfeld', 'Wodefield' and Middlefield, which all lay near Winthill.[11] Nine selions in Middlefield were known collectively as 'Weteland' ('wheat land').[12] In 1346, a common field called 'Tyckeleinsfeld' in The Hyde contained at least six selions.[13] In Hanley, before 1300, selions existed in 'Colwrecroft' (10), Woodcroft (8) and the field of 'Ruggeley' (30).[14] Nothing is known of the organisation of Cradley's medieval fields, but there is evidence of complex open-field systems utilising three-course rotation in neighbouring parishes.[15]

7 HAS, AH73/69, pp. 93–6.
8 HAS, HD2/1/30.
9 HAS, R13/10537.
10 WCM, B233.
11 WCM, B231, B236.
12 WCM, B236.
13 HCA, 3295.
14 TNA, C 146/9734, 20 and 10 are recorded separately at '*Ruggeleye*'. Ruggeley is recorded on Tithe Map (1839) next to Homehouse.
15 See *VCH Herefs. Bosbury*, 30–1; *VCH Herefs. Colwall*, 46–7, 54–5.

In 16th-century Storridge, two pieces of land – Storridge Birchwood and Storridge Hill – were presumably common ground.[16]

Agricultural expansion through assarting was under way in the 1220s and 1230s, when there were 2 a. of assarts 'near the embankments' above Cowleigh.[17] By *c.*1288, five of the bishop's tenants held assarts ranging from 6 a. to 21 a.; with one exception, all were freeholders already holding full yardlands.[18] In Barrow, before 1300, Robert of the Barrow granted a messuage and curtilage 'completely surrounded by hedges' called 'Herdingestockynge'. The word 'stokkyng' frequently denoted an assart that extended an existing field into surrounding waste- or woodland.[19] Evidence of later assarting is limited, possibly because of 14th-century population decline. In 1496–7, Adam Hill rendered account for 6 a. of assart.[20]

Enclosure of common fields may have begun before 1300. In Barrow, seven selions of land in 'Morfelde' were conveyed with hedges *c.*1275,[21] and in Hanley the selions at 'Colwrecroft' and Woodcroft were described as hedged.[22] In 1515, Overbarrow manorial court convicted Richard Morton of unjustly enclosing a parcel of land at 'Rastheall' in Barrow; it was seized and handed to the manor's farmer, John Pichard.[23]

Glebe terriers of 1589, 1607 and 1635 show the rapid spread of enclosure: in 1589, most land parcels were not described as enclosed, but in 1607 almost all were.[24] The speed of enclosure seems to have depended on the land's location (close to Cradley village, or peripheral), its quality and its use (whether arable, pasture or woodland). The enclosure of glebe land (then largely arable and pasture) was concentrated largely in the ancient field system of Churchfields. This contrasts with Overbarrow, a manor on the parish's sparsely populated northern border, which was mostly woodland and pasture. In 1649, there was reportedly no enclosure at Overbarrow because the underwoods were worth little and were eaten continually by cattle depastured there.[25] Thereafter, sub-division and probably enclosure of land gathered pace, and Overbarrow's ten fields in 1649 had increased to 28 by 1776.[26] Because of surviving accounts, agricultural changes in Overbarrow can be studied in detail. In 1649, almost half was woodland, with the remainder being pasture (mostly rough or furzy) with some arable.[27] By 1776, most woodland had disappeared (although many pastures retained some trees), and the estate was almost all pasture and arable, in roughly equal acreages.[28] By 1839, hardly

16 HAS, AA59/A/2, f. 56v.
17 *English Episcopal Acta: Hereford 1079–1234*, no. 363.
18 HAS, AA59/A/1, pp. 148–52.
19 *Et cum haycio undique vallato*, WCM, B231, B236; A.J. Roderick, 'Open-field agriculture in Herefordshire in the Middle Ages', *TWNFC* 33 (1949), 62–3.
20 HAS, AM33/13, rot. 21d.
21 WCM, B231, B236.
22 TNA, C 146/9734.
23 WCM, E182.
24 HAS, HD2/1/30–2.
25 Thomas Cave and Rowland A. Wilson (eds), *The Parliamentary Survey of the Lands and Possessions of the Dean and Chapter of Worcester Made in or about the Year 1649* (1924), 111.
26 Cave and Wilson (eds), *Parliamentary Survey*, 111; WAAS, f009:1, 5403/2.
27 Cave and Wilson (eds), *Parliamentary Survey*, 111.
28 WAAS, f009:1, 5403/2.

any woodland remained, and the estate was approximately a third pasture and two thirds arable.[29]

After Charles I converted a third of Malvern Chase into the King's Third, the uncontested remainder in Cradley, nearly 30 a., remained as common pasture. This extended from the northernmost prominence on End Hill to Old Hollow near its junction with Cowleigh Road.[30] Old Hollow as far as Lamb Bank formed the boundary between the commoners' 'two thirds' and the old enclosures (Cradley Ingrounds) to the west. From Lamb Bank southwards the boundary was with the King's Third, but higher up the hill it followed the future line of Ebrington Road to the Mathon boundary just before the West Malvern Road junction.[31]

By 1692, illegal enclosure of waste ground and building of cottages had begun at Birchwood.[32] In May 1793, a number of parishioners assembled at the church and perambulated the parish, removing some of the encroachments on, and enclosures of, Cradley's common land. The parish subsequently agreed, as a consequence of threats of litigation, to defend those involved and pay all necessary expenses.[33] But despite resentment, most encroachments were legally recognised after a while, rather than being removed. When, in 1846, Joseph Jones illegally built a cottage on parish land and enclosed a piece of common as a garden, it was agreed that he would become a tenant of the parish.[34]

In the 1820s, 37 newly enclosed allotments were made on Birchwood and Merryhill Commons, where there were already several pre-existing encroachments and enclosures.[35] By 1838, only 90 a. of the 5,666 a. of tithable land in Cradley was common,[36] and the only sizeable commons were Bearswood, Birchwood and Merryhill. Land still technically common at the north end of Malvern Hill was in fact almost entirely covered by 56 enclosures.[37] Extensive squatting and encroachment took place on Cradley's 'two thirds' of the chase between 1834, when 18 cottages were mapped, and 1891, when there were over 100.[38] In 1845 and 1849, land (not open-field arable) at Birchwood and Merry Hill was enclosed under general acts.[39] In 1966, most of the surviving common land was at Eastbury Hill, Conveyant Hill and Bearswood;[40] in 1967 and 1969, Crumpton Hill Green and other unspecified land was registered as common land.[41] In 2023, of what was once Cradley's 'two thirds' of the chase, only about one third of the area remained open, a triangle of steep land rising to the northernmost eminence on End Hill.

29 Tithe Map (1839).
30 Above, Other Estates: Malvern Chase.
31 WAAS, 705:24, BA81/366.
32 HAS, AA63/3, p. 131.
33 HAS, N37/34 16 May 1793.
34 HAS, N37/35 4 July 1846.
35 HAS, AH73/69, pp. 51–9.
36 HCA, 6437/II/1. Cradley was 5,756 a.
37 HAS, B9/35–6.
38 OS Map 1:2500, Worcs. XXXIX.8 (1888 edn); Census, 1881 – the Cradley part of District 5.
39 W.E. Tate, 'A hand list of English enclosure acts and awards. Part 15 Herefordshire', *TWNFC* (1939–41), 193.
40 CHC, Parish Council Minutes, I, p. 276.
41 CHC, Parish Council Minutes, I, pp. 313, 324; II, 16 Sep. 1969.

Medieval Landholdings

In 1086, unfree tenants on the bishop's manor had 28 ploughs, with a further three held in demesne by the bishop.[42] In addition, the priest, the reeve, the two knights and the *radman* together held five ploughs between them, and their unspecified number of sub-tenants a total of six ploughs. In Hanley, there was one plough in demesne, and four bordars had two ploughs and could have employed a third.[43] These figures suggest a total of *c*.4,500–*c*.5,400 a. of land under arable cultivation.[44] By *c*.1288, an additional 56 a. of cultivated land had been gained by assarting.[45]

Herefordshire custom, as stated *c*.1580, computed a yardland as 60 a., and a statute acre was 1½ Herefordshire acres.[46] Evidence from rentals of Bosbury and Colwall episcopal manors *c*.1288 suggests that 60 a. yardlands were more likely than 40 a. ones, although that from Cradley is ambiguous.[47] Cradley's annual rents per acre were only around half those of Colwall, Bosbury and Ledbury Foreign if based on a 60-a. yardland; but also the annual rent paid by customary half-yardland holders was variable, ranging from 4 to 10*s*.[48] Rents continued to vary: a yardland was 13*s*. yearly *c*.1288, but anywhere between 8*s*. and 14*s*. in 1533, by when a half-yardland ranged from 6*s*. 8*d*. to 12*s*. 6*d*. By then all recorded holdings included at least one messuage.[49] It is unclear whether these variations were the result of differing acreage, land quality, yardland size or some other factor.

In 1086, the bishop's demesne land – in line with many well-established church manors – was proportionately smaller than that of the peasant tenants.[50] Thereafter, demesne arable was reduced, from three ploughlands in 1086 (*c*.300–*c*.360 a.), to 96 a. by *c*.1288. By the latter date, nine tenants held between them 28½ a. of former demesne called forlet land,[51] and the bishop had followed the general trend and commuted labour services for money.[52] By 1404 the demesne had apparently gone entirely.[53] A customary yardland called 'bisshopeslond' *c*.1496 and later may have been former demesne.[54]

The bulk of the manorial rents were those from customary land.[55] Around 1288, the free and customary tenants rendered £6 11*s*. 8*d*. and £18 18*s*. 1*d*. respectively. The Black

42 *Domesday*, 502.
43 *Domesday*, 502, 514.
44 This figure is based on the evidence that a single plough could cultivate about 100 a. in a year; see Dyer, *Making a Living*, 92. For Herefordshire acres and the ambiguities surrounding Cradley, see paragraph below.
45 Below, Woodland and Forest.
46 HAS, AA59/A/2 f. 69v.; *VCH Herefs. Colwall*, 45. See also P. Williams, 'Land tenure in the bishop's manor of Whitborne', *TWNFC* 40 (1972), 338–42. Note that Cradley was no longer an episcopal manor by the time of Butterfield's Survey.
47 *VCH Herefs. Colwall*, 45; HAS, AA59/A/1, pp. 153–67.
48 HAS, AA59/A/1, p. 151.
49 HAS, AA59/A/1, pp. 148–53; R13/10537; TNA, SC 6/HENVIII/1511, rot. 8d.
50 Dyer, *Making a Living*, 96–7.
51 HAS, AA59/A/1, pp. 148–53.
52 Below, Agriculture: Arable farming; Livestock and pasture; HAS, AA59/A/1, p. 148; Dyer, *Making a Living*, 132–3.
53 *Domesday*, 502; above, Manors and Principal Estates: Cradley manor before 1562.
54 HAS, AM33/13; TNA, SC 6/HENVIII/1511, rot. 8d.; HAS, AA59/A/1, pp. 149–53.
55 Below, Social Character: Before 1550.

Death's impact on Cradley manor's rents is likely to have been severe. On another manor within the parish, The Hyde, annual rents declined sharply, from £1 18*s.* in the period 1314–18 to only 2*s.* 6*d.* in 1349. Two holdings totalling between them 1½ yardlands, a messuage and a noke of land lay uncultivated and in the lord's hands. The sole rent received was for one messuage and 8 acres.[56]

There is evidence of a marked recovery by 1404, when Cradley manor customary rents had risen to £22 12*s.* 1*d.*, though rents from free tenants had decreased from their *c.*1288 total to only £6, the average for Herefordshire.[57] Records of transfers before and after 1500 suggest that customary land was increasingly concentrated in the hands of a small group of wealthier tenants. Whereas two men held a yardland through customary tenure *c.*1288, by 1496–7 at least seven held a messuage and a yardland, and five in 1536,[58] suggesting an overall decrease in the amount of customary land held per tenant. By 1533, total annual rents had fallen to £26 19*s.* 3*d.*, mostly from customary land.[59] The bishop also received 2*s.* 8*d.* rent from two parcels of customary land in the garden/orchard of Cradley church, named 'Bargeyne'.[60] By 1559, rents had risen to £29 19*s.* 3*d.*, before falling back to £26 9*s.* 2*d.* in 1562 after the transfer to royal control.[61]

Arable Farming

The limited evidence of medieval land use and agriculture in Cradley does not suggest that the parish differed substantially from its neighbours.[62] Around 1288, the bishop's 96 a. of arable, 5 a. of pasture and 3 a. of orchards/gardens rendered £7 6*s.* 6*d.* for the year.[63] In 1536, the manorial court levied 11*s.* from a Robert Shepherd for a third of grain and green rye which he had sown on the lord's waste without permission, perhaps indicating pressure on agricultural land at the period.[64]

In the early modern period, most Cradley farmers and landowners cultivated arable crops and kept livestock; even those who were primarily craftsmen also engaged in some agriculture, such as a mason whose 1680 probate inventory included seven sheep and a variety of crops.[65] Between 1550 and 1700, 29 per cent of wills and inventories referred to wheat (often called corn), either growing, in the barn, or stored in the house.[66]

56 Hillaby, *St Katherine's*, 98; HCA, 7018/2, ff. 77–82. An antiquarian account (to be treated very cautiously) references a 1581 rent book which declares that in 'A.D. 1349, Anno 23, Edward III., there died in Bosbury, Colwall, Coddington, and Cradley, 158 Tenants': Francis T. Havergal, *Fasti Herefordenses and other Antiquarian Memorials of Hereford* (Edinburgh, 1869), (http://www.melocki.org.uk/MelockiFasti.html) (accessed 7 Feb. 2020), 203.

57 HAS, AA59/A/1, pp. 149–53; *Cal. Inq. Misc.* VII, 152.

58 HAS, AM33/13, rot. 21d.; TNA, SC 6/HENVIII/1511, rott. 8d., 9; HAS, R13/10537.

59 HAS, R13/10537.

60 *Gardius*, HAS, R13/10537.

61 *Cal. Pat.* 1558–60, 440; *Cal. Pat.* 1560–3, 285.

62 See, e.g., *VCH Herefs. Bosbury*, 30–9, and *VCH Herefs. Colwall*, 45–57.

63 HAS, AA59/A/1, p. 153.

64 TNA, SC 6/HENVIII/1511, rot. 17; below, Agriculture: Livestock and pasture.

65 See below, Appendices, Sample 2, 93.

66 These, and the following statistics in this chapter (Economic History), are based on detailed analysis of a sample of 100 wills from 1550–1700, balanced so as to have (as far as possible) a similar number of wills for each 50-year period within the overall time period. See below, Appendices, Sample 1.

In addition to corn,[67] Lent grain,[68] muncorn, barley, oats and rye were grown, and a 1677 inventory includes a pulse of peas.[69]

Alcohol production (mainly cider) and cultivation of fruit were significant in the area, particularly from the early modern period onwards, but with medieval roots. This included viticulture and hopyards, as well as orcharding throughout the parish.[70]

Most crops in Cradley were grown for human or animal food, but 13 per cent of wills and inventories between 1550 and 1700 refer to the raw materials of textiles being grown or processed to produce cloth. A 1575 will refers to 8lb. of 'hacheled' hemp, and a 1684 inventory to linen yarn. Two documents mention spinning wheels. Crops include flax and tow for linen manufacture, hemp for ropes and canvas, and wool.

Farming dominated Cradley's economic landscape in the 19th century. Labourers accounted for 61 per cent of fathers recorded in the 1813–47 baptismal register, with farmers a further 11 per cent.[71] In the 1841 census, 55 per cent of occupations listed were agricultural labourers (275) or farmers (46).[72] The 1941 national farm survey returned 82 farms and smallholdings in Cradley, averaging 52 acres. A total of 4,176 a. was under agriculture. Labourers (three on average) were employed on 48 per cent of farms.[73]

Documentary and architectural evidence reflects the diversity of produce farmed in Cradley since 1800. Many farms had both crops and livestock, and alcohol production was ubiquitous. Wheat (811½ a.) was the most common crop in 1801, with oats (196½ a.) and barley (67½ a.) also grown. Average yields did not exceed 14 bushels of wheat per acre.[74] The importance of corn growing is seen in surviving 19th-century buildings. Fixed threshing machines were installed at Beanhouse and Hill House farms, as indicated by their horse-engine houses. The large brick barn at Batchcombe, of *c.*1850, was built on a stream, with a water wheel, apparently to power a fixed threshing machine.[75] By 1876, a portable steam-driven threshing machine had become available to hire from Preston's at Ridgeway Cross.[76] Sales particulars mention a granary (22 per cent), and a chaff room or house (18 per cent).[77] In 1931, Beanhouse also had a bakehouse.[78] In 1941, 29 per cent of farms produced wheat, 29 per cent oats, 16 per cent barley and 20 per cent mixed corn. [79]

Apart from cereals and hops, in 1801 beans (124½ a.), peas (85 a.), turnips (56¾ a.), potatoes (26 a.) and rape (13 a.) were cultivated.[80] In 1941, 43 per cent of farms grew

67 HAS, 8-3-10, will of Thomas Bullock, 1548; HAS, 65-2-42, will of Catherine Bullock, 1680; see below, Appendices, Sample 1, 87, and Sample 2, 97.

68 'Lent grain' meant grain sown in the spring, around Lent (*OED*).

69 See below, Appendices, Sample 2, 88.

70 Below, Agriculture: Vineyards; Orchards; and Hopyards.

71 HAS, MX182.

72 Census, 1841.

73 TNA, MAF 32/6/15.

74 TNA, HO 67/12.

75 J.E.C. Peters, unpubl. report on the architectural history of Cradley's agricultural buildings.

76 *Kelly's Dir.* (1885–1934 edns).

77 The statistical analysis here and below in Economic History is based on a sample of 50 sales particulars from the period after 1800: see Appendices, Sample 3.

78 HAS, M5/6A/4.

79 TNA, MAF 32/6/15.

80 TNA, HO 67/12.

Figure 10 *Harvest and hopkilns 'near Cradley', 1930s or 1940s. (Photo by Miss Marjorie Wight, HAS, K80/205)*

potatoes, 24 per cent mangolds, 23 per cent turnips and swedes (mostly for fodder), 9 per cent kale and 9 per cent beans (both often for stock feeding) and 7 per cent sugar beet. Churchfields, besides poultry and fruit, grew 2 a. of tomatoes. Only Birchwood (146 a.) and Taswolds (36 a.) grew crops under glass, and only Batchcombe produced peas.[81] Just over 70 per cent of farms had grass for mowing or grazing, and 22 per cent for rough grazing.[82]

Many farms also grew fruit for consumption, jam making or alcohol production. Two sales particulars (from 1919 and 1929) mention fruit rooms,[83] and two (from 1929 and 1931) mention vineries.[84] By 1931, Beanhouse had adapted some of its hopkilns into a jam-making plant.[85] In 1941, 7 per cent of farms produced small fruit.

During the 20th century, some farmers used advances in technology and transportation to access new markets with different crops; Frank Jones at Churchfields in 1927 grew roses, shrubs, perennials and other plants, which were dispatched by rail from Colwall.[86] Hidelow Farm illustrates the impact of the depressions between the wars. Reports described the farmhouse as in need of repairs and many of its fields as 'very

81 TNA, MAF 32/6/15.
82 TNA, MAF 32/6/15.
83 HAS, M5/6A/5; HAS, M5/6A/3.
84 HAS, M5/6A/3; HAS, M5/6A/4.
85 HAS, M5/6A/4.
86 Edwards, *Cradley*, 46.

foul' and uncultivated,[87] while surviving correspondence indicates that tenants found it impossible to make a profit during the 1920s, and there appears to have been a rapid turnover during the 1930s.[88]

A significant – albeit slow – agricultural change was, of course, the arrival of tractors. In the 1920s, wealthier farmers began buying tractors and, consequently, owning fewer horses.[89] In 1941, however, 54 per cent of farms still had two horses on average, and only 16 farms (18 per cent) had wheel tractors; most had just one (usually a domestically produced Fordson), but Birchwood (146 a.), Summerville House (23 a.) and Winthill (166 a.) had two, and a track-laying tractor (a US-made Caterpillar). Birchwood and Winthill nonetheless still had horses, four and eight respectively. Almost all farms with tractors had larger than average acreages, and many were over 100 a., but not all large farms had tractors; Batchcombe (114 a.), The Vineries (125 a.), Cowleigh Gate (100 a.) and Seed Farm (218 a.) relied exclusively on horses.[90]

In 2023, most land in the parish remained agricultural, and (with very few shops and non-agricultural businesses) farming continued to play an important role in its economy. Many residents, however, were retired, and most of the working-age population commuted to work elsewhere or worked from home. Some of the agricultural land was also used for grazing horses.[91]

Livestock and Pasture

Unsurprisingly, given its well-drained terrain, numerous meadows and pastures existed in Cradley from the medieval to modern periods.[92] In 1086, the manor possessed 7 a. of demesne meadow,[93] and *c.*1288 the bishop held 5 a. in demesne. Between 1496 and 1536, the bishop held pasturage rights over two land parcels called 'Holmede' and 'Titbath', each rendering 12*d.*, as well as two hillside (*montnar*) pasturages called 'Eastlemynde', for 8*s.*, and 'Hokylmynde' for 3*s.*[94] A pasture called 'Somerlond', newly rendered in 1496–7 and 1506, may have been seasonal.[95] The Hill family appear to have held meadows and pasturages in Cradley, including at Westfield and 'Wylleyesino' in 1393, and possibly several near Stifford in the 14th and early 15th century, including a meadow called 'Styffordshom' in 1306, and an unspecified 16 a. in 1411.[96]

Customary pasturage existed in 1533 at 'Bokesbary Land' and 'Penypleck/Pernay Placke', and a tenant was accused of wrongfully holding 20 a. of pasturage and 6 a. of

87 HCA, 6065 (vii)/1–2.
88 HCA, 6065 (vii)/1–2.
89 Edwards, *Cradley*, 43.
90 TNA, MAF 32/6/15.
91 Inf. from local resident.
92 Above, Landscape.
93 *Domesday*, 502.
94 The '*mynde*' may well be derived from the Welsh *mynydd*, suggesting the names were of some long standing: HAS, AM33/13, rot. 21d.; BL, Add. Roll 27311, rot. 5d.; TNA, SC 6/HENVIII/1511, rott. 8d., 16d.
95 HAS, AM33/13, rot. 21d.; BL, Add. Roll 27311, rot. 5d.
96 Some of the 16 a. was probably that mentioned at Westfield and 'Wylleyesino': HAS, R13/10531; CF 54/1/16; P66/1, 5; TNA, CP 25/1/83/52, 43.

meadow.[97] Freehold meadows in the period 1533–8 included a 'Tatwelle Meadow' and a meadow lying below 'Combwell Hill'.[98] In 1839, of the 5,666 a. of the parish subject to tithe, 1,585 a. were meadow or pasture.[99] They were scattered throughout the parish, but concentrated along the banks of the Cradley brook, which was almost entirely bordered by pastures, including meadows. The largest pasture ground was Cowleigh Park.[100]

Cradley manor in 1086 may have required 336 oxen to provide full teams for its ploughs, of which *c.*224 would have been needed by the villeins, bordars and boors of the manor, an average of seven per tenant.[101] Hanley would have required 24.[102] Animals are listed in 16th-century wills, including a two-year-old bullock, a heifer and two kine, belonging to Richard Taylor in 1546; in 1548, Thomas Bullock bequeathed a cow named Silk and a bullock named Burnett.[103] Between 1577 and 1581, a 'Horseland' helped mark the boundary between Storridge and Cradley manors,[104] and in 1589 stock on the glebe land included four oxen, four kine and 20 sheep.[105]

Sheep and cattle were the most common livestock: 33 per cent of wills and inventories from 1550–1700 refer to sheep, and 32 per cent to cattle. Two 1671 inventories suggest a relationship between social status and flock size: Dorothea Pichard, who rented Overbarrow manor, had 64 sheep, whereas John Crisp, a husbandman, had only 17. When he died in 1681, William Hall the younger possessed five calves, three yearling beasts, four two-year-old beasts, seven cows and two bullocks. Dairy production or products (including milk, butter, cheese or equipment such as cheese presses, a milk board and a cheese ring) occur in 8 per cent of probate records.

Pig farming in Cradley, although probably common beforehand, may have become more important after *c.*1670, when it first occurs in wills and inventories. In 1681, Eleanor Stowers, a wealthy spinster, had a sow, three hog swine and 14 other swine, whereas in 1673, John Hill, a husbandman, had only one hog. Poultry 'of all sorts' occur in 13 per cent of probate records (all after 1680), and hives or stalls of bees are mentioned in 1678 (Anne Comby), 1680 (Richard Griffiths) and 1683 (Richard Clarke). Oxen occur in 10 per cent of wills and inventories, 1550–1700, tack of team in 19 per cent and horses in 14 per cent; equipment included wains, ploughs, yokes, ox and horse harrows, saddles and bridles.

Sales particulars after 1800 mention cowhouses (56 per cent) and dairies (52 per cent); several also mention cheese rooms. Cattle farming remained important in 1926, when 24 farms registered under the Milk and Dairies Orders.[106] In 1941, 65 per cent

97 William Bullock held a large amount of customary land in the 1533 rental. The 6 a. in dispute may have been the two meadows held by Christopher Wheler in 1533 and may have been customary land. Penypleck is also recorded as a cottage in 1533 belonging to William Bullock: HAS, R13/10537; TNA, C 1/696/3; SC 6/HENVIII/1511, rot. 8d.

98 The name of the third meadow is damaged: TNA, C 1/831/62.

99 HCA, 6437/II/1. The parish was 5,756 a.

100 Tithe Map (1839); above, Manors and Principal Estates: Cowleigh.

101 The total includes 24 for the bishop's demesne and 88 for the sub-holders and their tenants: *Domesday*, 502. There would usually be eight oxen in a team: Dyer, *Making a Living*, 92.

102 *Domesday*, 514.

103 HAS, 40/1/7, will of Richard Taylor, 1546; also HAS, 8/3/10, will of Thomas Bullock, 1548.

104 It can be found bordering Suckley on the Tithe Map (1839); HAS, AA59/A/2, f. 55v.

105 HAS, HD2/1/30.

106 HAS, BW15/1/5, 19, 26, 38, 46, 53–4, 66, 74, 102, 111, 139, 162, 191.

of farms had cattle, averaging 14 cows, and the largest herd was no more than 62 (at Cradley Hall).[107] The scale of cattle farming subsequently increased; in 1991, Woodend Farm, a dairy and stock farm, had 250 cows, and its agricultural buildings included a milking parlour and slurry store.[108] In 2022, Winthill, Old Upper House, Ridgeway Cross, Hollings Hill and Ridgeway were dairy farms.[109]

Pigsties or houses are mentioned in 54 per cent of post-1800 sales particulars, and this frequency is borne out by architectural evidence.[110] In 1941, Winthill and Birch farms specialised in pig farming, with more pigs (84 and 36 respectively) than other livestock; but 51 per cent of all Cradley farms had pigs, an average of five per farm.[111] Poultry buildings occur in 18 per cent of sales particulars, and The Sturts in 1933 had a pasture poultry holding.[112] In 1941, most farms (76 per cent) had poultry, with 91 chickens on average. Grittlesend (12 a.) then had 500 chickens, and Bourne Villa (2 a.) 210.[113] Sheep were kept on 38 per cent of farms, with an average flock of 65, although Nupend, Cradley Hall, Hill and Seed farms all had over 200. Only three farms (Wold House, The Combe, Batchcombe) had any goats, and then only between one and three.[114]

Stables or loose boxes figure in 62 per cent of sales particulars, including donkey stabling on the Hill estate[115] and an ox house at Cradley Hall Farm in 1842.[116] Two particulars refer to slaughterhouses on farm premises,[117] and Seed Farm had a wooden dovecote.[118]

Vineyards

Philip of 'Vineges' resided in Cradley before 1230,[119] and there was a vineyard in the parish by *c.*1288, when the customary tenants collectively had to pay 5*s.* 6*d.* quarterly for the works of the vineyard (probably replacing former labour services).[120] Robert Wyneward, who held Buriend, may have been the bishop's official overseeing the vineyards in 1346.[121] A 'Vyneghus' is recorded in 1354, and probably survives as Old Vinesend.[122] Three possible medieval sites include Great Vineyard Wood and Little Vineyard Coppice, located on a south-facing site to the south-east of Upper and Lower

107 TNA, MAF 32/6/15.
108 HAS, CO7/3.
109 https://directory.gloucestershirelive.co.uk/search/cradley%2Cgreat-malvern/dairy-farmers (accessed 17 Nov. 2022).
110 J.E.C. Peters, unpubl. report on the architectural history of Cradley's agricultural buildings.
111 TNA, MAF 32/6/15.
112 HAS, M5/6A/8.
113 TNA, MAF 32/6/15.
114 TNA, MAF 32/6/15.
115 HAS, K68/8.
116 HAS, K68/8.
117 HAS, M5/6A/4; HAS, M5/6A/8.
118 Hunt, *Cradley*, 75.
119 *English Episcopal Acta: Hereford 1079–1234*, no. 363.
120 Above Vinesend. How the tenants were to divide the payment of this sum among themselves is not specified: HAS, AA59/A/1, p. 153; Bishop Thomas Cantilupe established a vineyard on his manor of Ledbury before 1289: Smith, *Malvern*, 89.
121 TNA, C 146/10351.
122 Above, Settlement.

Figure 11 *Cutting hay at Seed farm, early 20th century. (CHC)*

Vinesend farms, and a field named The Vineyard in Storridge on the northern border of the parish. The names cannot, however, be traced before 1839.[123]

Orchards

Frequent references to cider, and a few to perry, occur in early modern probate records. A 1612 will (Anne Bullock) bequeathed three bushels of apples, and a 1671 inventory (Dorothea Pichard) included fruit. In 1839 orchards were concentrated around individual farms and settlements.[124] After 1800, most farms had apple orchards,[125] and other types of orchard were also fairly common, including a cherry orchard at Hanley's End (by 1839 a large field),[126] and an orchard planted with cherries and damsons at Pullins Pit in 1920.[127] In 1941, 35 per cent of farms had orchards.[128] Despite a nationwide decline in orcharding, and fewer fruit varieties, Cradley still contained many orchards

123 C.H.I. Homes, 'Herefordshire vineyards', *TWNFC* 41 (1973), 9. Homes incorrectly describes them as lying to the north of Upper and Lower Vinesend; Tithe Map (1839).
124 Tithe Map (1839).
125 E.g. *HJ*, 27 Apr. 1814 (auction of smallholdings at Seven Stars), and HAS, BK13/1/15.
126 Tithe Map (1839).
127 HAS, M5/6A/12.
128 TNA, MAF 32/6/15.

in 2023.[129] On the western border an area of orchards extended from Cowleigh north as far as the New Inn at Storridge, and just beyond was a small pick-your-own orchard at Norrest growing apples, plums, pears and damsons.[130]

Hopyards

Hop cultivation is first mentioned in probate records in 1667 (Richard Hales), and 11 per cent of early modern wills refer to hops or a hopyard. A 1680 will (Richard Griffiths) refers also to 'an old kilnhouse', probably the earliest reference to a hopkiln in Cradley. In 1706, William James owned at least five hopyards,[131] and in 1710 Richard Fawkes owned two.[132] Land and buildings sold in 1775 included a hop ground, orchards, a cider mill, a kiln and a brew house.[133] In 1801, there were 390 a. of hop grounds in Cradley,[134] and in 1839, there were *c.*50 hopyards, scattered throughout the parish; many farms had a hopyard reasonably near the farmhouse and sometimes adjacent to their orchard(s).[135] Hopyards then comprised 250 of the 5,666 a. subject to tithes.[136] Of sales particulars since 1800, 46 per cent mention hopkiln(s) and 30 per cent other hop-related buildings (such as hop rooms, hop-pickers' barracks and hop barns). In 1941, 13 per cent of farms grew hops.[137]

Surviving hopkilns are either circular, so later than *c.*1840, or square, a pattern appearing in the area from the 1870s.[138] Most farms with hop-drying arrangements had two kilns, but a few had only one, or three; Nupend had four, and Beanhouse and Winthill six each, but of these only those at Beanhouse, of the 1890s, survived in 2022. Shew's Patent Drying System was in use in some by 1931.[139] Hop pocket holes were found in a few farm buildings where there was no evidence of kilns: hops here may have been dried on an upper floor without any artificial heat.[140] Hop production declined in the 20th century. A small kiln was built at Brookhouse Farm after 1903, but by 1920 Batchcombe's hopkilns were disused, and by 1931 part of the facilities at Beanhouse had been converted to jam-making quarters.[141]

129 T. Williamson, 'English orchards in history: Production, aesthetics, and myth', *Studies in the History of Gardens and Designed Landscapes* 40:3–4 (2020), 197–215.
130 Inf. from local resident.
131 HAS, AH73/69, pp. 31–2.
132 HAS, AH73/69, pp. 37–41.
133 HAS, AH73/69, pp. 93–6.
134 TNA, HO 67/12.
135 Tithe Map (1839).
136 HCA, 6437/II/1.
137 TNA, MAF 32/6/15.
138 J.E.C. Peters, 'Hop kilns in the West Midlands', *Historic Farm Buildings Group Revd.* 12 (2010), 10–11.
139 OS Maps 1:2500, Herefs. XXIX.5 (1904) and Herefs. XXIX.1 (1905); CHC, sale catalogues of Winthill (1926) and Beanhouse (1931).
140 Since it has not been possible to inspect most of the farmhouses, it is not possible to say whether there is any similar provision in any of them.
141 OS Map 1:2500, Herefs. XXIX.5 (1904); CHC, sale catalogues of Batchcombe (1920) and Beanhouse (1931).

Figure 12 *Hop pickers at Seed farm, c.1900. (CHC)*

Woodland and Forest

In 1086, woodland on Cradley manor was assessed as one league long and half a league broad, and included a *haia*, probably an area of wood pasture rather than a hunting ground.[142] Cradley's woodlands were a significant part of its economy, though they shrank over the centuries. Woodland rights and products featured in many wills and indentures. In 1458, an indenture of Robert Polayn for a messuage at 'Hetheplace' and at 'Raynoldes' stipulated that he should not sell or surrender trees or underwood, but he retained the right to *housebote* (timber for house building), *fuyrebote* (firewood) and *haybote* (wood for hedging).[143] The Hill family charters mention *hays* several times in the 14th and 15th century, including one near Stifford in 1402–3.[144] Around 1289, the bishop's reeve collected charcoal from the woods at Storridge for carriage to Bosbury.[145] Storridge also possessed a piece of common woodland called Vallett wood in the 16th century.[146] The bishop retained the right to a render from wood sold from Cradley manor, though in 1536 Bearswood rendered nothing.[147] Chiminage was also collected

142 *Domesday*, 502. For a discussion of hays in Domesday, see S.J. Wager, *Agric. Hist. Rev.* 65:2 (2017), 167–93.

143 HAS, CF 54/1/25.

144 HAS, R13/10531; R13/10534–5.

145 *Expenses of Swinfield*, 29.

146 HAS, AA59/A/2, f. 9v.

147 TNA, SC 6/HENVIII/1511, rot. 8d.

Figure 13a *Photo of the probable seal impression of Thomas Hill, 1458. An equestrian figure turned face towards the viewer, a bird of prey in the left hand, a hunting horn held in the right. (HAS, CF54/1/25)*

in the bishop's manor.[148] In 1515, the prior and convent of Worcester fined Peter Hall for cutting down branches without the lord's permission in Overbarrow.[149]

The bishop employed a *woodward* (forester) for Cradley, both to prevent depredation of the underwood and timber, and to guard the resident young *eyesses* (unfledged hawks) and falcons; he was paid £6 17*s.* 6*d.*[150] A messuage called Woodward is recorded between 1577 and 1581 in Storridge, which had until recently been in the hands of the Woodwarde family.[151] Other evidence of falconry in the parish, particularly in the more heavily wooded region east of Cradley brook, may be a 1458 seal which probably belonged to the Hill family. Its impression displays a rider bearing a bird of prey on his wrist.[152] The motif was unlikely to have been randomly chosen, and the continued use

148 HAS, AM33/13–15; TNA, SC 6/HENVIII/1511 rot. 8d.; BL, Add. Roll 27311, rot. 5d.

149 WCM, E182.

150 *Expenses of Swinfield*, 179; HAS, AH73/38, p. 132.

151 This probably became Woodhouse, found on field names in the Tithe Map (1839); HAS, AA59/A/2, ff. 25v, 55v.

152 HAS, CF 54/1/25. While there is no legend, evidence within the charter points firmly towards the seal impression belonging to Thomas Hill.

Figure 13b *Sketch of the probable seal impression of Thomas Hill. (Fergus Eskola-Oakes)*

of the matrix suggests that hunting with birds had some enduring family connection, whether hunting rights granted by the bishop or other responsibilities.[153]

Hawks were reportedly trained for hunting in the land westwards down towards Cradley brook,[154] where Hawkhurst Cottage and House are situated; the cottage possessed a hawker's bothy until relatively recently. After 1300, Henry of Cowleigh held 'Hulcroft' from Philip of Vyneges in return for one barbed arrow rendered at Easter. 'Hulcroft' probably lay in the parish's heavily wooded east, and the arrow signified hunting in the area.[155]

At Crumpton Oaks, south-east of Storridge, there are signs of a ring boundary partly encircling the farm, which may denote a park pale; the feature is most evident less than 500m. north of the farm.[156]

Woodland and coppices continued to be an important part of Cradley's economy. Overbarrow manor in 1649 possessed woodland including 600 timber oaks worth £300,

153 Pers. comm. Dr Elizabeth New, who observes that the matrix appears to be 14th-century in origin, with indications that it was originally a sophisticated screw-out design. On screw-out matrices, see P.D.A. Harvey and A. McGuiness, *A Guide to British Medieval Seals* (Toronto, 1996).

154 Hawkhurst Cottage, SO 73534 47436; Hawkhurst House, SO 73561 47466; inf. on the bothy and hawking from local resident Jeff White.

155 TNA, C 146/9708.

156 Personal observations by Keith Ray from historical maps and ground inspection, Jan. 2019.

Figure 14 *Sawing at Seed farm, c.1905, with Mr Preston's engine. (CHC)*

and rent was paid partly in timber, valued at 10*s*. a year.[157] Several wills mention wood or its cultivation, and a blacksmith (William James), between 1695 and 1710, bought many parcels of woodland[158] and reserved the trees and wood for his own use on arable land he rented out.[159] Cradley's coppices presumably provided fuel for his trade and an additional source of wealth. In 1801, there were 600 a. of coppices in the parish.[160]

Timber might be auctioned in quite large quantities, such as the 70 maiden oak timbers from the Barrow Mills estate sold at the Seven Stars in 1807.[161] Tree bark was harvested and sold in the early 19th century.[162] Coppices constituted part of the income of Richard Hill's charity.[163] In 1814, tithes on woodland on The Hyde's Low estate were the subject of a protracted legal dispute.[164]

In 1839, Cradley's woodlands were mostly in the east of the parish, and concentrated in the north-east. In the west the numerous woods were small and scattered, apart from a larger area formed by the neighbouring coppices of Blackhouse, Park Barrow, Barrow and Barley hill. Relatively large areas of woodland lay in the east of the parish. Coppices from the parish boundary to Halesend wood connected with more coppices adjacent

157 Cave and Wilson (eds), *Parliamentary Survey*, 111.
158 Some of this was in 'Lumbry Hill', probably the modern day Lumbridge Hill wood.
159 HAS, AH73/69.
160 TNA, HO 67/12.
161 *HJ*, 25 Mar. 1807 (auction at the Seven Stars).
162 WAS, b705:1224 11516(ii).
163 Below, Social Welfare.
164 HAS, F35/RC/iv/E/2092–3008; *HJ*, 14 Sept. 1814 (coverage of the dispute).

to woodland on Whitman's hill; woodland ran from Ryefield to Oaken Grove; Mallins Coppice, High wood and Bough Fell were also wooded. In 1839, of the 5,666 a. of Cradley subject to tithe, 910 a. was woodland.[165] In 2023, the east of the parish remained the most wooded, with a large area of woodland including Halesend wood, Whitman's hill's coppice, and Six Acre wood, which ran uninterrupted from the northern parish boundary to the southern. Another broken stripe of woodland stretches north to south, including Mallins wood, Deep Leasow, Limekiln coppice, Oaken coppice, and Rough Hill wood.[166] The west of the parish has only scattered small areas of woodland, apart from the larger Riley hill and Blackhouse Rough wood.

Mills, Crafts and Industry

Corn Mills

In 1066, the bishop of Hereford had a mill in Cradley which in 1086 rendered 32*d*.[167] The bishop's mill had either been lost or removed from the demesne by *c*.1288, when two mills were held freehold, one by Geoffrey of Cradley and the other jointly by William de la Morendo and Robert Palmer. They cannot be reliably identified with other mills, and no demesne mill is recorded later.[168]

Stifford Mill is recorded *c*.1330 and seems to have belonged to the Hill family.[169] It is probably the mill granted in 1411 by John and Alice Hill to William and Ellen Walwyn.[170] It plausibly stood near present-day Mill Bank, where a leat is recorded in 1890.[171]

Barrow Mills: A mill is first recorded in Barrow *c*.1275 and again in the 14th century.[172] In 1521, John Pichard of Suckley specified a corn mill in his will,[173] and this may have been the water mill of Thomas Pichard when he died in 1533.[174] His son John sold it back to his uncle, also John Pichard, later in the 1530s.[175] Barrow Mill featured on a map of 1754.[176] After 1800, the millers' names are known, including William Smith and his sons from 1851 to *c*.1920. The mill belonged to the Barrow Mills estate but was tenanted separately.[177]

165 Tithe Map (1839); HCA, 6437/II/1.
166 OS Map 1:25000, Explorer Sheet 190 (2015 edn).
167 *Domesday*, 502.
168 HAS, AA59/A/1, p. 148; TNA, SC 6/HENVIII/1511, rot. 16d.
169 HAS, P66/5.
170 TNA, CP 25/1/83/52, no. 43.
171 HAS, N37/74; HAS, BJ2/1.
172 WCM, B231; the mill's name is partially damaged, but began 'War. . .'; WCM, B243b.
173 Above, Landownership: The Barrow and successors; *The Picards or Pychards of Stradewy (now Tretower) Castle and Scethrog, Brecknockshire* (1878), 141; TNA, C 1/866/83. It is unclear whether these are the same two mills mentioned in John's possession in 1495: TNA, CP 25/1/83/58, no. 8.
174 See Manors and Principal Estates: Netherbarrow, Beanhouse, Barrow Mills; *The Picards*, 141; HAS, R13/10537.
175 TNA, C 1/866/83.
176 Smith, *Herefordshire Maps*, pl. 22.
177 *HJ*, 31 Aug. 1814 and 19 July 1820 (sale of Barrow Mills estate).

Figure 15 *Beanhouse Mill, mid 20th century. (CHC)*

Heath Mill is first recorded in 1345–6 as *Geffemulle*, probably from the Middle English *geffe* or *yeven*, meaning gift.[178] Described as a water mill, the 'Gift Mill' belonged to the Cowleigh family *c.*1345, who granted it with land to Alan Charnes for life at a nominal rent.[179] Its name suggests that the generous terms may have been customary, though their origins are unknown. On a 1754 map, the mill on this site (on the Cradley and Mathon boundary) is unnamed,[180] but by 1834 a map records it as Yeaffe Mill, and by 1839 its name had become Heath Mill.[181] John Turner ran it in the 1850s, then F.D. Bowen in the 1860s and Samuel Smith (son of William Smith of Barrow Mill) from the 1870s to *c.*1900, followed by his wife until *c.*1920. James Faulkes had taken it over by the early 1920s, and it still existed in 1950, but was no longer operational in 2022.

The mill was rebuilt during the 19th century. It has two floors plus a loft, with a malt kiln attached. The leat runs under the buildings and yard.[182]

Beanhouse Mill (see figure 15), named 'Nether Mill' on a 1754 map,[183] and also known as Archer's Mill and Cradley Mill,[184] was a flour and grist mill with an undershot water wheel.[185] It is probably the mill run by a Mr Morris in 1799.[186] The miller was Thomas Archer, between the 1850s and 1880s, then his son – Thomas William – until *c.*1900, and

178 This can have the sense of alms, https://quod.lib.umich.edu/m/middle-english-dictionary/dictionary/MED53944 (accessed 1 Aug. 2023).

179 The rent of one rose for the term of his life, to be delivered on the feast of the Nativity of John the Baptist (24 June), TNA, C 146/9769, C 146/3218; it is mentioned again in 1393: HAS, C96/1.

180 Smith, *Herefordshire Maps*, pl. 22.

181 Hunt, *Cradley*, 152; Tithe Map (1839).

182 J.E.C. Peters, unpubl. report on the architectural history of Cradley's agricultural buildings.

183 Smith, *Herefordshire Maps*, pl. 22.

184 HER, 4821.

185 HAS, M5/6A/5; HER, 4821.

186 *HJ*, 16 Jan. 1799 (sale of Seed estate).

the latter's son until the 1950s or later.[187] It belonged to E.B. Archer until *c.*1970, when it was bought by Bernard Higgins of Halesend.[188] The mill building is an 18th-century, four-storey limestone-rubble structure, with slate roof and brick dressings to windows and lintels.[189] The mill functioned in 1971,[190] but not in 2023. There is also a small, 17th-century timber-framed cottage on the site.[191] The buildings are now used for The Clover Mill spa and wellness centre as an Ayurvedic retreat.[192]

Rectory mill: First recorded in 1589, a water-driven corn mill belonging to the rectory was still operating in 1635.[193] Its location is uncertain, but potential sites include Bason Croft (now Jubilee Fields), where a pond and traces of a leat are located, or just north of the rectory and church.[194] Lying next to a leat, the land upon which the post office sits was in 1839 named Big Run, and was adjacent to Mill Meadow, suggesting they served this 16th-century mill, of which the post office may originally have been part.[195]

Wold mill: Depicted as 'Cradley Mill' on a map of 1754,[196] by *c.*1800 Wold mill was ruinous.[197] Surviving buildings in 2022 include a Georgian or Victorian house and an arrangement of farm buildings.[198] The leat, extant in 1886, came off the Cradley brook south of Pound bridge.[199]

Unidentified mills: In 1330, an unnamed mill with a messuage and carucate belonged to John Biyendenhe.[200]

A 1655 indenture between Cradley manorial lord James Hopton and Richard Fawke the younger of Mathon conveyed land and buildings, including a millhouse[201] which may have been the manorial mill. Fawke's will of 1661 leaves to his wife Amy two 'waterborne mills' in Cradley which were formerly in the possession of John Loggin;[202] whether either was the mill bought from Hopton is uncertain.[203]

A parcel of ground called 'Mill Croft' belonged to William James in 1696, and in 1747 was held by Edward Miller, a tenant of Thomas James. A 1775 indenture refers to a former mill on a parcel of land called the Dingle, apparently next to Mill Croft.[204] A Mill Croft (perhaps the same) was located in 1839 adjacent to Whippets brook, just south of Cowleigh Gate.[205]

187 HAS, CL82.
188 HER, 4821.
189 HER, 4821; inf. from local resident; NHLE, no. 1082273, Beanhouse Mill (accessed 1 Aug. 2023).
190 HER, 4821.
191 Hunt, *Cradley*, 59; NHLE, no. 1349659, Beanhouse Mill Cott. (accessed 1 Aug. 2023).
192 https://www.theclovermill.com (accessed 1 Aug. 2023).
193 HAS, HD2/1/30–2.
194 HAS, HD2/1/30; *Cradley Conservation Area Appraisal Draft* (2007), 8 (accessed 17 Nov. 2022).
195 Above, The Built Character.
196 Smith, *Herefordshire Maps*, pl. 22.
197 HAS, N37/74; HAS, BJ2/1, II-191.
198 NHLE, no. 1349667, Wold Mill ho. (accessed 1 Aug. 2023); inf. from local resident.
199 OS Map 1:10560, Herefs. XXIX.SW (1886 edn).
200 TNA, CP 25/1/82/37, no. 22.
201 HAS, AH73/69, pp. 13–14.
202 These may have been a double mill.
203 HAS, AH73/69, pp. 15–16.
204 HAS, AH73/69, pp. 49, 93–6.
205 Tithe Map (1839).

A 1674 deed refers to a former mill on a parcel of ground called Millclose,[206] and a lease of 1812 mentions that a mill formerly stood by Little Meadow in Cradley.[207]

Quarrying[208]

William Bullock of Cradley is referred to as 'of the quarrey' in the period 1532–8.[209] A map of 1754 seems to depict a quarry accessed from a small road running south from the Ridgeway.[210] By the late 19th century, *c.*70 quarries or 'old' quarries, several gravel pits and one 'old sand pit' appear on Ordnance Survey maps. Only one 'old clay pit' is shown, perhaps indicating the inferiority of Cradley's clay compared with that extracted in neighbouring parishes.[211] Quarrying was then widespread throughout the parish, for sandstone on the western side and limestone on the east. On the south-eastern tip of the parish, Malvern granite was taken from the hillside, and Raglan Mudstone Formation was quarried at one site.[212]

Cradley stone is sandstone of the Freshwater West classification (previously known as St Maughan's Formation).[213] As a freestone (easily worked in any direction and shaped into neat ashlar blocks), it was in great demand after *c.*1850 in the Malvern area, where much building was taking place, and many significant Victorian and Edwardian buildings were constructed from Cradley stone. In 1841 and 1855, maps depict small-scale workings predominantly for local building work, but by *c.*1880 quarrying had become a substantial commercial venture.[214]

The most significant quarry was that to the north-west of Ridgeway Cross. In 1855, it was owned by George McCann, the most important builder in the Malvern area in the 1840s to the 1870s, who built several workers' cottages and used the quarry stone for his building projects.[215] He built not only houses, but also Storridge church (from 1856),[216] St Mary's church in Guarlford (Malvern) and the railway station at Malvern Link. By 1876 the quarry had been taken over by William Hopkinson (a former stonemason),[217] and by 1905 passed to his sons; shortly after 1913 it closed, as the extraction of the remaining stone was no longer viable.[218] The last building constructed of Cradley stone was the Elim College in West Malvern (then a mansion house: St James's).

206 HAS, AH73/69, pp. 65–8.
207 HAS, W9/32.
208 Valerie Goodbury is the primary author of this section.
209 TNA, C 1/696/3.
210 https://digitalarchive.mcmaster.ca/islandora/object/macrepo%3A81082 (accessed 18 Sept. 2023). This was no longer operational by 1886 but may be the site of 'Quarry Farm': OS Map 1:10560, Herefs. XXVIII.SE (1886 edn).
211 OS Map 1:10560, Herefs. XXVIII.NE; XXVIII.SW; XXVIII.SE; XXIX.NW; XXIX.SW (1886, 1906 edns).
212 http://www.buildingstones.org.uk/search (accessed 1 Aug. 2023).
213 http://www.buildingstones.org.uk/search (accessed 1 Aug. 2023); J. Payne (ed.), *Herefordshire's Rock & Scenery: A Geology of the County* (Eardisley, 2017), 200.
214 HAS, AK19/20; HAS, BO80/16; OS Map 1:10560, Herefs. XXVIII.SE.
215 HAS, Cradley tithe map & apportionment; HAS, AK19/20; HAS, BO80/16.
216 Hunt, *Cradley*, 8. Below, Church Architecture: Storridge St John the Evangelist.
217 *Cassey's Dir.* (1858); Census, 1871; *Littlebury's Dir.* (1876/7).
218 OS Map 1:2500, Herefs. XXVIII 12 (1903 edn); Hunt, *Cradley*, 72.

The limestone found in Cradley is classified as Much Wenlock and was used principally for aggregate and for lime;[219] this was used primarily by local farmers to improve the acidic soil, but also to limewash buildings, in construction (as mortar, and as an ingredient in daub for timber-framed structures) and by local tanners for preparing their hides.[220] By *c.*1750, it was quarried at Halesend, and after *c.*1800 at Whitman's.[221] Nine field names with limekiln elements are recorded in 1841 and six (all but one on different sites) in 1887. Three of those depicted in 1905 remained in 1992, but one was in very poor condition.[222]

Malvern granite was quarried from a small area at the northern tip on North hill that lay within Cradley parish, but no quarry is shown there on maps of 1841 or 1855. By 1887, and still in 1905, a quarry is shown reaching to the edge of the road opposite the Redan public house, but quarrying had probably ceased by the latter date, as several properties had been built within the area of the quarry.[223]

In 1920, one of the two limekilns on the Vinesend estate was still in hand.[224] In 1937, it was proposed that Lime Quarry at Vinesend (one of Cradley's many disused 19th-century quarries) be reopened.[225] In 1950, Whitman's hill limestone quarry at Storridge was extended.[226] In 1970, Huntsman Quarries Ltd were owners,[227] and blasting occurred twice weekly in 1971, despite complaints from nearby residents.[228] By 1988, the quarry had been worked out.[229]

Before 1856 (but probably after 1800), 'anthracitic shale' was found between Whitman's hill and Halesend, and 'credulous speculators . . . at various times made trials for coal on the western side of the Malvern Hills'.[230] Coal was discovered under the Vinesend banks and a mine shaft sunk at Lower Vinesend. Badsey Coal Company bought out the rights, but the mine was never worked. By 1913, the abandoned mine shaft was used by the farmer as a dumping hole.[231]

Crafts

Surname evidence suggest that Cradley's woodland landscape had a significant role in shaping the occupations of its inhabitants. Robert Turner and Robert Wheelwright (*Rotarius*) were customary tenants *c.*1288, the latter holding 16 a. and 9 a. of *forlet*.[232]

219 http://www.earthheritagetrust.org (accessed 17 Nov. 2022). For the extraction and use of Cradley's limestones, see, *inter alia*, HAS, N37/32 and HAS, N37/36.
220 V. Goodbury, 'Herefordshire limekilns' (unpubl. dissertation; Univ. of Birmingham, Ironbridge Institute, 1992).
221 HAS, N37/32; HAS, N37/36; HER, 4817.
222 Goodbury, 'Herefordshire limekilns'.
223 OS Map 1:2500, Herefs. XXIX 10 (1887 and 1905 edns).
224 HAS, M5/6A/2.
225 HAS, BW15/1/7, p. 8.
226 HAS, BW15/1/8, p. 286.
227 CHC, Parish Council Minutes, II, 24 Nov. 1970.
228 HAS, BW15/3/2, p. 273.
229 CHC, Parish Council Minutes, II, 21 June 1988.
230 E. Lees, *Pictures from Nature* (Malvern, 1856), 130–1.
231 Edwards, *Cradley*, 6.
232 See Glossary. By 1400 surnames do not necessarily denote occupations.

A *seaver* (sieve maker), John Albard, and a turner, Richard Knyght, are recorded in 1460,[233] and a turner, Thomas Drayton, in 1615. When Rowland Barrett died in 1683, his possessions included 'tools belonging to his trade and some timber', suggesting that he may have been a carpenter. In 1596, Richard Reynolds described himself as a collier, which, in the absence of coal mines, probably meant that he was a charcoal burner.[234]

After 1800, baptismal registers show evidence of woodmen, sawyers and charcoal burners alongside carpenters and other craftspeople. Fifteen carpenters are recorded in the period 1813–47,[235] and 16 in 1841,[236] and according to the baptismal registers, the profession was the third most common in Cradley in the first half of the 19th century.[237] Throughout the century, 4–5 per cent of Cradley men were carpenters, with eight recorded over the period 1875–1909.[238] Six lath cleavers (who made laths for building) are recorded 1813–47, and two wheelwrights and one fitter 1875–1909.[239] A hurdle-maker is recorded in 1839,[240] and two coopers, a handle-maker, two hooper shavers, two lath cleavers, a turner and six wheelwrights were listed in the 1841 Census.[241] There were at least three wheelwrights in 1913,[242] and two in 1927.[243] Two sawyers and a woodman are recorded 1875–1909.[244] It is probable that the carpenters, wheelwrights and fitter worked with Cradley wood.

Smithing in the parish is suggested by John Smith, a half-yardlander *c.*1288.[245] A husbandman in 1570 passed two iron towels (the nozzles of a blacksmith's bellows) to a son, implying a trade passed down through the family.[246] In 1722, Henry Dixon was an ironmonger.[247] Smiths are recorded in the 17th and 18th century.[248] William Smith, a blacksmith who died in 1679, was deemed sufficiently important to warrant burial and a monument within the parish church.[249] Blacksmiths constituted 3 per cent of entries in both the 1813–47 and 1875–1909 baptismal registers;[250] six blacksmiths are listed in the 1841 census.[251] In 1898, a smithy stood by the river next to the Seven Stars Inn and

233 TNA, CP 40/796.
234 See Appendices, Sample 2, 45, 105, 19.
235 HAS, AH73/5; HAS, BM72/1.
236 Census, 1841.
237 HAS, AH73/5; HAS, BM72/1.
238 HAS, AH73/5; HAS, BM72/1.
239 HAS, AH73/5; HAS, BM72/1.
240 HAS, W9/3.
241 Census 1841.
242 Edwards, *Cradley*, 29–34.
243 Edwards, *Cradley*, 54–6.
244 HAS, BM72/1.
245 HAS, AA59/A/1, p. 150.
246 See Appendix, Sample 11.
247 CHC, Copy of pre-nuptial settlement, 31 Dec. 1772 between Richard Hill and Henry Dixon.
248 Thomas James in 1695: HAS, 122-1-23; William James in 1690s and 1700s: HAS, AH73/69, 21–44; Richard Yapp in 1708: HCA, 4799.
249 HAS, MB81/1/19.
250 HAS, AH73/5; HAS, BM72/1.
251 Census, 1841.

another at Stony Cross.[252] At least three blacksmiths are recorded in 1913.[253] The decline in blacksmiths and wheelwrights in Cradley in the 1920s was attributed to the advent of tractors.[254]

The ready supply of bark from its woodlands and access to flowing water made Cradley an attractive location for tanning. Tanners are recorded in 1657,[255] 1699[256] and 1754.[257] In 1839, at least eight fields were called Tanhouse Field, in addition to Tanhouse Lane and Tanhouse Farm, suggesting five possible tannery sites close to flowing water. Storridge also had a Tanner's Cottage.[258] But the lack of tannery workers in the Victorian censuses implies that little tanning was taking place during the later 19th century, although a bender (meaning a leather cutter) appears in 1822,[259] and a tanner 1875–1909.[260]

Leather working is represented in 1354 by Hugh 'Jonesservant *Le Glovere*', and in 1418 John of Cradley was described as a *corviser*, a leather worker or shoemaker.[261] A glover is recorded in 1690.[262] These crafts sometimes passed down the family: William and John Archer were shoemakers in 1745 and 1785 respectively. [263] Lists of apprentices survive dating back to 1740, but do not specify the trade.[264] Directories list 13 boot- and shoemakers between *c.*1841 and 1909, and a further seven, and two shoe binders (both women, as was usual), were enumerated in the 1851 and 1861 censuses. In 1913 and 1927 there was at least one shoemaker, and a harness maker in 1913 also.[265] Frank Badham was a boot repairer in the period 1926–34, but then became a coal merchant.[266]

Henry Tailor is recorded *c.*1230.[267] Tailors are recorded in 1521, 1614 and 1624,[268] and three are enumerated in the 1841–61 censuses.[269] John Pichard in 1521 bequeathed a walk or fulling mill to his son Thomas together with the corn mill;[270] both mills were sold back before 1540.[271] The location of the fulling mill is unknown and it is not recorded after the 16th century.

252 OS Map 1:63360, Worcs., sheet 199 (1898 edn).
253 Edwards, *Cradley*, 29–34.
254 Edwards, *Cradley*, 43.
255 See below, Appendices, Sample 2, 72.
256 See below, Appendices, Sample 2, 115.
257 TNA, PROB 11/808/154, will of Daniel Racster, 1754.
258 Tithe Map (1839).
259 HAS, AH73/5.
260 HAS, BM72/1.
261 Above, Manors and Principal Estates: Cowleigh; *Reg. Trillek*, I, 207; *Cal. Pat.* 1354–8, 56; TNA, CP 40/629.
262 See Appendices, Sample 1, 99.
263 HAS, W9/15, W9/21.
264 HAS, N37/33.
265 Edwards, *Cradley*, 29–34, 54–6.
266 *Kelly's Dir. Herefs.* (1926–34 edns).
267 *English Episcopal Acta: Hereford 1079–1234*, no. 363.
268 Richard Tomlyns in 1521, TNA, CP 40/1031; see below, Appendices, Sample 2, 40 and 56.
269 Censuses, 1851–1901.
270 *The Picards*, 141; TNA, C 1/866/83.
271 TNA, C 1/866/83.

A weaver, Nathaniel Hill, is recorded in 1591.[272] One draper appears in the 1875–1909 baptismal register.[273] Fifteen dressmakers are recorded between 1851 and 1901,[274] and in 1913 there were at least two working in the parish.[275] Two seamstresses were active in the period 1851–61, and in 1881 one plain sewer and one needleworker.[276] By 1841, there was one spinster (age 30) and one wool spinner (age 75) as well as a wool carder (age 85), suggesting that, as elsewhere, these were now roles taken primarily by elderly women, perhaps widows.[277] In 1879, a laundress was listed in a directory.[278]

Legislation in 1765–6 encouraged the import of foreign kid and lamb skins, and this led to the rapid expansion of the glove trade in Worcester and nearby parishes.[279] In 1816, the trade was said to afford 'employment to numbers of industrious poor in the parishes of Ledbury, Cradley, Bosbury and various other parts of the adjoining county of Hereford'.[280] Cradley women may have learned to sew gloves for local manufacturers, and then passed the skill on to subsequent generations. They may also have found employment from Ledbury, where a glover is recorded in 1838.[281] No detailed information is available on the number of gloveresses in Cradley at this period, although the parish registers record 37 illegitimate children born to gloveresses between 1818 and 1838.[282] Laws passed in 1826, removing all prohibitions on imported gloves,[283] and 1860, removing all import duty on gloves,[284] were catastrophic blows. A writer in 1868 claimed that, although some three quarters of the trade had been destroyed in about the previous 50 years, there were still thousands of persons employed, including the female seamstresses in rural districts.[285] The 1851 census records 144 gloveresses in Cradley, of whom 13 were described as paupers. By 1861, the number had fallen to 80, two of whom were described as 'cloth glove maker', with six women were classified as 'former gloveress'. The decline continued, with 61 gloveresses being recorded in 1871, and 65 in 1881, but only 29 in 1891. Where it is possible to trace former gloveresses on subsequent censuses, most record no employment, and a number are described as 'pauper gloveress'.[286] Gloveresses lived throughout the parish, often in groups, with concentrations in two distinct and rather isolated areas, Bearswood Common and Birchwood Common, where almost every property housed at least one gloveress. Their age range was wide, from 10 to 76, and most were the wives or daughters of agricultural labourers.[287]

272 See Appendices, Sample 2, 17.
273 HAS, BM72/1.
274 Censuses, 1851–1901.
275 Edwards, *Cradley*, 29–34.
276 Censuses, 1851–1901.
277 Census, 1841; see *VCH Herefs. Bosbury*, 47–8.
278 Censuses, 1851–1901.
279 S.W. Beck, *Gloves: Their Annals and Associations* (1883), 162. Valerie Goodbury is the primary author of this material on gloving.
280 W.R.T. Eaton, *A Concise History of Worcester* (Worcester, 1816), 43.
281 *Robson's Dir.* (1838); *Ledbury: A Market Town and Its Tudor Heritage*, pp. 99–102.
282 HAS, AH73/5.
283 D.C. Lyes, *The Leather Glove Industry of Worcester in the Nineteenth Century* (Worcester, 1973), 24.
284 Beck, *Gloves: Their Annals and Associations*, 171.
285 J. Noake, *Guide to Worcestershire* (1868), 370.
286 Censuses, 1851–91.
287 Censuses, 1851–91.

A mason is recorded in Cradley in 1653,[288] and another in 1680.[289] Thomas Apperley, a stonemason living near Stifford's Bridge, was responsible for some monuments in the churchyard in the late 18th century.[290] The numerous quarries in the parish provided significant employment in the 19th century;[291] the 1851 census listed 11 masons, two quarrymen, eight mason's labourers, five quarry labourers, a stone cutter, a stone sawyer and a bricklayer.[292] Other men employed in quarrying when needed are described as labourers or agricultural labourers in the census returns. The censuses also show that quarrying was an occupation followed by several generations of the same family.[293] In 1913, there were four builders and a memorial sculptor.[294]

In 1929, Gibbs & Co. was listed in a directory as a jam manufacturer at Ridgeway Cross. In 1965, seven people from Cradley worked at the Worcester porcelain works.[295]

Crafts encompassed 19 per cent of occupations listed in the 1841 census, highlighting their importance in the parish economy.[296] The 696 entries for fathers' occupations in the parish baptismal register for 1875–1909 encompassed a wide range of crafts. Many, but by no means all, centred on stone, wood, leather and cloth. There were also bricklayers, hoop makers, a brazier, a glazier, a chandler, builders, plumbers, machinists, a machine maker, a roadman and watchmakers.[297] The diversity gradually diminished during the 20th century, and traditional crafts, such as blacksmithing, wheelwrights and shoemakers, had entirely disappeared by the 21st century.

In 1913, Cradley had at least five grocers, two butchers, two laundresses, a florist, a market gardener, a fruit grower, four undertakers and a village stores (previously the Bullshead pub).[298] In 1927, there were at least three builders and two taxis.[299] In 1971, there was a car repair workshop at Birches filling station.[300] In 1982, Birchwood Lodge changed from a blacksmith's forge to livery stables.[301] In 2023, there were two shops – a general stores and a garden supplies store; there were also car workshops and an art gallery.[302]

Between 1984 and 1991, small-scale production industries were established in redundant agricultural buildings and on new premises. The barn at Nethergreen Farm became a workshop for the restoration of vintage cars, and an agricultural storage building at Pullens Farm was used to produce horticultural containers. Norburys Norrest

288 TNA, PROB 11/253/575.
289 Below, Appendices, Sample 2, 93.
290 *HJ*, 17 Mar. 1790 (auction stonemason's premises); Apperley's signed monuments of 1785, 1790 and an unknown date can be seen in Cradley churchyard; J.I. Currie, *Three Centuries of a Herefordshire Village: Putley, 1685 until Now* (Putley, 2009), 93.
291 Above, Mills, Crafts and Industry: Quarrying.
292 In the censuses 'mason' was applied to anyone working with stone, and someone raising or breaking the stone was not necessarily described as a 'quarryman'.
293 Censuses, 1841–1911.
294 Edwards, *Cradley*, 29–34.
295 HAS, BL20/2, p. 548.
296 Census, 1841.
297 HAS, BM72/1.
298 Edwards, *Cradley*, 29–34. Below, Mills, Crafts and Industry: Retail; Communal Life: Inns.
299 Edwards, *Cradley*, 54–6.
300 CHC, Parish Council Minutes, II, 16 Nov. 1971.
301 CHC, Parish Council Minutes, II, 20 July 1982.
302 Inf. from a local resident.

Fruit Farm & Cider Company opened a new building for cider making and storage, two industrial units were built at Ashvale[303] and a bottling plant was established at Seed Farm.[304]

Services

Servants figure in 13 per cent of the early modern wills, and of these, two thirds were women.[305] Bequests to servants ranged from the fairly modest to the extremely generous, with two individuals leaving most of their messuages and goods to a servant.[306] In the 1841 census, services account for 19 per cent of occupations, although some individuals probably worked in neighbouring parishes. A large majority (97 in total, with fairly equal numbers of men and women) were servants.[307]

Some residents offered services elsewhere, including many laundresses in the late 19th and early 20th century servicing the growing number of hotels in the Malvern area.[308] In the early 1900s, five travelling hawkers had their official place of abode as Cradley.[309] One railway guard and one railway porter (perhaps employed at the nearby station of Suckley) occur in the 1875–1909 baptismal register.[310]

The redundant farm buildings at Upper House Farm Greenhill were converted for the use of Halesend Investments Ltd in 1988.[311]

Retail

A tinker in 1572 and a victualler in 1616 are recorded in probate records.[312] From the 1670s to the 1690s, the relatively wealthy Francis Pengrifte was a butcher.[313]

In the early modern period many households produced alcohol, either for domestic use or perhaps to sell. Malt mills occur in 10 per cent of probate records between 1550 and 1700, beer in 4 per cent, must mills in 7 per cent and cider mills in 10 per cent. In 1558, Rychard Hallis bequeathed his recently built must mill and a broache to be used as a standard in it.[314] Roger White's farmhouse in 1681 included a malthouse.[315] Cider is mentioned in 17 per cent of inventories, and there are two references to cider presses. A 1667 inventory (of Richard Hales) includes a perry mill stone and all appurtenances, and four wills and inventories refer to perry. After 1800, 46 per cent of farms had facilities for cider production or storage.[316] In 1920, Lower Vinesend had a cider house with a stone

303 CHC, Parish Council Minutes, II, 15 Nov. 1988.
304 HAS, CO7/3. 18 Sep. 1990.
305 See Appendices, Sample 1.
306 See Appendices, Sample 1, 78 and 87.
307 Census, 1841.
308 *Kelly's Dir.* (1979); censuses, 1871–1921.
309 HAS, MX321.
310 HAS, MX321.
311 CHC, Parish Council Minutes, II, 23 Feb. 1988.
312 See Appendices, Sample 2, 8 and 46.
313 See Appendices, Sample 2, 111; HAS, S82/3; HAS, AH73/69, 65–9; TNA, C 6/287/107.
314 HAS, 20-5-7, will of Rychard Hallis, 1558.
315 See Appendices, Sample 2, 92.
316 See Appendices, Sample 1, 71; Sample 3.

Figure 16 *Cradley Stores c.1897. (CHC)*

cider mill and press, and a cider storeroom.[317] In the 20th century, two farms had malt kilns; one at Mill Bank was a large building much altered since then, the other a single kiln attached to Heath Mill.[318]

Shopkeepers recorded in 1841 included four butchers and three grocers, and five individuals working in pubs.[319] Of fathers' occupations given in the 1813–47 baptismal register, 5 per cent worked in retail trades. This includes blacksmiths, butchers, innkeepers, grocers and tailors, as well as unspecified shopkeepers, not all of whom would have had shops.[320] In the period 1875–1909, 8 per cent of fathers in the register worked in retail, and the variety of shops had therefore probably expanded.[321] This is corroborated by the directories and censuses, which show the range of Cradley's retailers. Five men operated as bakers and grocers between 1879 and 1909, 11 individuals (including at least one woman) worked as butchers between 1863 and 1950, and 11 were grocers 1876–1929. Three men operated as clock-/watchmakers between 1879 and 1950, four as florists between 1851 and 1950, and two as coal merchants between 1868 and 1950. Six men and three women listed themselves simply as shopkeepers in the directories between 1851 and 1950 (one man was also a beer retailer). There were also provisions dealers.[322]

317 HAS, M5/6A/2.
318 J.E.C. Peters, unpubl. report on the architectural history of Cradley's agricultural buildings.
319 Census, 1841.
320 HAS, MX182.
321 HAS, MX321.
322 Census, 1841–1901. *Pigot's Dir. Herefs.* 1833–68; *Littlebury's Dir Herefs.* 1867–77; *Kelly's Dir. Herefs.* 1900–41.

There were at least two butchers' shops at Cradley in 1951.[323] In 1901, Cradley Stores opened in the former premises of the Bullshead.[324] In 1961 and 1973, the Stores in Cradley village was licensed to sell wine and spirits.[325] By 1970, there were general stores in both Storridge and Cradley.[326] In 1981, Mill Bank Garage changed from a café into a furniture shop.[327] There was a farm shop – Crumpton Oaks – in Storridge in 1981.[328] In 1985, there was a butcher's shop on the Bosbury road, both of which were still in operation in 2023, although the butcher's had become a general stores.[329]

There was also in 2023 the Crumpton Hill farm shop and a garden supplies store, and in west Cradley an establishment that sold packing.[330] On the A4103 there were two vehicle repair shops, and an art gallery and coffee shop located in Home End farmhouse.[331] There were also an outdoor activity organiser near Ridgeway Cross, a riding school near Stony Cross and a clothing supplier in the Ashvale Business Centre.[332]

Tourism and Hospitality

Cradley's proximity to Malvern meant that it was regarded as a resort village, and properties were sometimes advertised as such during the 19th century.[333] Two lodging houses operated in Cradley from 1879, as well as three in the West Malvern area by 1873.[334] An 1895 directory lists four apartments, and the 1871 and 1891 censuses show that two ladies (perhaps successively) were operating as landladies at Stifford's Bridge.[335] At least five tea rooms traded in the parish between 1922 and 1941.[336] In 1948, there was also a hotel (the Red Lion) at Stifford's Bridge.[337]

In 2022, Cradley had a small hospitality sector. In 1988, the Nupend was converted to a small guesthouse.[338] The Old Rectory became a hotel *c.*2006,[339] and was renovated in 2019 to become a wedding venue.[340] In 2023, Larchgrove, near the Countess of Huntingdon chapel, and Queenswood, near the parish church, offered accommodation, and there were holiday apartments near Stony Cross, Ridgeway Cross[341] and Stifford's

323 HAS, BW15/2/4, pp. 329–30.
324 Hunt, *Cradley*, 100; below, Communal Life: Inns.
325 HAS, Lic. Reg. BT 25/20; Lic. Reg. Bromyard Division, 1828–75.
326 CHC, Parish Council Minutes, II, 20 Jan. 1970; HAS, BW15/1/11, p. 343.
327 CHC, Parish Council Minutes, II, 17 Mar. 1981.
328 CHC, Parish Council Minutes, II, 19 May 1981
329 CHC, Parish Council Minutes, II, 20 Aug. 1985.
330 Inf. from local resident.
331 NHLE, no. 1349663, Home End fm ho. (accessed 1 Aug. 2023); https://www.primelocation.com/for-sale/details/57280693 (accessed 1 Aug. 2023).
332 Inf. from local resident .
333 *HJ*, 21 Jan. 1801 (advert. for Crumphill Farm); *HJ*, 15 Jan. 1806 (advert. for Hill House); *HJ*, 10 Feb. 1817 (advert. for Hill House).
334 *Littlebury's Worcs. Dir.* (1873 edn).
335 *Kelly's Dir.* (1879–1917 edns); censuses, 1871, 1891.
336 *Kelly's Dir.* (1922–41 edns).
337 HAS, BW15/2/4, p. 87.
338 CHC, Parish Council Minutes, II, 23 Feb. 1988.
339 www.tripadvisor.co.uk The Old Rectory Cradley (accessed 17 Nov. 2022).
340 https://www.theoldrectorycradley.com (accessed 17 Nov. 2022).
341 https://www.hopeendholidays.co.uk (accessed 23 Feb. 2022).

Bridge.[342] There was also a (residential) spa and wellness centre at The Clover Mill,[343] while Cowleigh Park Farm operated as a hospitality business, offering bed and breakfast in the historic farmhouse, and self-catering apartments, including in the converted cider press building.[344] The Boundless Outdoors sports and activities centre in Old Hollow (now Malvern, formerly Cradley) ran a range of activities for children and groups, who could stay in on-site accommodation.[345]

Markets and Fairs

In 1284, Bishop Richard Swinfield obtained a royal charter granting the right to hold a weekly Tuesday market at Cradley and a yearly fair, to be held on the vigil, feast, morrow and day after the feast of St Barnabas (10–13 June).[346] There is no surviving documentary evidence for either the market or fair subsequent to the charter, and it is not clear what if anything came of the grant.

342 https://www.airbnb.co.uk/rooms/4147636?source_impression_id=p3_1735826132_P3LCuGuvVthTeWnT (accessed 15 Mar. 2022).

343 https://www.tripadvisor.co.uk/Attraction_Review-g1509008-d5221158-Reviews-The_Clover_Mill-Cradley_Herefordshire_England.html (accessed 17 Nov. 2022); above, Mills, Crafts and Industry: Beanhouse Mill.

344 https://cowleighparkfarm.co.uk (accessed 1 Aug. 2023); above, 'Cowleigh' and 'Madresfield estate'.

345 https://boundlessoutdoors.co.uk (accessed 1 Aug. 2023).

346 *Cal. Chart.* 1257–1300, 281.

SOCIAL HISTORY

UNTIL THE 17TH CENTURY, a small number of gentry and lesser nobility owned or leased the parish's manors, and the rectors were consistently men of quite high social status; aside from these, the wealthiest tended to be prosperous yeomen. Thereafter, many Cradley landowners came to identify as gentlemen, and this is reflected in the range of leisure activities in the parish. Although Cradley enjoyed modest prosperity overall, poverty was also present, and, by the 19th century, this was concentrated on North Hill. Several charities for the poor were created between the 17th and 20th centuries, and some continued into the 21st. A boys' school was endowed in 1667, the first recorded educational establishment; several other schools existed in the 19th and 20th century, and one still functioned in 2023.

Social Character

Before 1550

In 1086, most of the bishop's tenants (23 of 42) were villeins, who owed him services, but whose landholdings were largely sufficient to support their households. Below them were three bordars and six boors, men of more modest means who would have augmented their meagre holdings by working for hire on the bishop's demesne (or home farm) alongside the five slaves. The boors, in fact, were probably freed slaves granted a small amount of land in return for heavy labour services.[1] The bishop, who probably resided only sporadically, had five principal tenants: reeve, priest, two knights and a *radman* (riding man or escort). Each possessed their own sub-holdings, with bordars as tenants and to provide labour. The reeve was a freeman, which was unusual on the bishop of Hereford's lands.[2] This may have reflected Cradley's comparative wealth and importance, or else that the reeveship of Cradley carried enhanced administrative responsibilities at this period.[3]

1 *Domesday*, 502 and 1431. For slaves and dependent labour, see Dyer, *Making a Living*, 36–8.

2 Cf. Bromyard (holder of one hide), Bishop's Frome (holding a mill) and Holme Lacy (an unfree tenant): *Domesday*, 501, 503. On Herefordshire reeves, see James Campbell, 'Some agents and agencies of the late Anglo-Saxon state', in J.C. Holt (ed.), *Domesday Studies* (Woodbridge, 1987), 206–7.

3 Reeves could be responsible for a group of manors. There is no clear evidence that Cradley's reeve did so, although Cradley and Bosbury may once have been administered together; see above, Storridge, manor of Bosbury, and below, Manorial Government: Manor of Cradley.

By *c.*1288, most tenants were self-sufficient peasants, with only a few smallholders and several larger principal tenancies.[4] Of the 90 tenants recorded, 17 were freeholders and 73 were customary tenants. Five freeholders held at least a yardland, of which one (with two yardlands) was held by knight service. Eight held half-yardlands, and three (18 per cent) were smallholders with 6 a. or less.[5] Among the 73 customary tenants, 33 held between half a yardland and a yardland, but only two a full yardland. Most of the remainder had 12 a. or sometimes 16 a., and only eight had 6 a. or less. These 11 free and customary smallholders were probably the successors of the five slaves and six boors of 1086.

Storridge, part of Bosbury manor, had nine or ten tenants, one holding a yardland by knight service, and the two free tenants and most of the customary tenants holding half-yardlands. The customary tenants paid a higher rent than those in Cradley, and some had to make additional payments. Two tenants held lands in both manors.[6]

On Cradley manor, by *c.*1288, the bishop received rent rather than services, suggesting that the tenants were expected to raise cash from a surplus.[7] They were also expected as a group to make a quarterly payment to the works of the vineyard, probably replacing previous forms of labour service or payments in kind.[8] Most of Cradley's yardlands, both free and customary, had by then been sub-divided, reflecting both the tenants' desire to provide holdings for their children, and the bishop's desire to increase his rental income.[9] Assarts probably also contributed to the creation of new tenancies. The smaller holdings – particularly those under 15 a. – left tenants vulnerable to poor harvests when they might need supplemental sources of income.[10] The subsequent social impacts of the Black Death in the mid 14th century included a reduced population, a surplus of work, increased holding sizes and a consequent rise in living standards. Evidence of this change can be found in the late 15th century, with greater numbers of customary tenants holding a whole yardland.[11]

Later medieval Cradley was a relatively prosperous farming parish. In 1334, its assessment for the lay subsidy (£3 12*s.* 6*d.*) exceeded those of Colwall, Coddington and Bosbury, but locally was dwarfed by Ledbury at £8 6*s.* 7*d.*[12] In 1379, most tenants paid 4*d.* poll tax, although John Hill, the farmer, paid 12*d.* and Roger Corbet, esq., paid 20*s.*[13] The 1542 muster roll suggests that 50 men in Cradley possessed goods worth at least 20 marks (£13 6*s.* 8*d.*) annually, up to lands worth £10, and in some cases more.[14]

4 This para: HAS, AA59/A/1, pp. 148–53.
5 For the uncertainty regarding yardland and/or acreage size in Cradley, see Agriculture: Medieval Landholdings.
6 HAS, AA59/A/1, pp. 153, 156.
7 HAS, AA59/A/1, p. 153.
8 For vine growing, see above, Agriculture: Vineyards.
9 See Dyer, *Making a Living*, 163.
10 See Dyer, *Making a Living*, 163.
11 See above, Population; and Agriculture: Medieval Landholdings.
12 For uncertainty over the methods of assessment, see R.E. Glasscock (ed.), *The Lay Subsidy of 1334* (1975), xxv–xxvi, 129.
13 *Poll Taxes of 1377–81*, ed. Fenwick, 370.
14 Three men were not classified, probably as they had to produce equipment instead: Faraday, *The Herefordshire Musters of 1539 and 1542*, 68–9. No parishioner possessed sufficient wealth to provide a war horse.

Within Radlow hundred, only Ledbury Foreign approached the number of men wealthy enough to be mustered that Cradley had.[15] Those lower down the social scale, however, go unrecorded. Of 64 taxpayers, including ten widows, in 1543 only three were assessed on land.[16] Nine were assessed at the minimum threshold of liability, on 20*s.* of moveable goods. Of the others, 18 were assessed at the 40*s.* threshold, and the remaining 37 paid more. In 1545, John Myntrigge, the manor's farmer, paid the most tax, twice that of the five next wealthiest men.[17] Cradley's assessment in 1547 was higher than Colwall, Bosbury and Ledbury Borough.[18]

There is little direct medieval evidence of migration into the parish, as surnames tend either to be local to Cradley, such as Batchcombe or Heath, or occupation-based, although that does not mean that the population was static. The 'alien subsidy' in the 1440s records a Janyn 'Frenschman' living in Cradley as a non-householder, his profession variously described as a common labourer and as a servant of John Hill.[19] In the 1397 bishop's visitation, an Amice Daniel was accused of practising sorcery. It was noted that she had died, however, before any apparent resolution to the case.[20]

1550–1800

	Husbandman	Yeoman	Gentleman
1550–1600	9	7	0
1600–1650	6	27	4
1650–1700	5	30	5

Table 1 *Wills identifying the testator's social status, 1550–1700.*[21]

Social status among Cradley's wealthier farmers gradually increased. After 1600, increasingly they identified as yeomen (see Table 1),[22] and the upward trend continued in the 18th century, when they shifted to describing themselves as gentlemen.[23] There was, however, great disparity in the farmers' wealth and social standing. Around 80 per cent of dwellings assessed for hearth tax in 1665 had just one hearth, and many more were exempt. It can be estimated that *c.*120 households, the vast majority, had a single

15 Faraday, *Herefordshire Musters*, 68–9; recorded as 45 and 40 respectively in *L&P Hen. VIII*, 1542, 501.

16 Thomas Wythe, Thomas Arundell and Rowland Longe, *Herefs. Taxes*, 24R3, 36R19, 45bR6, 46R14, 45R26.

17 Apart from Elisabeta Falke and John Arundell, who both paid 2*s.* on the basis of land, the remainder were assessed at over 3*s.* 4*d.*: *Herefs. Taxes*, 46R14.

18 *Herefs. Taxes*, 47R1.

19 *England's Immigrants 1330–1550* (https://www.englandsimmigrants.com), 57330, 56822, 57104.

20 I. Forrest and C. Whittick (eds), *The Visitation of the Diocese of Hereford* (Woodbridge, 2021), 106–7.

21 See below, Appendices, Sample 2.

22 On the distinction in early modern English society between yeoman and husbandman, see J.V. Beckett, 'The peasant in England: A case of terminological confusion?', *Agricultural History Review* 32:2 (1984), 113–23.

23 HAS, AH73/25.

hearth.[24] In contrast to these cramped living conditions, surviving inventories show that, by the late 17th century, Cradley's wealthiest families had at least seven rooms in their houses, with furniture and goods worth more than £100.[25] Valuations in inventories of yeomen's wealth range between £3 and £353, whereas the few surviving husbandmen's inventories total between £18 and £39.

Most land and wealth was concentrated in the hands of a small number of families and the rector, and they dominated parish offices and charity trusteeships.[26] In 1798, five individuals[27] together paid almost half (46 per cent) of Cradley's land tax.[28] Some owners of estates, such as the Hereford and Worcester deans and chapters, and many of Cradley's rectors, were absentee landlords, renting their manors out to gentlemen who usually came from outside the parish.[29] Hyde was leased in this way, often to gentry from nearby parishes.[30]

Wills and inventories give some insight into the parish's social character. Before 1700, books are rarely mentioned, and many testators and witnesses signed with 'their mark' (suggesting illiteracy); it seems that, overall, educational levels in Cradley were poor. There were exceptions – the inventory of Thomas Wood, a tanner who died in 1699, includes books, and his will makes careful provision for the education of both his son and daughter.[31] Dorothy Pichard of the Barrow (a widow, d. 1671) also possessed books.[32]

Since 1800

By 1800, the title of gentleman was ubiquitous among those who owned Cradley's largest farms.[33] Those of high social status dominated the parish offices,[34] although exceptionally one parish clerk was a blacksmith.[35] 'We have no castle nor even a mansion but there are quite a lot of gentleman's houses,' observed two parishioners in 1913. 'They are well maintained with attractive flower gardens, lawns and usually tennis courts.'[36] Some were fine properties. Beanhouse, described in 1931 as 'a medium size gentleman's residence', had around 25 rooms, including nine bedrooms; adjoining the house were a conservatory and vinery, and in the grounds were a summer house, swimming pool, two ornamental lakes (one with trout) and heated glasshouses.[37]

24 TNA, E179/119/487; the hearth tax related to households, and even small houses might be subdivided into two or even three separate domestic units.
25 No earlier inventories survive.
26 HAS, S82/3–7.
27 Revd D.H. Ford; Thomas Racster; Richard Racster; Mr Lechmere, esq.; Mr Hill.
28 CHC, copy of Land Tax 1798.
29 In many cases this included the demesne as well as the manor house.
30 HCA, 1839; 3505/1–5.
31 See Appendices, Sample 2, 115.
32 See Appendices, Sample 1, 77.
33 HAS, S82/8.
34 HAS, S82/8; HAS, S82/10.
35 HAS, AH73/12; HAS, MX 183; HAS, S82/4.
36 Edwards, *Cradley*.
37 HAS, M5/6A/4.

In 1818, of East Cradley's population of 695, 38 were recorded as poor, and 59 of West Cradley's 688.[38] The poorest part of the parish seems to have been on and around North Hill, transferred into West Malvern in 1897. Although a few wealthy, gentry residents lived in this area,[39] it also had a number of convicted criminals.[40] School logbooks highlight the impoverished and squalid living conditions of some Cradley families during the 19th and early 20th century; teachers complained of a lack of hygiene and cleanliness, and sent children home because they had ringworm or were so dirty that they were 'totally unfit to be with other children'.[41]

For those who reached adulthood, life expectancy was much better in rural Cradley than in industrial parishes during the 19th century. Between 1815 and 1835, of residents who survived to age 20, 58 per cent lived to 70 or older. On average between 1800 and 1850 a Cradley resident died in their nineties every other year, and some lived over a century, such as Mary Reynolds (d. 1818 at 101) and Sarah Kent (d. 1834 aged 100).[42]

In the 18th and 19th century, the social character of the parish, like much of the surrounding area, was marked by an annual wave of temporary migration for the hop harvest. The baptismal registers show that, by the early 20th century, hop pickers (including heavily pregnant women) were coming from as far away as the Midlands, Teesside, Lancashire and South Wales.[43]

Between 1813 and 1908, around 8 per cent of recorded births in Cradley were illegitimate. The proportion born to servants increased from 51 per cent to 64 per cent during this period, but to gloveresses declined from 39 per cent to 12 per cent, with none after 1876, as the gloving industry declined. Conversely illegitimate births to women paupers or others who were not glovers or servants rose from 10 to 24 per cent during the century.[44]

Several notable musical figures have had connections with Cradley. Edward Elgar and his family rented Birchwood Lodge, in Storridge, 1898–1903; he continued to use Birchwood as a peaceful retreat for composing while living elsewhere.[45] Another composer, Arthur Bliss, also visited the parish, and once performed in the Old Rectory.[46] In the 1970s, Bill Ward, drummer of Black Sabbath, lived at Summerville House in Cradley, and often frequented the Crown pub with his band.[47]

38 *Select Cttee on Educ. of Poor* (1818); *Digest of Parochial Returns* vols I, II and III, 331.

39 *Littlebury's Worcs. Dir.* (1873), 471.

40 Valerie Goodbury, *West Malvern: A history of the village* (Worcester, 1994), 72–3.

41 HAS, BP20/5 March 1900.

42 HAS, AH73/12.

43 HAS, AH73/12; HAS, BM72/1.

44 HAS, MX182; HAS, MX321. Percentages are taken from 1813–38 (earlier period), 1875–1908 (later period).

45 J.N. Moore, *Edward Elgar: A creative life* (Oxford, 1984), 232, 287, 317, 322, 350, 352, 373.

46 CHC, The Old Rectory – House Records; Andrew Grant, Sale Catalogue: 'The Old Rectory', 2019.

47 http://www.bbc.co.uk/herefordandworcester/musicmap/artists/black_sabbath_the_wharf/content/index.html (accessed 1 Aug. 2023); https://www.bbc.co.uk/herefordandworcester/content/articles/2008/06/03/bill_ward_house_david_tangye_feature.shtml (accessed 17 Nov. 2022).

Communal Life

A prosecution in the bishop of Hereford's consistory court, in 1587, featured a man in Cradley on a cowlstaff, along with blowing of horns and throwing of grains. It seems to have been a charivari, and may have been a Shrovetide observance.[48] The curate, Thomas Higgins, brought the episode before the court, complaining that the noise made by those involved had hindered worshippers from hearing the prayers.[49]

Little evidence survives concerning the impact on Cradley of the Civil Wars. With Mathon and Leigh Sinton, the parish provided some members of the Malvern Hills Clubmen,[50] and may have experienced skirmishes, since cannon and musket balls have been found in Seedwood, Hopyard and Butcher's Field as well as at the Seven Stars.[51] Moreover, Canon Frome was held by Royalists, and the Hereford–Worcester road through the parish was the obvious transit route for their campaigns in Malvern and Worcestershire.[52] There was a claim for compensation connected to Cradley.[53] No Cradley wills survive for 1637–46, and only six up to 1660, which highlights the disruption to local society and government caused by the Civil Wars and interregnum, even in rural parishes.[54]

Cradley had many recreational clubs, associations, occasions and facilities in the later 19th and 20th century; only the more significant are included here.

Many larger estates had facilities for fishing, hunting and shooting.[55] The local hunt tended to meet at Coddington Cross (in Coddington parish).[56] By the late 18th century, around five men a year (often including the rector or curate) purchased game duty licences,[57] and Robert Cotton, lord of the manor, and John Ballard, tenant of Overbarrow manor, also purchased licences for gamekeepers, 1787–91.[58] In 1806, concern about poaching at Cradley manor and elsewhere[59] led to the formation of an association for the preservation of game.[60]

48 D.N. Klausner (ed.), *Records of Early English Drama: Herefordshire and Worcestershire* (Toronto, Buffalo, London, 1990), 15. Comparable cowlstaff customs are also found in the Worcester records in the same title.

49 Ibid., 72.

50 An organisation formed in 1644 to protect local families and their property.

51 Hunt, *Cradley*, 99.

52 J. Webb, *Memorials of the civil war . . . as it affected Herefordshire . . .* (1879), ii, 90–1, 116, 209–20, 421, 247.

53 CHC, Document currently lost.

54 See below, Appendices, Sample 2, 70, 71, 72, 73, 74; TNA, PROB 11/224/311, will of Thomas Arundell, 1652; TNA, PROB, 11/207/323, will of Mary Holland, 1649.

55 https://www.worcesternews.co.uk/news/7657416.chance-to-be-lord-of-the-manor (accessed 17 Nov. 2022).

56 E.g. cf. *HJ*, 7 Apr. 1838.

57 E.g. *HJ*, 22 Feb. 1787, 9 Sept. 1789, 4 Oct. 1809 (purchases of game duty licences).

58 *HJ*, 20 Sept. 1787 and 21 Sept. 1791 (gamekeeper licences).

59 *HJ*, 17 Sept. 1806 (letter concerning poaching at Cradley manor).

60 *HJ*, 12 Nov. and 10 Dec. 1806.

By the 19th century, Cradley had a cricket team, which continued into the 20th century;[61] by the 1920s, there was a cricket ground in New Meadow.[62] In 1878, a football club was formed, and continued until 1995/6.[63] By 1927, Storridge also had a football club, which was still running in 1952.[64] A quoits team won a local trophy in 1907. In 2022, Cradley Sports Club provided sports facilities for local children and people with disabilities; there were four boys' football teams (divided by age) and one girls' team.[65] A tennis club was set up in the 1920s, and from 1923 there were tennis facilities in the paddock opposite Rectory House. In 2023, there was a Mathon, Cradley and Storridge Tennis Club, located in Mathon.[66] The part of Cradley transferred to West Malvern had a playing field from the 1930s, and a West Malvern Football Club played there until *c.*2010. There was also a bowling green and tennis courts.[67]

There were also fêtes, shows, concerts and dances. In 1847, the Cradley and Colwall Horticultural Show was founded (also involving neighbouring parishes);[68] Cradley's involvement may have petered out after 1876.[69] In 1890, however, the parish had a (possibly annual) flower festival, and by 1920 a joint flower show, with Storridge and Mathon, was held in Cradley parish hall. In the same year, the parish council agreed to run a monthly dance, combined with a whist drive on alternate months.[70] In 1973, the barn at the Crown Inn was made into a skittle alley and dance floor.[71] In 2023, there was a choir – Cradley Singers.[72]

In 1894, a monthly parish magazine began,[73] and was still published in 2022.[74] Woodwork classes were provided in 1895 by the county council, and a course of lectures on nursing was offered.[75] In the early 20th century, there was a carving class held in the parish,[76] and the rector, Thomas Ayscough, gave talks on the history of Cradley and the surrounding area.[77] He wrote short pieces, mainly on the architecture of the church, for Cradley's parish magazine, 1907–11, and these were issued as an illustrated booklet in or after 1917.[78]

61 HAS, N87/61; CHC, Parish Council Minutes, II, 17 Oct. 1978.
62 HAS, AH73/61, 23 May 1922; AH73/71 (1907).
63 HAS, AH73/36 1878; HAS, BK13/1/15; inf. from local resident.
64 HAS, N37/45, 27 Oct. 1927; HAS, BL20/2, 11 Nov. 1952.
65 https://www.charityinfo.co.uk/charity/cradley-sports-club-1118245 (accessed 17 Nov. 2022).
66 https://www.mcstennisclub.co.uk (accessed 17 Nov. 2022).
67 Inf. from local resident.
68 *HT*, 20 July 1867 (Horticultural Show).
69 *HT*, 7 Sept. 1868 (Horticultural Show).
70 HAS, AH73/60.
71 CHC, Parish Council Minutes, II, 13 Mar. 1973.
72 http://cradleysingers.org.uk (accessed 1 Aug. 2023).
73 HAS, BO80/17.
74 Inf. from local resident.
75 HAS, BO80/17, April 1895.
76 HAS, AH73/71, 1907.
77 E.g. to the Birmingham Archaeological Society *c.*1907: HAS, AH73/71, loose letter (4 Apr. 1907) in cover.
78 HAS, AH85/1.

Figure 17 *Cradley's victorious quoits team in 1907. (CHC)*

In 1913, there was a Girls' Friendly Society, as well as a Boys' Club and Men's Club.[79] Cradley Scouts troop had formed by 1973,[80] and was still functioning in 2023 but only for Beavers and Cubs.[81] Cradley Women's Institute was founded in 1938, and was in the Herefordshire Federation until the Second World War, and then in the Worcestershire Federation until it reverted to Herefordshire in the 1980s.[82] Storridge Women's Institute was founded in 1936, initially in the Herefordshire Federation, but moved to the Worcestershire Federation after the Second World War, where it remained.[83] In 1956, there was a Cradley Women's guild.[84]

In the 19th century, Cradley had a Loyal Lodge of Oddfellows (still meeting in the 1920s).[85] West Malvern's Lodge of Oddfellows met at the Lamb Inn.[86] In the early 20th century, there was a branch of the Pure Order of Britons, which met at the Seven Stars, Stifford's Bridge.[87] A branch of the Royal British Legion existed in 1938,[88] and continued in 2022.[89]

79 Edwards, *Cradley*, 11.
80 HAS, BW15/1/11, p. 406.
81 https://register-of-charities.charitycommission.gov.uk/charity-search/-/charity-details/1043075 (accessed 1 Aug. 2023).
82 HAS, BW15/1/10; HAS, BK13/1/15.
83 Inf. from local resident.
84 HAS, BW15/1/9, p. 765.
85 HAS, BM81/1/19.
86 Inf. from local resident.
87 Hunt, *Cradley*, 103.
88 HAS, BW15/2/1.
89 Inf. from local resident.

Figure 18 *Oddfellows at the rectory of Cradley St James, c.1920s. (CHC)*

There were no allotments in Cradley,[90] although there are allotments in the area transferred to West Malvern.[91] In 1981, a recreation ground was created at Chapel Lane,[92] and there is a playground in Buryfield at East Cradley.[93] In the early 20th century, there was a parish library, and in 1948 libraries were opened in both Cradley and Storridge.[94] In the 1960s, the village library was in the Countess of Huntingdon chapel,[95] but this apparently had closed by 1971, when Cradley was served by a weekly mobile library, which was later discontinued.[96]

In 1953, to commemorate the coronation of Elizabeth II, the parish council proposed to build a village hall serving Cradley and Storridge, but then decided to use the Cradley share of the Coronation Fund surplus to convert the old boys' school, and give Storridge's share to its village hall committee.[97] Since becoming Cradley parish hall, the old boys' school has been used for a wide variety of community societies, including the Women's Institute, fitness classes, Christmas fayres, amateur dramatics and whist

90 CHC, Parish Council Minutes, I, p. 299.
91 Inf. from local resident.
92 CHC, Parish Council Minutes, II, 21 July 1981.
93 Inf. from local resident.
94 HAS, BL20/2, p. 269.
95 See below, Protestant Nonconformity.
96 Inf. from local resident; CHC Parish Council Minutes, II, 16 Nov. 1971.
97 HAS, BL20/2, p. 485.

drives.[98] Storridge village hall is owned by the village,[99] and in 1966 the parish council became a trustee of the Storridge Village Hall Committee, and a Cradley Village Hall Committee was formed.[100] In 2022, Cradley and Storridge both had functioning village halls registered as charities.[101]

The war memorial on the village green (next to the church) is dedicated to members of the Maclean family; in 1920, Mrs Maclean of Hereford, formerly of Halesend, erected it to commemorate her two sons and two grandsons who had all died in the war.[102]

Cradley's millennium celebration included a 'Millennium Book', which related some of the history of the parish and what life was like there in the year 2000.[103]

The Old Rectory once welcomed numerous guests from the local religious and cultural elites; most notably, one of the first-floor bedrooms was reserved for the bishop of Hereford.[104]

Inns

Cradley has had many inns and pubs, of which only the principal ones are discussed here. The Red Lion at Stifford's Bridge is first recorded as an inn in 1841,[105] although the building dates from the 17th century.[106] It became the Oddfellows' meeting place and displayed a painted board of officers, 1872–1910.[107] It was also a frequent location for auctions (often of houses, shops and farms) in Cradley,[108] and was the only pub which remained open in the parish in 2023.[109]

The Seven Stars at Stifford's Bridge was the other common location in the parish for auctions of buildings and land.[110] First recorded in 1790, when it belonged to George Nott, innholder,[111] it was owned by the Royal Well Brewery by 1906,[112] and closed in 2009.[113]

98 WAAS, 474:02 BA10235/2 (xv).
99 CHC, Parish Council Minutes, I, p. 283.
100 CHC, Parish Council Minutes, I, p. 304.
101 https://www.charityinfo.co.uk/charity/cradley-village-hall-508710; https://www.charityinfo.co.uk/charity/storridge-village-hall-520987 (accessed 17 Nov. 2022); below, Education: Cradley Boys' School (old boys' school).
102 NHLE, no. 1462191, Maclean War Memorial (accessed 1 Aug. 2023).
103 http://www.ajcopp.plus.com/MilleniumBook.html (accessed 17 Nov. 2022).
104 CHC, The Old Rectory – House Records; Andrew Grant, Sale Catalogue: 'The Old Rectory', 2019.
105 Census, 1841.
106 NHLE, no. 1082284, Red Lion Inn (accessed 1 Aug. 2023).
107 Edwards, *Cradley*, 13; Hunt, *Cradley*, 103.
108 E.g. *HJ*, 4 Dec. 1816 and 30 July 1828 (sale of messuages), 8 Mar. 1815 (sale of timber).
109 Inf. from local resident.
110 E.g. *HJ*, 17 Mar. 1790, 16 Jan. 1799, 4 May 1796 and 27 Apr. 1814 (sales of messuages and estates), 16 Jan. 1813 (sale of farmland), 25 Mar. 1807 (sale of timber).
111 HAS, N37/34, 1 June 1790.
112 HAS, BL20/1, p. 142.
113 CHC, Parish Council Minutes, I, 12 Apr. 1994; T. Hobbs, *Pubs of the Malverns, Upton & Nearby Villages* (Little Logaston, 2012), 17.

Figure 19 *The Seven Stars, Stifford's Bridge c.1916. (CHC)*

Drinking establishments proliferated after the 1830 Beerhouse Act was passed. They included Monkhall, established at Ridgeway Cross, renamed 'The Quiet Woman' after 1851,[114] and still open in 1966.[115] A public house, later known as the Bullshead, opened *c.*1830, but by 1871 had become a grocer's shop, the Cradley Stores, and seems no longer to have sold beer.[116] Cradley's New Inn was open by 1841;[117] called at various times Ridgeway House, Mobbleplecks and (after 1960) the Stable,[118] it closed in 1972,[119] and was demolished in 1999.[120] The Crown, a 17th-century, single-storey building with timber framing and painted-brick nogging,[121] had opened as an inn by 1851,[122] and was closed in 1988 and converted to a house.[123] The New Inn, Storridge, was open by 1901,[124] and still running in 2012,[125] but by 2017 had closed and in 2023 was being converted

114 HAS, Q/SR/39–41; HAS, B9/35–6.
115 CHC, Parish Council Minutes, I, p. 296.
116 Hunt, *Cradley*, 100.
117 Census, 1841.
118 Hunt, *Cradley*, 102–4; J. Eisel and R. Shoesmith, *The Pubs of Bromyard, Ledbury & East Herefordshire* (Almeley, 2003), 174–81.
119 HAS, Lic. Reg. BT 25/20, Licence Reg. Bromyard Division, 1828–75.
120 Hunt, *Cradley*, 104.
121 NHLE, no. 1082250, Crown Inn (accessed 1 Aug. 2023).
122 Census, 1851.
123 https://www.worcesternews.co.uk/news/7663227.cradley-crusaders-fighting-for-the-crown (15 Mar. 2022).
124 Census, 1901.
125 Hobbs, *Pubs of the Malverns*, 202.

to a dwelling.[126] After the 1830 Act, the Happy Jack opened in the West Malvern area of Cradley;[127] it was renamed the Lamb by 1873[128] and closed in 2011.[129] The Redan Inn, also in the West Malvern area, was allegedly built in the 1850s,[130] and certainly in operation by 1873;[131] it stood on the North Malvern Road, where the road turns towards West Malvern;[132] although the inn was demolished in 1980,[133] the site is still known as the Redan Bend.[134]

Many of these establishments functioned as side businesses.[135] In 1851, the beerhouse Monkhall was also a farm owned and occupied by the master shoemaker Timothy Hill senior, who employed four men and two journeymen cordwainers.[136] Most were on the main roads through the parish, which would have provided them with passing trade. The Red Lion and Seven Stars at Stifford's Bridge and Monkhall at Ridgeway Cross were on the Hereford–Worcester road, while the Bullshead and Crown Inn were on the Ledbury–Bromyard road via Stony Cross.

Education

There was an endowed boys' school in Cradley in the 17th century, which merged in 1909 with a National school for girls, founded in 1855. The combined school continued as a mixed, Church of England school, became a primary school in 1944, and in 2004 moved to a site at the north end of East Cradley, where it continued in 2023. There was a mixed school at Storridge 1871–1946. There were also other, smaller educational initiatives, including an open-air school founded in 1914.

Cradley Boys' School (old boys' school)

By his will dated 1667, James Turner bequeathed the sum of £20 a year for ever for maintenance of a free school within the parish of Cradley to be paid to the schoolmaster. Payment was charged on the bulk of Turner's lands in Cradley,[137] and by the 19th century was being charged on Vinesend estate.[138] At some periods the school was free (as the founder originally intended), but intermittently pupils were charged a small fee.[139]

126 Inf. from local resident.
127 HAS, Q/SR/39–41; HAS, B9/35–6.
128 *Butcher's Worc. & Mal. Dir.* (1873).
129 Inf. from local resident.
130 http://www.visitoruk.com/GreatMalvern/west-malvern-C592-V10448.html (accessed 1 Aug. 2023).
131 *Littlebury's Worcs. Dir.* (1873).
132 OS Map 1:10560, Herefs. XXIX.SW (1886 edn).
133 Hobbs, *Pubs of the Malverns*, 109.
134 http://www.visitoruk.com/GreatMalvern/west-malvern-C592-V10448.html (accessed 1 Aug. 2023).
135 Eisel and Shoesmith, *The Pubs*, 174–81.
136 Hunt, *Cradley*, 102–3.
137 TNA, PROB 11/327/309.
138 HAS, AH73/36.
139 TNA, PROB 11/327/309; HAS, N37/33; *Select Cttee on Educ. of Poor* (1818). *Digest of Parochial Returns* vols I, II and III, 331.

At what date its building, probably originally a church house,[140] began to be used as a school is unknown. Turner described it as the church house or school house when he left £10 for its repair in 1667. In 1674, it was repaired and the projecting north wing was probably added, with accommodation on the first floor for the schoolmaster and his family. A stone in the rebuilt chimney stack records the 1674 churchwardens, Richard Turner and William Bullock, who presumably oversaw these alterations.[141] Richard may have been a relative of James, the school's founder.

William Cowell, curate of Cradley in 1674, was schoolmaster 1673–7.[142] In 1759, Tychias (*alias* Tychieus)[143] Whitting, son of a cleric from Thruxton and curate of Coddington, was schoolmaster.[144] He may have continued until 1766 or later but was dead by 1773.[145] In 1818, the school had an attendance of 37.[146] For much of the 19th century, the schoolmaster was William Jones, a shoemaker.[147] First appointed *c.*1806, he taught the school for 58 years, until he was over 80, retiring in the 1860s.[148]

To meet the requirements of the 1870 Education Act, the school became a National school.[149] A certificated master was appointed, and the maximum number on roll was increased to 100. The schoolroom was enlarged at a cost of £420 by removing the ceiling which separated it from an upper room and combining it with the room previously occupied by William Jones.[150] In 1878, when it started taking infants as well as older boys, the school had over 70 pupils, and offered a very wide curriculum,[151] including poultry keeping in the 1910s–20s.[152] In 1901–2, there were 122 children on the roll but the school had an average attendance of 34 and an annual grant from Parliament of £35 14*s*.[153]

During the 19th century, the building was used for various purposes besides schooling. By 1870, Hill's charity trustees met and distributed clothing to the poor there.[154] In 1886 and 1888, the school was used as a polling station for elections,[155] and in 1900 for drills by Cradley and Mathon members of the Herefordshire Rifle Volunteer Battalion.[156]

In 1909, the managers decided that they could not adapt their building to meet current requirements.[157] Cradley boys' and girls' schools were therefore merged under

140 TNA, PROB 11/327/309; below, Church Architecture.
141 HAS, N37/55.
142 *CCED*, no. 170325.
143 HCA, 3364.
144 *CCED*, no. 180189.
145 HCA, 3364.
146 *Select Cttee on Educ. of Poor* (1818). *Digest of Parochial Returns* vols I, II and III, 331.
147 HAS, AH73/36
148 HAS, AH73/36.
149 HAS, AH73/67.
150 HAS, AH73/36.
151 HAS, BP20/4.
152 Edwards, *Cradley*, 37.
153 Board of Educ., *Lists of Schools Under the Administration of the Board, 1901–2*, 95, https: archive.org/details/listschoolsunde00educgoog/page/94/mode/2up (accessed 26 Nov. 2023).
154 HAS, BL20/3 11 Oct. 1870.
155 HAS, BP20/4.
156 HAS, N37/45 27 Mar. 1900.
157 HAS, N37/52.

Figure 20 *Teaching in Cradley Boys' School, c.1900. (CHC)*

the headship of the former, and the boys' premises were no longer used as a school.[158] From 1909, James Turner's charity divided the (former) school site and buildings from the residue of Turner's endowment and administered them as a separate foundation. The rector and churchwardens became trustees of Turner's old school, and it was agreed that the building could be used for education, or for other purposes subject to a charge.[159]

Subsequently, and until 1939, the building seems to have been used by the Royal British Legion.[160] In 1952, it housed a school canteen, and a kitchen was proposed in 1953,[161] but in that year Cradley parish council decided to convert it into a village hall.[162] Through a Millennium Heritage Lottery Grant the building was renovated and extended in 2002–3, to provide a resource and heritage centre, including an archive of sources relating to the history of the parish. These have been donated by residents past and present, and include a substantial collection of photographs, written sources such as parish council minutes, and artefacts.[163]

158 HAS, BL20/4 1 Sept. 1909.
159 HAS, AH73/67.
160 HAS, AH73/62 22 May. 1939; John Ellison *et al.* (eds), *The Old Rectory, Cradley: Former Inhabitants Remembered* (Cradley, priv. printed, 2021), 11.
161 HAS, BW15/2/5, 414.
162 HAS, BL20/2, 485; above, Communal Life.
163 Inf. from local resident.

Cradley Girls' School (later Cradley School)

A National school for girls was founded in 1855,[164] and built very near to the boys' school on glebe land (Edcroft field)[165] at a cost of £692 3*s*. 5*d*.[166] Entirely under the rector's supervision,[167] it comprised initially a single schoolroom that could be divided by interior curtains into up to four units. The headteacher's house and yard were adjacent to the school.[168] The school building was extended 1857–8 to add a new classroom, presumably for younger children,[169] thus accommodating *c*.100 girls and 50 infants.[170] In 1867, there were 131 children on the roll, with an average attendance of 82.[171] In 1888, a kindergarten was also introduced. In 1901–2, the school had an average attendance of 67, and received an annual grant from Parliament of £61 2*s*.[172]

In 1909, when the boys' and girls' schools combined,[173] the joint school was renamed Cradley Church of England School (also known as the National school), and was a public elementary school.[174] Average attendance at each school was then around 110 pupils, so that the former girls' school's capacity, 140, was insufficient,[175] and the building was therefore enlarged.[176] Hereford Archdeaconry Association advanced £120 towards enlargement in 1909,[177] and the Board of Education allowed the trustees to borrow up to £200.[178] This school, and the £20 rent charge from Turner's school, were administered by the trustees of the National school as a single foundation, and the income was used for support and maintenance.[179]

Wartime evacuation in 1940 caused an influx of children, swelling class sizes to the point of overcrowding.[180] The school meals service started during the war, all children being required to go to the old boys' school each day to get lunch. In 1944, the leaving age was lowered from 15 to 11, transforming it into a primary school, which required children over 11 to attend secondary schools outside the parish.[181] In 1966, there were 100 children in attendance.[182]

164 HAS, AH73/67.
165 OS Map 1:10560, Herefs. XXIX.SW (1886 edn); Hunt, *Cradley*, 41.
166 This figure included the schoolmaster's/mistress's house.
167 HAS, AH73/36.
168 HAS, F21/14ii.
169 HAS, F21/14i. *Report of the Cttee of Council on Educ.*, 1871, HC201, 269.
170 HAS, HA73/36.
171 *Littlebury's Dir.* (1867).
172 Board of Educ., *Lists of Schools Under the Administration of the Board, 1901–2*, 95, https: archive.org/details/listsschoolsunde00educgoog/page/94/mode/2up (accessed 26 Nov. 2023).
173 HAS, N37/52.
174 HAS, N37/52.
175 HAS, N37/52.
176 HAS, N37/51; HAS, N37/52 23 Aug. 1909; Edwards, *Cradley*, 11.
177 HAS, N37/51.
178 HAS, N37/52.
179 HAS, AH73/67.
180 HAS, BW15/1/7, p. 169.
181 HAS, BK13/1/15.
182 CHC, Parish Council Minutes, I, 20 Sept. 1966.

Post-war improvements included altering the classrooms (1957),[183] and constructing a new classroom block (1968),[184] swimming pool (1971)[185] and library (1992).[186] By 2003 the chair of governors deemed the buildings 'substandard' for 'a modern method of education', and too small. Hereford diocese sold the old school to offset the costs of its replacement, and the government grant for the new school took into account the value of the old.[187]

The new school in Buryfield, a Church of England voluntary-aided primary school with capacity for 140 pupils, was opened in 2004.[188] Construction was 90 per cent government-funded, the governors and diocese providing the remainder. The school was rated 'Outstanding' by Ofsted in 2022,[189] and was judged to be among the top ten best state primaries by *Tatler* magazine in 2018.[190] The on-site nursery closed *c.*2010.[191] The school's maintenance costs are supported by a small charity, which in 2019 had an income of £660 and an expenditure of £241.[192]

Storridge School

Storridge school, which opened in 1876 with accommodation for 59 pupils, was built by Earl Beauchamp on Taswold farm land,[193] and administrated by a committee of ratepayers.[194] Until 1891, when the school decided to follow the Free Education Act,[195] some children's school fees were paid by Cradley's wealthy inhabitants, including Miss Little.[196]

In 1882, the Cradley parish schools managers agreed that boys ten (reduced to nine in 1893) and older should move from Storridge school to Cradley Boys' School; from 1894, girls who reached the 4th standard moved to Cradley Girls' School.[197] In 1901–2, average attendance was 70 and the annual grant from Parliament was £79 16*s.*[198] Additional funding was provided to structure many lessons around topics relating to farming and agriculture, such as the clover plant and its cultivation. Clover was milled at two of the mills along the Cradley brook.

183 HAS, BW15/7/1, p. 725.
184 HAS, BW15/3/2 18 Apr. 1968.
185 CHC, Parish Council Minutes, II, 15 June 1971; HAS, BW15/8/2, p. 109.
186 CHC, Parish Council Minutes, II, 21 July 1992.
187 https://www.herefordtimes.com/news/5673856.work-under-way-on-new-school (accessed 17 Nov. 2022).
188 https://www.herefordtimes.com/news/5673856.work-under-way-on-new-school; https://www.herefordtimes.com/news/5654130.Cradley (accessed 17 Nov. 2022).
189 https://reports.ofsted.gov.uk/provider/21/103846 (accessed 7 Mar. 2025).
190 https://www.tatler.com/article/best-state-primary-schools-uk-2018 (accessed 17 Nov. 2022).
191 https://reports.ofsted.gov.uk (accessed 17 Nov. 2022).
192 https://www.charityinfo.co.uk/charity/cradley-church-of-england-school-charity-527234 (accessed 17 Nov. 2022).
193 HAS, R9/52/7; HAS, AH73/36; HAS, N37/35 26 Sept. 1873; 8 Jan. 1874; 6 May 1876.
194 HAS, N37/35 8 Jan. 1874; 4 Feb. 1875.
195 HAS, N37/44 21 Aug. 1891.
196 HAS, BP20/1 20 Oct. 1876, 23 Mar. 1877. The Little family were major landowners in the Storridge area, owning the Storridge estate. See above, Storridge, manor of Bosbury.
197 HAS, N37/45 5 July 1894.
198 Board of Educ., *Lists of Schools Under the Administration of the Board, 1901–2*, 95 https: archive.org/details/listsschoolsunde00educgoog/page/94/mode/2up (accessed 26 Nov. 2023).

Figure 21 *The open-air school, West Malvern, c.1915. (Malvern Gazette, 13 June 2014)*[199]

In 1919, Earl Beauchamp sold most of his Cradley properties, including the school buildings,[200] although the school continued as before. There were 40 pupils in 1935. The school closed in 1946.[201] By 1948 the schoolroom had become a parish hall.[202]

Other Schools

From *c.*1850, a National school was attached to St James's church, Mathon (the chapelry which included the North Hill area of Cradley),[203] and in 1877 some children attended there instead of the Cradley schools.[204] By 1872, it had 101 pupils.[205]

A girls' school managed by the sister and daughters of the Revd Charles Scott Luxmoore was held from 1841 or earlier in a room over an old hopkiln in the rectory kitchen gardens. It had about 40 pupils at any one time, admitted free of charge.[206] As of 2005, what may have been its school bell survived, attached to an outside wall of

199 From Malvern Gazette, 'Outdoor centre celebrates 100 years of healthy schooling for county's children', 13 June 2014: http://www.malverngazette.co.uk/news/11276474.outdoor-centre-celebrates-100-years-of-healthy-schooling-for-countys-children (accessed 14 Aug. 2024).

200 HAS, AH72/2.

201 HAS, BP20/3, p. 204.

202 HAS, BL20/2, p. 306.

203 This para: Goodbury, *West Malvern*, 7–11.

204 HAS, N37/35 17 Sep. 1872; WAAS 468 BA12235 1(i), e.g. 14 Dec. 1877.

205 Goodbury, *West Malvern*, 10.

206 HAS, AH73/36; HAS, K42/3.

the Old Rectory.[207] A dame school for infants at Green Hill was run for many years in the 19th century by Mary Philpotts, replacing a short-lived infants' school held in a cottage.[208]

An open-air school (see figure 21) was established in 1914, in Old Hollow.[209] Disabled girls certified incapable of benefiting from an ordinary elementary-school education were drawn from across the country; a boys' section opened in 1922. The school aimed to improve pupils' health by exposing them to as much fresh air as possible (even sleeping outdoors in fine weather) and giving them good, plain food. The school was replaced in 1967 by an establishment with similar aims, the Worcestershire County Field Study Centre. It became the West Malvern Outdoor Education Centre in 1990, and was renamed Boundless Outdoors in 2019.[210]

Sue Lim of 'Blue Ginger' established a school for overseas children at Home End farmhouse in 1986, later discontinued.[211] In 1975, 46 pupils from Cradley were attending Ledbury Grammar School.[212]

Social Welfare

Richard Hill Charity

In 1673, Richard Hill of Braces Leigh (Worcs.) left the rents and profits from his land 'Tashold' (Taswolds) in Cradley[213] to fund the distribution of 16*d*. of bread every Sunday and clothing at Michaelmas to 'such honest Poor People . . . as should have most need therefore', at least half of whom should not be receiving other relief.[214] He appointed six leading Cradley inhabitants as trustees of the charity and feoffees of the land, with instructions for choosing replacements when they died.[215] Trustees were usually wealthy men, from Cradley or elsewhere.[216] In 1847 it was ordered that only people having an actual settlement in the parish should be relieved.[217]

Hill's charity maintained a workhouse and land on Barley hill (part of Taswolds) in the early 19th century, and derived much of its income (£40 annually 1811–25) from letting them to the parish overseers.[218] After poor law unions were established, the workhouse closed in 1837 and the building and land were let to tenants for £30 annually.[219]

207 CHC – Notes on the Old Rectory.
208 HAS, AH73/36; Goodbury, *West Malvern*, 14.
209 Located within the area transferred from Cradley to West Malvern in 1897.
210 https://boundlessoutdoors.co.uk (accessed 17 Nov. 2022); inf. from local resident.
211 https://www.primelocation.com/for-sale/details/57280693 (accessed 17 Nov. 2022); inf. from local resident.
212 CHC, Parish Council Minutes, II, 17 June 1975.
213 HAS, S82/5.
214 HAS, S82/5.
215 HAS, S82/3.
216 HAS, S82/4–14.
217 HAS, BL20/3.
218 HAS, BL20/3.
219 HAS, BL20/3.

Repeated financial mismanagement during the 19th century created problems.[220] Parts of Taswolds, most importantly Poors Coppice, were sold in 1838,[221] and the remainder in 1903, raising £1,030, which was invested in East Indian Railway Co. stock. Interest on its investments was henceforth to be spent annually on clothing for poor people in Cradley.[222] By 1909, it owned £600 of stock plus an additional £4 10*s.* 11*d.* of consols.[223]

The parish council, in 1938, sought to combine five charities,[224] including Richard Hill's, into a single entity under five trustees which it would appoint.[225] In 1947, the council ruled that beneficiaries must have been Cradley residents for six years and with a verifiable need for relief.[226] The parish council still administered the charity accounts in 1958,[227] and in 1984 the Cradley combined charities gave £5 each to 39 people.[228] In 2023, the trustees of the combined charities, described simply as Richard Hill's, met annually to distribute its accrued interest to elderly Cradley residents; its income in that year was £609, and it donated £600.[229]

Other Charities for the Poor

Several 17th-century legacies benefited the parish poor, including those of Christopher Long (£5 in 1634), Eleanor Stowers (£4 in 1681)[230] and John Long of the Barrow Mills (£5 in 1682).[231] In 1662, Anthony Turner of Stone House gave rent from Mellin's estate in Castle Frome to be distributed among the most deserving poor of the parish;[232] by 1894, his charity's annual income was £1 6*s.* 8*d.* and the money was used to buy bread for the poor.[233] Another Anthony Turner left an annuity of 25*s.* 8*d.* in 1836 for the poor of Cradley, the income coming from his mill; in 1860, 51 widows received 1*s.* and 21 received 6*d.*[234]

By an agreement in 1718, rent worth 20*s.* from a house and land was to be used for good causes after Emma, widow of a carpenter, John Watkins, had died. The bequest provided twopenny loaves to be distributed at the church porch on four feast days annually. By 1837, this rent was taken from an estate called the Mills, and the charity's

220 HAS, S82/10.
221 HAS, N37/10. The coppices were the charity's main source of periodic surplus income, which was invested in stock: HAS, AH73/65.
222 HAS, S82/20; HAS, N37/10.
223 HAS, AH73/65.
224 Richard Hill's, Anthony Turner's, Richard Chambers', Emma Watkins', Poor's Meadow.
225 HAS, BL20/2, p. 118.
226 HAS, BL20/2, pp. 219–20.
227 CHC, Parish Council Minutes, I, p. 80.
228 CHC, Parish Council Minutes, II, 1 May 1980.
229 https://register-of-charities.charitycommission.gov.uk/charity-search/-/charity-details/218935 (accessed 1 Aug. 2023).
230 See Appendices, Sample 1, 63, 87.
231 HAS, N37/60.
232 HAS, N37/60.
233 HAS, BL20/1, p. 5.
234 HAS, AH73/66.

trustees were the rector and churchwardens.[235] Its funds *c.*1913 derived from renting out Poors Meadow (also called Brown Meadow) near Poors bridge, and annual charges on the Mill Bank estate and the Mill End portion of the Canon Frome estate.[236]

In 1772, Richard Chambers, rector of Cradley, who owned land in Herefordshire (including Cradley) and Worcestershire, bequeathed £2 12*s.* annually for a weekly dole of penny loaves to be distributed to 12 elderly poor, to be funded by the tenant of Cradley Hall Farm at Whitsuntide and Christmas.[237] During the 19th century, the loaves were given monthly rather than weekly, though the amount was sometimes augmented from surplus funds of the Hill charity.[238]

In 1894, the recently founded parish council appointed six trustees to all the Cradley charities,[239] including in 1897 two who were parish councillors.[240] Annual income in 1894 included £2 10*s.* from Poors Land in Cradley to provide bread for the poor,[241] and £1 for charitable purposes from Hills Cottage (or Goodyears) and its orchard on Miss Little's estate.[242] Cradley Provident Dispensary, an unendowed charity, existed in 1907, when an appeal for increased support secured 22 new subscriptions.[243] In 1904, there was a St Thomas's Day Charity,[244] likely a precursor of the Emily Julia Purser charity that existed from 1961 to 1971.[245] The Charles Purser charity (founded 1918) was actively supporting elderly people in Cradley in 2022.[246]

In 1913, some North Malvern residents still claimed help from Cradley charities, because they lived in areas within the parish before the boundary changes.[247]

Clubs for the Poor, and Refugee Welfare

A coal club existed in 1895 to encourage poor parishioners to save up sufficient coal in the summer for the winter. From the 1890s, some children from the Bromyard union were boarded out to Cradley,[248] and the Cradley schools all ran charitable enterprises for their own pupils. The Revd Mr Hampden encouraged thrift and savings by running a penny bank at the boys' school, and a clothing club and (in 1892) a lending library, which rewarded good attendance. In 1900, Storridge School began a 'boot club' to procure strong and useful winter boots and shoes for the children.

During the Second World War, Lower Nupend estate hosted refugees in connection with the International Commission for War Refugees in Great Britain.[249]

235 HAS, AH73/64.
236 HAS, N37/10.
237 HAS, AH73/34.
238 HAS, BL20/3.
239 HAS, BL20/1, p. 9.
240 HAS, BL20/1, p. 48.
241 HAS, BL20/1, p. 8.
242 HAS, BL20/1, p. 8.
243 HAS, AH73/71.
244 HAS, BL20/1, p. 131.
245 HAS, AH73/67.
246 https://www.charityinfo.co.uk/charity/the-charles-purser-charity-241464 (accessed 17 Nov. 2022).
247 Edwards, *Cradley*, 11.
248 HAS, AH73/36.
249 CHC, 'International Commission for War Refugees in Great Britain', 14.

Medical Services

In 1841, Cradley had a midwife, and in 1891 a (female) chemist. After 1900, it had midwives,[250] nurses, a resident public vaccinator (1922–9) and several doctors, including A.G. Ede (1938–40) and W.J.A. Webster (1933–58).[251] Webster, a trained surgeon as well as physician, submitted plans for a waiting room, surgery and examination room in 1937.[252] He is commemorated on a plaque in the parish church, along with his wife and his dispenser.[253] There was also a 'club doctor' (Dr Cowen in 1913, Dr Meikle of Malvern in 1929), with surgery and dispensary at Stifford's Bridge, and a private doctor whose surgery was at Stoney Villa. During the First World War, Dr Howe began a practice at Howeyland; it subsequently belonged to Dr Drew (surgeon), and then Dr Drake.

Cradley's first district nurse, before 1929, had been a Protestant nun.[254] There had been two midwives,[255] but by this date there was only one, semi-retired. Nurse Edwards had her surgery in the field opposite St Katherine's drive gate.

In 2022, Cradley had a surgery on Bosbury Road, with two general practitioners, two nurses, a healthcare assistant and dispensers.[256]

250 E.g. cf. *Kelly's Dir. Herefs.* (1917 edn).
251 Hunt, *Cradley*, 118; inf. from local resident.
252 HAS, BW15/1/7, p. 18.
253 HAS, BS37.
254 Edwards, *Cradley*, 42–3.
255 Edwards, *Cradley*, 14.
256 https://www.cradleysurgery.nhs.uk (accessed 25 June 2021).

RELIGIOUS HISTORY

St James's church is medieval, on the site of a pre-Conquest antecedent, but heavily altered by Sir George Gilbert Scott in the late 19th century. Cradley has always been in the gift of the bishops of Hereford.[1] It has been a wealthy benefice since the medieval period, attracting well-educated incumbents of high social status, but often absentee pluralists employing curates to serve the living. Cradley's Old Rectory, one of the finest houses in the parish, reflects this affluence. Cradley village hall, the old boys' school, was built in the 16th century originally as a church house (also known as the church ale house). Barrow Manor had a chapel in the medieval period, and chapelries were established at Storridge and North Hill (St James's) in the later 19th century,[2] so that briefly three ecclesiastical territories existed within Cradley ancient parish; the modern civil parish still contains Cradley and Storridge ecclesiastical parishes. Apart from Robert Gower, Cradley's manorial lord, little evidence of recusancy survives, and Protestant Nonconformity has not been found before 1815; thereafter, several congregations and places of worship rapidly emerged.

Church Origins and Parochial Organisation

According to tradition, Hereford cathedral received a large grant of lands in the Malvern hills from Mildfrith, possibly a sub-king of the *Magonsaete*,[3] in the late 7th century, and this may have included Cradley.[4] A suggestion that it was a daughter church, founded *c.*1000 within Ledbury minster's *parochia* (parish),[5] is weakened on architectural and archaeological grounds, since there are possible indications of an 8th-century church or family minster preceding a late Anglo-Saxon building on the site.[6] Cradley, like Bosbury, may have originated as a proprietary church of the manorial lord.[7]

1 HAS, AA59/19/3.
2 The chapelry was created in 1844. Although the ecclesiastical parish of St James's originally encompassed a small part of Cradley civil parish (on North Hill), the church building was in Mathon civil parish. Following boundary changes in 1897 St James's ecclesiastical parish no longer lay partly inside Cradley civil parish: *London Gaz.*, 7 June 1844; V. Goodbury, *West Malvern: A history of the village* (Worcester, 1994), 1.
3 A minor sub-kingdom of the greater Anglo-Saxon kingdom of Mercia, centred on Hereford.
4 *Fasti Eccles. Ang. Hereford, 1066–1300*, VIII, ed. J. Barrow (2002), xxi–xxv.
5 S.K. Waddington, 'The origins of Anglo-Saxon Herefordshire: A study in land antiquity' (Univ. of Birmingham PhD thesis, 2013), 102–6; S.K. Waddington, 'The Anglo-Saxon mother-churches of eastern Herefordshire', *TWNFC* 62 (2014), 76–7.
6 Below, Church Architecture: Church of St James: Anglo-Saxon and Norman.
7 *VCH Herefs. Bosbury*, 67.

In 1086, a priest held 1½ yardlands of land in Cradley,[8] and the 11th-century parish boundaries seem to have remained unchanged through the medieval period. The dedication of the medieval church is unknown.

In 1844, a consolidated chapelry district was formed for the new St James's church, North Hill in Mathon, from parts of four adjacent parishes, including a small area of Cradley on and near North Hill (part of West Malvern civil parish from 1897).[9] In 1857, the district chapelry of Storridge was formed, so that Storridge became a separate ecclesiastical parish from the majority of Cradley civil parish; Storridge St John, designed by Frederick Preedy, became its parish church. In 1982, Cradley was joined with Mathon and Storridge as a united benefice, served by a rector.[10]

Advowson and Church Endowment

The bishops of Hereford held the advowson throughout the Middle Ages, and presented regularly, except during a vacancy in 1317, when Edward II presented Richard de Hale.[11]

Cradley was the third-wealthiest benefice in Frome deanery in 1291, assessed at £23 6*s*. 8*d*. for the papal tithe.[12] In 1428, Cradley church had the third-highest tax assessment in Radlow hundred (35 marks, providing a subsidy of 46*s*. 8*d*.), behind only Bosbury and Ledbury Foreign.[13] By 1535, Cradley rectory's total value was assessed at £18 2*s*. 12*d*. (sic). The tithe of grain accounted for £10, and the rector also received tithes from hay, lamb, wool, calves, piglets and geese, fruit, linen and sheep, as well as oblations and pasturage, rents of assize from the manor (36*s*. 4*d*.) and glebe (13*s*. 4*d*.), altogether providing a total annual income of £17 2*s*. 19*d*. The rector rendered payment to the bishop (7*s*. 9*d*.), dean and chapter (12*s*.), Great Malvern abbey (4*s*.), the archdeacon of Hereford (7*s*. 8*d*.) and the commissioner general (6*s*. 8*d*.).[14]

From before 1200, the dean and chapter were entitled to a tithe of Cradley church demesne to pay for bread for the poor on the anniversary of Bishop Robert Foliot's death (9 May) each year.[15] In 1291, however, only the prior of Hereford (probably St Guthlac's) is recorded as having a portion.[16] By 1535, both the dean and the precentor were drawing portions from Cradley, although the dean's portion was only 6*s*. from a total of £24 11*s*. 2*d*. obtained from portions.[17]

8 *Domesday*, 502.

9 https://www.history.ac.uk/research/victoria-county-history/county-histories-progress/herefordshire/herefordshire-vol-iii-radlow-hundred-ledbury-and-malvern-hills (accessed 23 Jan. 2025).

10 *London Gaz.*, 2 Nov 1982, 49157, p. 14281.

11 *Cal. Pat.* 1313–17, 670.

12 *Tax. Eccl.*, 160.

13 *Feud. Aids.*, II, 403.

14 *Valor Eccl.*, vol. 3, 42.

15 *English Episcopal Acta: Hereford 1079–1234*, no. 196; *Charters and Records of Hereford Cathedral*, ed. W. Capes (Hereford, 1908), 34–5.

16 *Tax. Eccl.*, 160.

17 *Fasti Eccles. Ang. Hereford, 1066–1300*, VIII, 13; *Valor Eccl.*, vol. 3, 4. There is no mention of a prior's portion by 1535.

Figure 22 *Drawing of Cradley St James's church, 1717, viewed from the south. (HAS, CF50/116, p. 417)*

Detailed records of the medieval rectory's lands do not survive, but by 1340 they totalled a carucate, and included a messuage (presumably the rectory), a curtilage and orchards or gardens, a dovecote and at least one fishpond.[18] Medieval fishponds survive near the church.[19] In 1397, there was also a house or hall (*domus*) of Blessed Mary in Cradley *sanctuarium* (probably churchyard). Its location and purpose are uncertain, though it was reputedly used regularly for trysts between a chaplain, Richard Sterre, and a local married woman, Alice Haket.[20] By 1393, the rector held lands from the Hill family,[21] and between 1478 and 1536 rectors rendered to the bishop's bailiff 6*d*. annually for six parcels of unspecified wasteland rented out.[22]

In the early 17th century, the glebe, which comprised 11 enclosures and 4 parcels of land in the common fields, was estimated at between 84 and 115 acres.[23] The parish tithe map and terrier, made by William Jones 1837–9, was not approved by the tithe

18 Cradley was not normally assessed in carucates, so it is unclear why that was used instead of the customary hide: *Nonarum Inquisitiones*, 152.

19 HER, 3804.

20 The building might have been a predecessor to the current village hall, though there is no evidence to support this, and the hall probably originated as an alehouse (see below, Religious Life: Village Hall): Forrest and Whittick, *Visitation of the Diocese of Hereford*, 106.

21 HAS, C96/1.

22 TNA, SC 6/HENVIII/1511, rot. 8d.; HAS, AM33/13, rot. 21d.

23 HAS, HD2/1/30–32.

commissioners because of changes in the parish since it was commissioned.[24] In 1839, almost all glebe land was the same as in earlier terriers, concentrated in a ring around the medieval Churchfields (except a parcel of coppice in High Grove) and comprising 110 a. (in 32 separate parcels). The church was the major landowner in the Churchfield area, much of it belonging to the rectory farm.[25] In 1839, when 5,666 a. (all but 90 a.) were tithable, the rector's total tithes were commuted for an annual rent charge of £1,023 17*s*., with £22 for tithe of glebe.[26] By 1884, the rector was letting out at least part of the glebe.[27] In 1913, some North Malvern residents (who had lived there before the boundary changes) still paid a tithe rent charge to Cradley.[28] In 1913, the endowment of the living included the 12-bedroom Glebe House with stables and outbuildings, and 73 a. of land elsewhere, including the site of the rectory and its gardens and outbuildings.[29] In 1967, Edcroft (opposite the rectory) was still glebe land.[30]

Former rectory estate buildings are characterised by dentilled eaves and segmental brick arches over windows and doors.[31] Two significant but unlisted probable examples are the single-storey Cider Barn in Rectory Lane, once probably an agricultural building, and Church House, a two-storey, painted-brick house with timber framing and wattle and daub under the brick exterior, probably of 17th-century origin, with substantial later alterations. The pond north of the rectory was once fed by a leat, traces of which survive in Jubilee Field (formerly Bason Croft); both may have served the corn mill which belonged to the rectory in 1607.[32]

Clergy Houses

In 1589, the parsonage house comprised a parlour, a hall, a kitchen and one cross-chamber on the ground floor, with other rooms above; its outbuildings included a dovecote.[33] In 1719, what may have been the same building was under repair;[34] the present Old Rectory is later, although almost certainly on the same site.

The Old Rectory occupies a large plot next to the parish church and has been described as the 'most significant' 18th-century building in the parish.[35] The three-storey house is large, of Flemish-bond red brick, with a hipped slate roof.[36] Attached is a long brick stable range, largely 18th-century, but perhaps 17th-century on the

24 HAS, N37/28.
25 HCA, 6437/II/1; Tithe Map (1839).
26 HCA, 6437/II/1.
27 HAS, N37/23.
28 Edwards, *Cradley*, 11.
29 HAS, N37/10.
30 CHC, Parish Council Minutes, I, p. 312.
31 This para: *Cradley Conservation Area Appraisal Draft* (2007), 8, 14–18, 20: http://councillors.herefordshire.gov.uk/documents/s11645/9%20Cradley%20CA%20RL2.pdf (accessed 17 Nov. 2022).
32 HAS, HD2/1/31–2. Above Mills, Crafts and Industry: Corn Mills.
33 HAS, HD2/1/30.
34 HAS, HD5/15/33.
35 *Cradley Conservation Area Appraisal Draft* (2007), 8. It has been a Grade II listed building since 1967: NHLE 1082301 (accessed 17 Nov. 2022).
36 *Cradley Conservation Area Appraisal Draft* (2007), 8, 15.

Figure 23 *The Old Rectory, mid 20th century. (CHC)*

south side.[37] Most of the house was probably built in the 1790s,[38] although Charles Scott Luxmoore (rector 1815–54) added a drawing-room wing extension and rebuilt part of the rear service area, which was probably a surviving part of an earlier house. In 1877, Renn Hampden was authorised to remove the long-disused tithe barn,[39] which probably adjoined the Old Rectory wall on Rectory Lane.[40] Its palatial nature, reflecting the exceptional wealth of the benefice, is illustrated by the accommodation. Until 1946, when it was converted into a parsonage and two flats,[41] it had 30 rooms, including ten bedrooms, three sitting rooms (two converted from bedrooms) and two living rooms.[42] In 1971, despite the rector's opposition,[43] Hereford diocese sold it at auction to Mrs H.U. Richards for £18,200, and permission was given to build a new rectory.[44] This stands on the opposite side of Rectory Lane, and is a large, two-storey brick building, behind a high brick wall;[45] it is accessed by a driveway through a grassed area of glebe land.[46]

37 *Cradley Conservation Area Appraisal Draft* (2007), 8; NHLE, no. 1177124, Stables immediately W. of rectory (accessed 4 Jan. 2024).
38 CHC, Notes on the Old Rectory.
39 HAS, N37/12.
40 Tithe Map (1839).
41 HAS, AA61/36; HAS, BW15/2/3, p. 2.
42 HAS, AA61/36.
43 HAS, BP37/4. The rector, C.T. Cottrell, told the estate agent that he was 'at war' with the diocese over it.
44 HAS, BW15/3/2, pp. 293, 304.
45 *Cradley Conservation Area Appraisal Draft* (2007), 17.
46 Inf. from local resident.

Religious Life

Table 2 *Known rectors of Cradley and known dates in office.*[47]

Known dates	Rector	Known dates	Rector
*c.*1178–98	Ralph Foliot	1678–9[48]	Edward Bosworth
*c.*1230–52	M. Gervase of London	1679–82[49]	George Benson
1295–?	M. William de la Gare[50]	1682–1713[51]	John Benson
1303–?	Robert de Kingswood[52]	1713–31	Thomas Bisse
1317–?	Richard de Hale[53]	1731–76	Richard Chambers
1320–48	Dm. Walter Carles[54]	1776–94[55]	Daniel Price
1348–54*	M. Adam Trewlove[56]	1794–1813[57]	Henry Ford
1366–93*	M. Thomas Birmingham[58]	1813–15[59]	John George Harrinton
1401–*c.*37	M. Maurice Dyby/Druy/Dewy[60]	1815–54	Charles Scott Luxmoore
*c.*1437–55	Maurice Trevenaunt/Trefnant[61]	1854–91	Edward Renn Hampden
1455–67*	M. William Chapmon[62]	1892–1917[63]	Thomas Ayscough

47 Rectors before 1300 are largely unrecorded. After 1560 there are numerous contradictions across the corpus of sources. The dates given here are those that best fit the evidence. The dates 1928–92 are taken from HAS, AS88/291, in conjunction with the other sources referenced.

48 See Appendices, Sample 2, 91.

49 HAS, AH85/1–2, I.

50 Cathedral Treasurer. Held prebend of Nonnington, *Reg. Swinfield II*, 530, 533, 535; *Cal. Pat.* 1292–1301, 277; *Expenses of Swinfield*, 220; *Fasti Eccles. Ang. Hereford*, 1300–1541 (2009), 10, 37.

51 HAS, BC79/2/52.

52 *Expenses of Swinfield*, 116–17, 209.

53 De Hale was presented by Edward II during the vacancy following Swinfield's death: *Cal. Pat.* 1313–17, 670.

54 Held prebend of Hunderton. Was appointed while in Avignon: *Reg. Trillek*, 374; *Cal. Papal Regs.* III, 322, 384; *Cal. Papal Pets.*, I, 204.

55 *CCED*, no. 159184. Note: some sources give date of death as 1791; cf. HAS, BS27.

56 Sole rector of Cradley recorded seeking papal dispensation for holding multiple benefices. Was also a canon at Wells and Lincoln cathedrals; *Reg. Trillek*, 374; *Cal. Papal Regs. III*, 322, 384; *Cal. Papal Pets.*, I, 204.

57 CCED, no. 17617; HAS, CA19/1–2.

58 *Reg. Lewis Charlton*, 71; HAS, C96/1.

59 CCED, no. 63370; HAS, CA19/2.

60 *Reg. Trefnant*, 185; *Reg. Mascall*, 69, 189; TNA, CP 40/705, CP 40/647.

61 *Reg. Stanbury*, 173; TNA, CP 40/705.

62 Held prebend of Bartonsham: *Reg. Stanbury*, 173; *Reg. Mayew*, 18; *Fasti Eccles. Ang. Hereford, 1300–1541*, 14. In TNA, CP40/861 in 1477 William is described as 'recently of Cradley', so it is unclear if he had perhaps resigned the rectorship by this date.

63 Edwards, *Cradley*, 47.

Known dates	Rector	Known dates	Rector
(1490?)–1508	Dr John Nans (D.Cn. & C.L.)[64]	1917–27[65]	William Langston Benest Janvrin
1508–24	M. Henry Martyn (B.Cn. & C.L.)[66]	1928–36[67]	Charles Edward Warner
1524–6	Dr William Burghill (D.Cn.)[68]	1936–42[69]	Robert Gallenters
1526–*c.*58	M. William Booth	1942–6	Tom Anstruther Wilkinson
*c.*1558–60	John Parfey	1946–61	John Wilfred Lewis
1560–71[70]	Thomas Greenwiche	1961–72[71]	Charles T. Cottrell
1571–83[72]	?	1972–83[73]	Mark Thompson McCausland
1584–7[74]	William Penson	1983–92[75]	Geoffrey P. Howell
1587–1621[76]	Morgan Powell		Samuel Ashton[77]
1621–9	Thomas Godwyn		Robert Ward
1629–78[78]	Edward/Edmund Skinner		

* indicates the last known date.

64 Held Putson and Gorwell as well as canonries at Exeter and Wells. He was a sub-dean at Wells and the Vicar General in Spirituals of Bishop Redman at Exeter from 1497, and Cardinal Hadrian at Bath and Wells from 1506: A.B. Emden, *A Biographical Register of the University of Oxford to* AD *1500* (Oxford, 1957), 1336–7.

65 HAS, BS37; HAS, AS88/291; Edwards, *Cradley*, 50.

66 *Reg. Mayew*, 276; *Reg. Bothe II*, 337; Martyn held Norton 1504–8, Warham, 1508, Gorwell & Overbury, 1508–12, Wellington, 1512, Inkberrow, 1512–24. He was treasurer from 1515–16 before becoming archdeacon in 1516. He was also commissary general, *Fasti Eccles. Ang. Hereford, 1300–1541*, 8, 12, 25, 31, 39, 49, 51; Emden, *Biog. Register*, 1234; *Calendar of Probate and Administration Acts 1407–1550*, 514/180.

67 HAS, BS37; John Ellison *et al.* (eds), *The Old Rectory, Cradley: Former Inhabitants Remembered* (Cradley, priv. printed, 2019), 10; Edwards, *Cradley*, 50.

68 Cathedral treasurer. Held prebend of Bartonsham, *Reg. Bothe II*, 337; *Fasti Eccles. Ang. Hereford, 1300–1541*, II, 12, 15, 40. For Burghill, see Emden, *Biog. Register*, 85.

69 Spelt 'Gallenters' in memorial inscription: HAS, BS37; Ellison *et al.*, *Old Rectory, Cradley*, 11.

70 *CCED*, no. 65110; HAS, AH73/1.

71 Ellison *et al.*, *Old Rectory, Cradley*, 12.

72 *CCED*, no. 134086; see Appendices, Sample 2, 8; *CCED*, nos 103018 and 10322.

73 HAS, BS37.

74 *CCED*, nos 65184 and 150578. It is unclear whether these relate to the same man.

75 HAS, BS37.

76 *CCED*, no. 132754; HAS, AH73/1.

77 Inf. from local resident.

78 *CCED*, no. 90921; HAS, BC79/2/52. The memorial in Cradley church which states that he died in 1676 is incorrect.

1000–1559

The valuable benefice of Cradley was generally presented to either senior diocesan figures or ambitious and well-connected younger clergy. Most, therefore, especially those holding multiple benefices or offices, were probably only sporadically resident. Consequently, Cradley's religious life would principally have been led by vicars assisted by chaplains.[79]

More than half the 17 identified medieval rectors definitely held canonries, at Hereford or elsewhere. Three were treasurers of the cathedral and two were archdeacons. One was referred to as *dominus* (i.e. held a bachelor's degree) and seven as Master, and two held doctorates.[80] A few rectors held office briefly, sometimes towards the end of their lives, but several remained for much of their careers. Only one is recorded as exchanging the benefice for another.[81] The earliest identified rector, Ralph Foliot, was a canon at Hereford by 1178 and became archdeacon of Hereford the following year. A senior royal servant, he served as Henry II's *sigilarius* in the Chancery and as a royal justice, as well as possibly holding a prebend in Salisbury cathedral and several benefices elsewhere.[82] Ralph's career was exceptional, but other rectors followed similar, if less heady, career trajectories.[83] But such absenteeism was not always deemed acceptable. In 1409, Bishop Mascall admonished the rector, Maurice Druy, to reside in his parish to carry out his pastoral duties.[84] Maurice had, however, in 1404 been granted leave for a year's absence 'for study'.[85]

No rector pursued a more colourful career than Gervase of London. A canon of Hereford cathedral, holding an unidentified prebend, he was rector of Cradley by *c.*1240. His activities provoked fractious relations with several parishioners, leading to two cases before the royal justices, which he lost. In the first, Edith de la Heath successfully sued him for taking wrongful custody of the heirs and lands of Robert de la Heath; the other was a clash over ownership of tithes and presentation rights of Barrow chapel.[86] His career in Cradley was cut short when he was outlawed for involvement in the murder of the bishop of Hereford's proctor, Prior Bernard of Campagne, before the cathedral high altar in 1252. Gervase managed to evade royal justice and was finally pardoned in 1256, although not restored to his Herefordshire benefices.[87]

79 Above, Table 2, and below, Religious Life 1000–1559.

80 Above, Table 2.

81 M. Richard Chaundos to M. Thomas Birmingham in 1366: *Reg. Lewis Charlton*, 71.

82 *English Episcopal Acta: Hereford 1079–1234*, no. 196; *Fasti Eccles. Ang. Hereford, 1066–1300*, VIII, 14n, 24, 82, 97, 156.

83 E.g. M. Adam Trewlove, M. Henry Martyn and Dr John Nans; above, Table 2.

84 *Reg. Mascall*, 69–70.

85 *Reg. Mascall*, 189.

86 Above, Manors and Principal Estates: Cradley manor before 1562, and see below.

87 *ODNB*, s.v. Aigueblanche, Peter D' [Peter de Aqua Blanca], bishop of Hereford and royal councillor (accessed 25 Jan. 2020); *Fasti Eccles. Ang. Hereford, 1066–1300*, VIII, 61–98; *Fasti Eccles. Ang. Coventry and Lichfield, 1066–1300*, 66, 69; Gervase eventually received a pardon, *Close* 1253–4, 13–14; *Cal. Pat.* 1247–58, 455, 475, 509.

Only two vicars are known by name – Walter, before 1300, and Henry Tanner, in 1557[88] – with a probable third, John the Priest of Cradley, in 1331.[89] It is not certain how vicars were maintained, but a pasture referred to as 'Vicaresland' was recorded in 1496–7.[90] A 1562 grant of the bishop's lands to Elizabeth I included the 'advowsons of portions, tithes, prebends and vicarages' belonging to Cradley, Ross and Colwall.[91] A vicar's portion is also recorded in 1557, when Henry Tanner granted William Druett all the lands, tenements and pertinences belonging to the vicarage of Cradley in Little Hanley for 50 years.[92]

In addition to a manorial chapel at Barrow and another belonging to the Hill family, two parish chaplains, Walter de Intebawe in 1330 and a *dominus* William in 1397, are recorded. At least one chaplain, therefore, was probably attached to a chantry or other chapel in the parish church, which may have been dedicated to the Virgin Mary.[93] In 1397, at least two chaplains served in the parish during the bishop's visitation, William and *dominus* Richard Sterre, both apparently graduates. They were accused by parishioners of fornication with local women and other behaviour unbecoming the dignity of the church.[94] Another chaplain, *dominus* Thomas Dagger, was recorded 1455–7, and *dominus* or Sir Christopher Heganbothen, clerk, was active 1547–8, though whether as chaplain or vicar is unclear.[95]

The Barrow family had established a private chapel at Barrow before 1200. A dispute in 1242 between Robert de Barrow and the rector of Cradley, Master Gervase of London, which reached the king's court, referred to two chaplains, William (before 1198) and Nicholas (before 1242).[96] The parties disagreed over entitlement to tithes and the right to present a chaplain. A local jury swore that traditionally two sheaves from Robert's demesne belonged to the chapel and one to the church. Furthermore, Robert's grandfather, Robert, had presented William the clerk to Bishop William de Vere. Robert was awarded damages and his right to present was confirmed.[97] By 1370, the chapel belonged to the prior and convent of Worcester cathedral. It was apparently well endowed, possessing fields and a manse of several buildings, and was farmed out to two chaplains, for two payments of 20 marks annually, conditional on paying for a chaplain, maintaining the fields, goods and buildings, and constructing a grange at a site

88 TNA, E 210/3775; HCA, 3339.

89 John was openly married to an Agnes, though he was dead by the time of the charter. Prominent families of the parish including John of the Barrow and Peter of the Hill, witnessed Agnes' charter; TNA, C 146/10056.

90 HAS, AM33/13, rot. 21d.

91 *Cal. Pat.* 1560–63, 288.

92 HCA, 3339.

93 TNA, C 146/9686.

94 The site of the alleged trysts, the *domus* of Blessed Mary (see Advowson and Church Endowment above), was probably related to a side altar in the church dedicated to the Virgin Mary which may have been used for intercessory masses. The house may have been the customary residence of the chaplain or chaplains attending the altar: Forrest and Whittick, *Visitation of the Diocese of Hereford*, 106–7. An Amice Daniel was accused of unspecified sorcery in the same proceedings.

95 *Calendar of Probate and Administration Acts 1407–1550*, 55/138, 547/138; HAS, 41/2/4, will of Margery Tomes alias Luley, 1546.

96 *English Episcopal Acta 35: Hereford 1234–75*, Appendix 1, VI and XVI.

97 *Cur. Reg.* 17, nos 697 and 1533.

of the prior and convent's choosing.[98] It is unclear whether the prior and convent were still required to present a chaplain to the bishop of Hereford. There is no subsequent reference to Barrow chapel.

Another, unidentified, chapel is recorded in 1393, probably as part of the Hill family's manor complex in the parish.[99]

William Booth or Bothe was presented to the rectory by Bishop Charles Booth in 1526, though their relationship is unknown.[100] A man with apparently reformist roots, he nevertheless remained discreetly in office through Mary's reign until his death *c.*1558. His high-profile career included roles as supervisor of the wines at Oxford in 1529 and keeper of the Winton chest.[101] Like his predecessors, he may have been absent during his early career, though he was probably involved in constructing the church house *c.*1530.[102] In 1537, he received dispensation to hold a second benefice, and became personal chaplain to the bishop of Rochester, John Hilsey.[103] Booth and Hilsey were fellow students at Oxford in the late 1520s, and Booth's appointment suggests sympathy with Hilsey's reformist stance and championing of the royal supremacy.[104] After Hilsey died in 1539, Booth seems to have resided in Cradley, since from 1542 he wrote and witnessed parishioners' wills and specified their debts.[105] When pensioned from the wardenship of a chantry at an altar in the church of St Mary Aldermary (London) before 1549, he was described as an honest man and unmarried.[106] He wrote his will in Cradley *c.*1558, enlisting prominent parishioner Rowland Longe as overseer and Richard Hill, gentleman, as witness. He instructed that he be buried in the chancel of Cradley church and left money to Hereford cathedral.[107]

Whether or not influenced by Booth, few parishioners' wills of the 1540s and 1550s expressed Catholic adherence. Richard Taylor in 1546 was exceptional in bequeathing 5*s.* for prayers for himself, specifically by Sir Christopher Heganbothen, although Booth witnessed the will.[108]

98 WCM, B240.

99 HAS, C96/1.

100 Booth was ordained as sub-deacon at Cradley on 15 June 1527. He obtained his MA at Oxford on 15 March 1529 and was ordained as a priest on 27 March. The published reg. incorrectly lists William as a Master of Arts, when the original refers to him as Bachelor; see *Reg. Bothe II*, 324, 339 and HAS, AL19/13, f. 128. After completing his BA at Oxford in 1525, he was given dispensation to go abroad for further study: A.B. Emden, *A Biographical Register of the University of Oxford,* AD *1501 to 1540* (Oxford, 1974), 61–2.

101 Emden, *Biog. Reg.* AD *1501 to 1540*, 61–2.

102 Above, Education: Cradley Boys' School (old boys' school).

103 Emden, *Biog. Reg.* AD *1501 to 1540*, 61–2; He received £6 13*s.* 4*d.* and his income for the rectorship of Cradley as £18, HCA 5602/12; From 1537 to *c.*1549, he was also warden of chantry at altar in St Mary Aldermary in London; *Cal. Pat.* 1547–8, 324.

104 Hilsey graduated B.D. in May 1527; Emden, *Biog. Reg.* AD *1501 to 1540*, 61–2; *ODNB*, s.v. Hilsey, John (d. 1539), bishop of Rochester (accessed 1 Aug. 2023).

105 HAS, 25/3/2, will of William Jones alias Fletcher, 1542; HAS, 40/1/7, will of Richard Taylor, 1546; HAS, 24/4/2, will of John James, 1547; HAS, 11/1/13, will of Thomas Carpenter, 1548; HAS, 8/3/13, will of John Balocke, 1549.

106 HCA, 5602/12.

107 See Appendices, Sample 2, 1.

108 HAS, 40/1/7, will of Richard Taylor, 1546.

In 1553, Bishop John Harley allegedly granted the right of presenting Booth's successor to Rowland Longe of Cradley, on condition that Rowland present John Harley's stepson, Thomas Bromald of London, to the rectory. After Harley was removed from office and Catholicism restored under Mary, such a presentation was politically unwise, so Longe and Richard Harford of Bosbury presented John Parfey instead. Bromald launched legal proceedings in 1559 under Elizabeth I to obtain recompense for the loss.[109]

1560–2023

Under Parfey,[110] Cradley may have seen a brief but enthusiastic period of counter-reformation Catholicism. No evidence survives regarding Parfey's education, but he probably graduated shortly before his earliest recorded office, as precentor at Hereford cathedral in 1557.[111] If typical of the high-calibre clergy appointed under Mary I, he would have experienced burgeoning counter-reformation Catholic ideology at university,[112] and he was certainly a firm opponent of Protestantism, since he was deprived of his precentorship in 1559 and of Cradley rectory in 1560, and had fled abroad by 1561.[113] Either he resigned his positions in protest at the Elizabethan settlement or was expelled because he refused to conform to the new practices.

Perhaps under Puritan influence a post of preacher was created at Cradley after 1600, presumably to provide more frequent or better-quality sermons. Thomas Godwyn, rector from 1621, resigned in 1629, but continued as preacher until 1635,[114] and in 1627 gifted a pulpit to the church.[115] Extant 16th-century carved choir stalls suggest some small-scale renovation of the church fabric during this period.[116] And their survival implies a fairly moderate response to the religious upheavals of the period, not veering towards radical Protestantism, despite the creation of the role of preacher and the national changes engendered by the Civil Wars. Cradley church seems to have escaped the upheavals of the Civil Wars and Interregnum, as Edmund Skinner remained rector throughout the period, serving from 1629 to 1677.[117]

In 1716, the church building was reported to be generally in good repair.[118] Sunday services were held at 10a.m. and 3p.m., communion was administered four times a year, and catechism was provided (for children and servants) during the season of

109 *Reg. Bothe II*, 327; HAS, 24/2/2, will of John James, 1547, 11/1/13, will of Thomas Carpenter, 1548; 40/1/7, will of Richard Taylor, 1546; TNA, C 3/15/20. This charter names John Harley's wife as Elizabeth. Presumably Bromald was the surname of her previous husband. For mention of Harley's marriage, see *ODNB*, s.v. Harley, John (d. 1557/8), bishop of Hereford (accessed 26 Jan. 2020).

110 Alias Parfrey, Parfew, Parfoye.

111 *CCED*, no. 171293. He was later also appointed prebendary at the Cathedral in 1559.

112 Cf. E. Duffy, *Fires of Faith: Catholic England under Mary Tudor* (2009), 22–8.

113 *CCED*, no. 171293. William H. Campbell (ed.), John Le Neve, *Fasti Ecclesiae Anglicanae 1541–1857: Hereford Diocese*, vol. 3 (2014), 16, 78.

114 *CCED*, no. 133970.

115 HAS, BC79/2/52. This may have been the same pulpit described as a 'triple-decker' in a 1736 seating plan: http://www.cradleychurch.org.uk/tour (accessed 17 Nov. 2022).

116 Below, Church Architecture: Church of St James: Anglo-Saxon and Norman.

117 *CCED*, no. 90921.

118 HAS, HD5/14/107.

Figure 24 *Engraving of Thomas Bisse, rector 1713–31. (HCA, B.03.65/1 © Hereford cathedral)*

Lent. The minister dutifully baptised, and visited the sick and dying; the parishioners abstained from work on Sundays, no public penances had been performed within the church in the last year, and no one refused to pay church rates. Such an exemplary state of spiritual affairs cannot be credited to the rector, Thomas Bisse, who in 1719 was non-resident and relied on a curate.[119] Bisse, rector 1713–31,[120] was persistently non-resident (holding six other livings simultaneously), and owed his preferment to nepotism, having been appointed in 1713 by the bishop, his brother.[121] Bisse was probably involved in small-scale renovation of the church fabric, as he donated the ornate font *c*.1722,[122] and probably commissioned the bells made in 1724 during his incumbency.[123] He was also involved in 1724 in establishing the charity that supported the placing-out, education and maintenance of the orphans of poorer clergy belonging to the dioceses of Gloucester, Worcester and Hereford. This went on to become the Three Choirs Festival.[124]

Despite pluralism and nepotism, some rectors gifted items, such as Edmund Skinner (rector 1629–78), who gave communion plate to the church.[125] Others were significant parish landholders, and thus had a stake in its socio-economic life. Edmund Skinner was from a local gentry family (nephew of Stephen Skinner and uncle of James Turner of Vinesend, and inheriting the bulk of both of their estates) and socialised with some of the parish elite.[126] Similarly, Richard Chambers (rector 1731–76)[127] held sizeable estates in the parish, from which he funded a charity for the poor.[128] Many pluralist rectors chose Cradley as their place of burial (suggesting it held particular importance to them among their benefices), including Thomas Greenwiche (d. 1571);[129] Morgan Powell (d. 1621); John Benson (d. 1713) and family members; Richard Chambers (d. 1776); Daniel Price (d. 1794); Edward Renn Hampden (d. 1892); Thomas Ayscough (d. 1920) and family members; and William Janvrin (d. 1927) and his wife.[130] The 18th century saw alterations to the church. The surviving south doorway in the tower was probably made *c*.1722, re-using much earlier material, including parts of a Norman font.[131] A west gallery seating 80 existed by 1789; it was probably built after 1736, and almost certainly after 1717; in 1841, the rector, Charles Scott Luxmoore, was authorised to enlarge it, which he did at

119 HAS, HD5/15/33. It is not known who this curate was.
120 *ODNB*, s.v. Bisse, Thos (1675–1731), Church of England clergyman and founder of the Three Choirs festival (accessed 1 Aug. 2023); HAS, AH85/1–2, I.
121 *ODNB*, s.v. Bisse, Thos (1675–1731), Church of England clergyman and founder of the Three Choirs festival (accessed 1 Aug. 2023); HAS, AH85/1–2, I; HAS, HD5/14/107; HAS, HD5/15/33.
122 HAS, BM81/1/19.
123 HAS, AH85/1–2, I; http://www.cradleychurch.org.uk/tour (accessed 17 Nov. 2022). The tenor bell bears Bisse's name.
124 A. Boden and P. Hedley, *The Three Choirs Festival: A history* (Woodbridge, 2017), 16–19.
125 HAS, BC79/2/52; *CCED*, no. 90921.
126 See Appendices, Sample 2, 67, 84, 88; TNA, PROB 11/327/309.
127 *CCED*, nos 180188 and 191835.
128 Tithe Map (1839); above, Social Welfare.
129 HAS, AH73/1.
130 HAS, BM81/1/19.
131 RCHME, 61–2.

Figure 25 *Edward Renn Hampden, rector 1854–91. (HCA, B.04.102/2 © Hereford Cathedral)*

his own expense.[132] The ring of six bells was cast by Abraham Rudhall in 1724, but the survival of a medieval bell frame in the tower demonstrates that the bells were replacements for an earlier ring.[133]

Charles Scott Luxmoore (rector 1815–54),[134] eldest son of the bishop of Hereford,[135] had an important impact on parish life, but was a notorious pluralist. He received £1,200 annually as dean of St Asaph; from Cradley rectory, £1,000; and from sinecure rectories at Bromyard and Darowen (Montgoms.), £200 each; he was also chancellor and a canon of Hereford cathedral.[136] In 1831, in response to a vituperative letter in the *Hereford Journal* complaining that he 'never resides in his parish', he acknowledged that he resided mostly at (nearby) Bromyard, but kept a curate at Cradley.[137] Under Luxmoore, Charles Thomas Pattrick was curate until 1831.[138] In 1832, John Humphrey Davies was engaged as curate for £150 annually, with use of the rectory house and garden (suggesting that Luxmoore was then non-resident), but his licence was revoked in the same year for dereliction of duty. Allen Robert Cliffe was licensed in 1833 for £150 p.a. with no mention of the rectory house, so perhaps Luxmoore was then more frequently in Cradley. William Dyke was licensed as curate in 1837.[139] In 1839, Luxmoore was one of the largest landowners in the parish, his glebe and other landholdings totalling 359 acres.[140] He was instrumental in creating Storridge church.[141] He died in 1854 at Cradley.[142]

Luxmoore's successor, Edward Renn Hampden (1854–91),[143] was an important influence on Cradley's religious life, including commissioning and taking an active role in restoring St James's church.[144] Another controversial pluralist, son of a bishop of Hereford, besides rector of Cradley, he was perpetual curate of Breinton and vicar of Eaton Bishop. In 1854, this blatant nepotism was criticised in an angry *Hereford Times* article: he nonetheless later added three more benefices.[145] A *Hereford Times* article of 1859, however, signed by a Cradley parishioner, responded to criticisms that pastoral care in large parishes was lacking, and cited Cradley as an exemplary exception, its 1,200 inhabitants having three places of worship and five Sunday services, with 'active, zealous and benevolent' ministers.[146] This is testament, perhaps, to the work of the several curates during Hampden's time as rector.[147]

132 HAS, N37/35 2 Dec. 1841.
133 Eisel, *TWNFC* 69 (2021), 108; HAS, AH85/1-2, vol. 1.
134 HAS, CA19/2.
135 *ODNB*, s.v. Luxmore, Charles Scott (1792?–1854) (accessed 1 Aug. 2023).
136 *CCED*, no. 112631.
137 *HJ*, 7 Mar. 1831, 23 Nov. 1831, 8 Aug. 1821. At least five curates are recorded during Luxmoore's time as rector: *CCED*, no. 112631; HAS, CA19/3; HAS, 8/13/51.
138 HAS, MX182.
139 HAS, CA19/3.
140 Tithe Map (1839); Hunt, *Cradley*, 90.
141 Below, Church Architecture: Storridge St John the Evangelist.
142 *CCED*, no. 112631.
143 F. Havergal, *Fasti Herefordensis and Other Antiquarian Memorials of Hereford* (Edinburgh, 1869); HAS, AW15/2.
144 Below, Church Architecture.
145 *HT*, 27 May 1854, 17 June 1854, 16 Sept. 1854; HCA, B.04.102/2; *Littlebury's Dir.* (1867).
146 *HT*, 5 Mar. 1859.
147 *Slater's Dir.* (1859); *Littlebury's Dir.* (1867); HCA, 6308/3/10.

When Hampden arrived in Cradley, there was no attempt at singing during services, and there were no musical instruments. He remarked that in an oak chest in the tower there were the remains of a cello which, with a violin and flute, had once led the singing.[148] Hampden's use of Latin for the biblical quotation in St James's east window may suggest he had high church leanings, in contrast to the more controversial, and liberal, views of his father.[149]

In 1855, Hampden rented Haywards barn on the Ridgeway road as a mission chapel.[150] His likely intention, given its position, was to counter the influence of the Mormon chapel in the same area.[151] Latterly it was used for Sunday afternoon services, but closed between 1917 and 1927,[152] and was subsequently converted to a dwelling.

Cradley's parish community included a missionary association, which raised funds for, and heard talks by, Anglican missionaries from across the world.[153] 'The Cradley Parochial Association for the Defence of the Church', a committee of parish churchmen, inspired Ledbury to form a similar association. In 1895, a Cradley petition to Parliament against disestablishing and disendowing the Church in Wales attracted a large number of signatures.[154] There were also Young Men's Bible Classes on Sundays, and a Bell Ringers' Guild.[155] Cradley had a Mothers' Union in 1895 and still in 1936,[156] when a branch was set up in Storridge, and meetings were held at several locations.[157] The surviving base of the medieval churchyard cross was made into a sundial to commemorate Queen Victoria's jubilee in 1887.[158]

Augmentations to the interior were made in the course of the 20th century, including the large cross hanging over the chancel, the central length of the brass communion rail and the front choir stalls (late 1980s) made by the Morgan Motor Co. of Malvern.[159] Peter H.G. Morgan, director of the company, lived in Cradley for 30 years until his death in 2003.[160] In 2009, a temporary installation of 59 angel images in and outside the church, by the English artist Celia Kilner, raised funds for church repairs. The bishop of Hereford attended the opening and a special celebratory cider was created. Five of the angels were bought by the churchwarden and his wife and donated to the church in 2014, where they are now displayed.[161] A Glastonbury Thorn was planted in the north part of the churchyard in 2019 to commemorate a tradition of villagers gathering on Twelfth Night to celebrate a similar tree flowering in the north of the parish.[162]

148 HAS, AH85/1–2, vol. 1.
149 http://www.cradleychurch.org.uk/tour (accessed 17 Nov. 2022).
150 The primary author of this paragraph is Edward Peters. Hunt, *Cradley*, 7; 'Mission Room' on OS Map 1:10560, Herefordshire, XXVIII.SE (1886 edn); 1:2500, Herefordshire XVIII.12 (1904 edn).
151 Below, Protestant Nonconformity.
152 Hunt, *Cradley*, 7; Edwards, *Cradley*, 47.
153 HAS, AH73/71.
154 HAS, BO80/17.
155 HAS, AH73/71.
156 HAS, N37/63.
157 HAS, BO80/17.
158 Edwards, *Cradley*, 10.
159 http://www.cradleychurch.org.uk/tour (accessed 17 Nov. 2022); inf. from local resident.
160 Plaque on south choir stalls.
161 http://www.cradleychurch.org.uk/tour (accessed 17 Nov. 2022).
162 http://www.cradleychurch.org.uk/tour (accessed 17 Nov. 2022); Edwards, *Cradley*, 27.

The rector in 2023 (Robert Ward) also served Mathon and Storridge, and was rural dean of Ledbury.[163] Services were held at St James's church on Sundays and Wednesdays.[164] The church remained important to parish life in the modern era, and was regularly being used for community events including concerts, plays and lunches.[165] Tombstones were cleared from the southern part of the churchyard to provide an outdoor space for community activities.[166]

Church Architecture

Church of St James: Anglo-Saxon and Norman[167]

The church of St James is sited on a slight hill, within a hedged enclosure with a medieval hollow way or ditch marking its north-eastern boundary.[168] Although considerably rebuilt in the second half of the 19th century, it contains decorative and structural elements in the west tower and south doorway that indicate a late Norman origin, but with Anglo-Saxon elements from an earlier phase.[169] The lower two stages of the west tower, undivided externally, date from *c.*1200, with the top stage added *c.*1500.[170]

The Pre-Conquest Church

The church retains several rare survivals of pre-Conquest decorative stonework. The earliest fabric is represented by several carved and otherwise distinctive stones visible in most external elevations of the walls, and individual uncarved blocks of local yellow mudstone of distinctive size and regular shape.[171] An elaborately decorated stone frieze or panel of pale buff sandstone is reset on the northern external elevation of the church tower. Such a panel or frieze might have stood as one of a pair of responds on either side of an elaborate Anglo-Saxon chancel arch. Alternatively, it may have formed one side of a square entablature panel providing the horizontally set first-stage separation of a freestanding churchyard cross, supported and surmounted by elaborately decorated shafts; such a cross has been reconstructed from fragments at Wroxeter (Shrops.).[172]

163 http://www.cradleychurch.org.uk/index_m.php (accessed 18 Feb. 2022); https://www.linkedin.com/in/robert-ward-0476a350 (accessed 18 Feb. 2022).
164 http://www.cradleychurch.org.uk/services_m.php (accessed 18 Feb. 2022).
165 http://www.cradleychurch.org.uk/tour (accessed 17 Nov. 2022).
166 http://www.cradleychurch.org.uk/tour (accessed 17 Nov. 2022).
167 The primary author of this section is Keith Ray.
168 Map ref: SO 735 471. HER, 31074. *RCHME Cradley*, monument 1; above, Settlement: Before 1000; HER, 31074.
169 RCHME, 61.
170 RCHME, 61; NHLE, no. 1082298, Ch. of St James (accessed 1 Aug. 2023).
171 These stones have all been observed and photographed, but none has been drawn *in situ*.
172 The sketches were discovered among the papers of the Shropshire antiquary William Mytton. The shaft and the other pair of stones were carved on Oolitic limestone from the Cotswolds. See R. Bryant, *Corpus of Anglo-Saxon Stone Sculpture, Volume 10: The West Midlands* (Oxford, 2012), 314–17. The possibility that the 'crocket stone' at Cradley was from a freestanding cross was first raised in K. Ray, 'Archaeology and the three early churches of Herefordshire', in Malpas *et al.* (eds), *The Early Church in Herefordshire* (Leominster, 2001), 99–148, at 137.

Figure 26 *Cradley St James; elaborately decorated Anglo-Saxon stone frieze or panel, built into the north face of the tower. (Photo by Keith Ray, 2022)*

The tower doorway and lower south elevation fabric are grey-green sandstone or mudstone. The south doorway has what has been described as a 'solid rounded arch', while a narrow round-headed window in the second stage is thought to provide its pre-Conquest date.[173] The doorway's arch stone is a single block of grey-green sandstone or mudstone with incisions marking 14 voussoirs. The stones forming the eastern jamb are typical Anglo-Saxon long-and-short work. The grooving of each jamb stone and the groove incised around the inner door-head stone produced a continuous cordon around the inner edge of the doorway.

Inspection in 2023 of the void between the inner facing of the tower fabric and the (inserted) timber and lath bell-frame structure revealed another single-stone door-head set into the upper inner face of the doorway (see Figure 26). This stone, apparently worked from a single Oolitic limestone block, is an almost exact parallel to one of the door-head stones remaining *in situ* at Deerhurst (Glos.), which probably date from *c.*1000.[174] Another feature of the outer doorway is the shadow of what was either an inverted V-shaped relieving arch above it, or a difference in build that indicates the former presence of a porch. Thus, both door-head stones were probably reused from elsewhere in the church to create a doorway into the tower. An 18th-century illustration appears to show the tower minus its doorway.[175]

A fragment of another carved arch, possibly formerly heading a window opening, is incorporated in the rubble walling just below eaves height in the north elevation of the

173 Brooks and Pevsner, *Herefs.*, 182.

174 H.M. and J. Taylor, *Anglo-Saxon Architecture*, vol. 1 (1965), 194–6.

175 See figure 22 above. http://www.cradleychurch.org.uk/tour/11 and 27 (accessed 15 Nov. 2022).

Figure 27 *Cradley St James; the tower south doorway with the probably reused Anglo-Saxon solid rounded arch. (Photo by Keith Ray, 2022)*

chancel. Five radiating lines are incised on the stone's surface which, on analogy with those on the tower doorway arch, mark out six faux voussoirs. The fragment's present position suggests that the masons responsible for positioning it knew that it was meant to be viewed this way up. Its presence here, with the two door-head stones reset in the tower, lends substance to the idea that there was once a small late Saxon minster or estate church here.

The simplest explanation for the other pre-Romanesque stones described here is that they all formed elements or decorative features of the Anglo-Saxon church, although the stone with the crockets in the north elevation of the tower may once have been a horizontal element in a freestanding churchyard cross. If this was the case, as at Acton Beauchamp (8km. north-west), where a fragment of the vertical shaft of such a cross exists, it is possible that another 8th-century 'family monastery' existed at Cradley comparable with that at Acton.[176]

176 See J. Blair, 'The Anglo-Saxon church in Herefordshire: Four themes', *The Early Church in Herefordshire* (Leominster, 2001), 5–7.

A yew tree in the churchyard east of the church may be around 1,000 years old and thus pre-Conquest, while another to the south is *c.*700 years old, dating from around 1300.[177]

The Norman Church

Major rebuilding apparently took place in the mid 12th century (*c.*1130–60), with additional work in the late 12th to perhaps early 13th century. The south doorway into the nave is a wholly later 12th-century Romanesque architectural element, featuring 'nook shafts with scallop capitals and arch with roll mould and chevrons'.[178] The lack of voussoirs of the kind described above in this doorway suggests that the shafts have been relocated and were once part of a chancel arch. The very small corbels indicate that the Romanesque parish church was relatively modest in size and elaboration.[179] Eight stones embedded into the visible fabric of the south elevation are of more durable grey sandstone. All eight are architectural components of a mid 12th-century church with apparent links to the so-called 'Herefordshire School' best represented by Hereford cathedral, Leominster priory and Kilpeck church. Four are fragments of voussoirs, characterised by a finely worked double-chevron.[180] The other four are corbels that would have been located under the church roof eaves. One is a human head ('face-puller') and the others are animal heads in a muted grotesque style, very similar to those at Kilpeck. Two were reused as corbels on either side of the east window after the chancel was rebuilt in 1870. Cradley was clearly linked to the major architectural (and church patronage) movement involving flamboyant figural sculptural features that swept Hereford diocese between 1130 and 1160, and is a strong indicator of both Cradley's episcopal patronage and the wealth of the benefice at the period.[181]

Inside the church, the pillars of the interior archway into the tower are late 12th-century with scallop capitals.[182] The slightly pointed arch may be early Gothic.[183] Although the medieval chancel was largely rebuilt in 1870, much of the old fabric was apparently reused. It appears to sit on its original foundations of *c.*1200 – visible

177 Edwin Lees, *Pictures from Nature* (Malvern, 1856), 131–2; the east was estimated as between 962 and 1002 years old, the south as between 650 and 700 in 2015; J.P. Ross, 'Report on yew trees at St. James the Great, Cradley: Based on a ground level inspection carried out 28th September 2015'; J.P. Ross, 'Yew trees at St James the Great Church, Cradley' (16 Apr. 2019); http://www.cradleychurch.org.uk/tour/23 and 31 (accessed 17 Nov. 2022).

178 NHLE, no. 1082298, Ch. of St James (accessed 1 Aug. 2023).

179 It is possible that the origins of the west tower at Cradley lie with the 12th-century church rather than its 14th-century rebuild. Just possibly, the upper stages of the tower were once timber-framed (but not using the frame subsequently installed to strengthen the tower for its heavier bells (see D. James, 'Saw marks in vernacular buildings and their wider significance', *Vernacular Architecture* 43 (2012), 7–18; 'The church of St James, Cradley, Herefordshire', *TWNFC* 67 (2019), 151–4 at 151–2), and that this frame was removed when the tower was taken up to its full height in stone.

180 These stones would, for most of the existence of this walling, have been rendered over and therefore both invisible and protected from weathering.

181 Malcolm Thurlby, *The Herefordshire School of Romanesque Sculpture* (Eardisley, 2013).

182 RCHME, 61–2.

183 Brooks and Pevsner, *Herefs.*, 182–3.

outside in the plinth beneath the east wall.[184] It is notable that the chancel is the same width as the original nave and as such quite large; perhaps it was originally designed to accommodate visits by the bishop and his retinue of attendant priests.[185] Before alterations were made in the 19th century, there were reportedly effigies of a bishop and a king with the church in one hand and a sword in another. The windows contained the arms of the see and deanery.[186]

Little can be known of the medieval nave, as most medieval fabric was lost in the restoration, while the windows in the south wall are reproductions. However, as with the chancel, the nave width seems to have been reduced when the north aisle was added.[187] A sketch from 1717 depicts a lancet window in the south wall of the nave which was later replaced.[188] The remains of 'an ancient image', almost certainly a medieval or early modern wall painting, are recorded in the nave, near the now lost 17th-century tomb of Richard Hill.[189]

In the tower, inside the south doorway, an arch is made from the halves of an octagonal font, possibly Norman in date.[190]

The 14th to 18th Centuries[191]

The church underwent further alterations *c.*1330, when windows were inserted or replaced in the north and south chancel walls. The two in the south wall were reset and much restored in 1870.[192] Dating to probably between 1280 and 1345, the church's medieval iron-bound, boarded-box chest is one of the earliest if not the earliest in the county, although with later repairs.[193] More significant work was carried out in the late 14th or early 15th century, when the top stage of the tower was added, probably during the rectorship of either Thomas Birmingham (1366–1393), or Maurice Druy (1401–*c.*1437). A late 14th-century (perpendicular) window with vertical tracery and three trefoiled lights survives in the west wall.[194]

In the 15th century, a wooden screen, at least part of which survives below the Victorian screen, was erected between the chancel and the nave.[195] Surviving fragments of timber work imply that stalls were placed in the chancel at around the same date.[196]

184 RCHME, 61–2.
185 http://www.cradleychurch.org.uk/tour/15 (accessed 15 Nov. 2022).
186 HAS, BC79/2/52.
187 RCHME, 61–2.
188 http://www.cradleychurch.org.uk/tour/11 (accessed 15 Nov. 2022).
189 HAS, BC79/2/52.
190 RCHME, 61–2.
191 This section is principally authored by Duncan James with contributions from David Whitehead.
192 There is also a priest's door in the south wall with possibly reset chamfered jambs and semi-elliptical head, RCHME, 61–2.
193 R.A. Sycamore, 'Church chests in Herefordshire revisited: New perspectives on their dates and construction', *TWNFC*, 70 (2022), 118.
194 Brooks and Pevsner, *Herefs.*, 182–3. For the dating of Thomas, see above, Table of Rectors.
195 RCHME, 61–2.
196 NHLE, no. 1082298, Ch. of St James (accessed 4 Jan. 2024); http://www.cradleychurch.org.uk/tour/15 (accessed 15 Nov. 2022).

Figure 28 *Cradley St James; the medieval plank chest inside church. (Photo by Barry Sharples, 2023)*

During the 15th or early 16th century an independent timber structure was raised inside the tower. Two timber-framed walls or screens were built parallel to but not embedded into the stonework of the north and south walls.[197] The frames, 20ft. high and 12ft. 6in. apart, support two large north–south beams which rest against or nearly against the internal face of the tower.[198] Both were later heightened by 4ft. to support a floor.[199] Diagonal saw-marks on the face of the primary components indicate a see-saw technique suggestive of a 15th- or early 16th-century date.[200] Carpenters' assembly marks comprising circles and lines were cut using a race knife and are similar to those found widely in Herefordshire.[201] This purposeful construction, made by experienced, professional craftsmen, uses methods seen in timber-framed house building of the period. The heartwood surfaces of the frames face inwards, indicating the higher status of the interior space.

197 The inspectors, later repeated without explanation by Brooks, assess the beams as being from the 17th century, *RCHME*, 61, Brooks and Pevsner, *Herefs*., 182.

198 The sill beams are now mostly hidden due to the raised floor.

199 The modern bell frame carried on steel beams is located above this.

200 Before the 15th century one might expect to see different jointing and timber conversion methods: James, 'Saw marks in vernacular buildings and their wider significance'; 'The church of St James, Cradley, Herefordshire'.

201 Other marks include taper burns and Marian marks in the form of a double V, for Virgin of Virgins. Taper burn marks on the timber are now thought to be apotropaic marks rather than the result of carelessness. J. Dean and N. Hill, 'Burn marks on buildings: Accidental or deliberate?', *Vernacular Architecture* 45 (2014), 1–16. There is no doubt that a more detailed scrutiny of the two frames would reveal more marks of interest.

The purpose of the frame is obscure: it cannot, as the RCHME suggested in the 1930s, have been intended to stiffen the structure of the tower, nor does it appear to have been designed to support a bell or bells (unless the clapper was the only moving part).[202] There are, furthermore, indications that a bell or bells were being rung prior to the frame's insertion.[203] It is unlikely that their sole purpose was to support a floor, as there are easier ways of doing that.[204] It is possible that the frame may simply have been intended to upgrade the church with a more comfortable bell-ringing chamber – perhaps when Cradley village hall was built *c.*1530.[205]

A medieval stone cross in the churchyard south of the tower was converted into a sundial in 1887.[206]

The 19th Century and Later Restorations[207]

The church was extensively restored, and in part rebuilt, in 1868–70 at the instigation of the rector, Edward Renn Hampden.

The chancel was largely rebuilt in 1868, at Hampden's expense, to plans by Sir George Gilbert Scott,[208] the money being raised through loans from Queen Anne's Bounty.[209] The roof and the south and east walls were rebuilt, and pulpit and pews removed to create a sanctuary at the east end.[210] Scott created new chancel stalls, incorporating some medieval woodwork, and a new screen above the low medieval one between nave and chancel.[211] The altar was presented by the curate, Arthur Constance.[212] In 1874, a Nicholson organ, given by Hampden, replaced a harmonium in the chancel.[213] The east window, depicting the resurrection, was made by Hardman & Co. of Birmingham,[214] and commemorates Thomas Webb (d. 1869), a crystal glass maker, who had retired to Cradley. The north stained-glass window in the chancel, depicting Francis of Assisi, was donated in memory of Thomas Ayscough (rector 1892–1917)[215] by his daughter-in-law.[216]

A.E. Perkins, a Worcester architect, restored the nave and constructed the north aisle in 1869–70,[217] the money being raised by a public campaign generously supported by Hampden. The north and south nave walls were rebuilt (though their original windows

202 For deeper discussions, see James, 'The church of St James, Cradley, Herefordshire'; J.C. Eisel, 'Mediaeval timbers in the tower of Cradley church, Herefordshire', *TWNFC* 69 (2021), 107–15.
203 Eisel, 'Mediaeval timbers', 107–15.
204 James, 'Saw marks in vernacular buildings and their wider significance'; James, 'The church of St James, Cradley, Herefordshire'; Eisel, 'Mediaeval timbers', 107–15.
205 See paragraph below.
206 HER, 3809.
207 David Whitehead made a substantial contribution to the research underpinning this section.
208 NHLE, no. 1082298, Ch. of St James (accessed 1 Aug. 2023).
209 HAS, AH85/1.
210 HAS, N37/11.
211 RCHME, 61–2; http://www.cradleychurch.org.uk/tour (accessed 17 Nov 2022).
212 HAS, AH85/1–2, vol. 1.
213 HAS, AH85/1; http://www.cradleychurch.org.uk/tour (accessed 17 Nov 2022).
214 NHLE, no. 1082298, Ch. of St James (accessed 1 Aug. 2023).
215 HAS, AH85/1–2, vol. 1.
216 HAS, BM 81/1/9.
217 NHLE, no. 1082298 Ch. of St James (accessed 1 Aug. 2023).

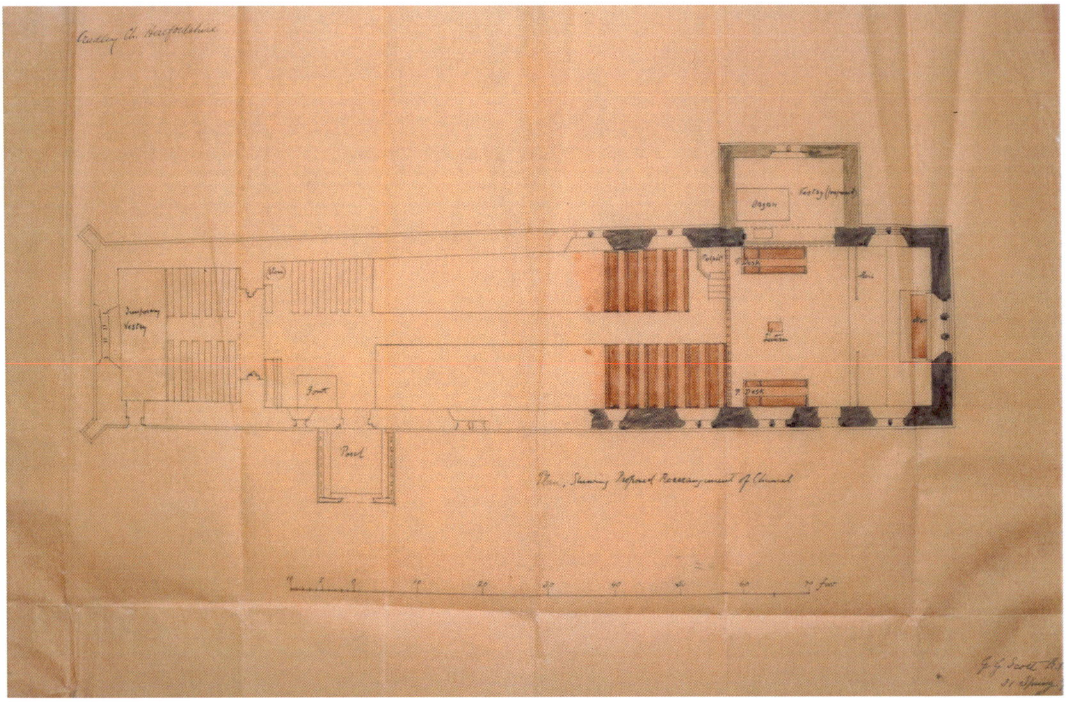

Figure 29 *George Gilbert Scott's plan for proposed work on the chancel of Cradley St James. (HAS, HD10/29a)*

were reset), and a new north aisle created.[218] The west gallery was removed, a tie-beam oak roof and oak chancel arch built, and stalls installed.[219] The work created seats for 350 people.[220] Hampden also donated a new font, of Cradley stone, modelled on the font in Bosbury church.[221] In 1893, the arcading in the nave was constructed.[222] Parishioners who died in the First World War were commemorated with a marble tablet in the south wall of the nave.[223]

In 1947, small-scale changes were made to the nave west end; some pews were removed, and Hampden's font was replaced with the 18th-century one given by the rector Thomas Bisse. In 1985, a Lady Chapel was created in the north aisle, in memory of Major John Lawrence Pilling and his wife Eveline. In order to facilitate community events, in the later 20th and 21st century minor alterations were made to the nave and north aisle.[224] Major repair and development work was carried out in 2019, funded largely by the National Heritage Lottery Fund, including a kitchen at the nave west end and a replacement north aisle floor.[225]

218 RCHME, 61.
219 HAS, AH85/1–2, vol. 1.
220 HAS, HD10/31/5.
221 HAS, AH85/1.
222 HAS, AH85/1–2, vol. 1.
223 HAS, AH73/40; HAS, BS37.
224 http://www.cradleychurch.org.uk/tour (accessed 17 Nov. 2022).
225 Inf. from local resident.

The upper stages of the tower, which were 'much dilapidated' in 1870, were repaired during Hampden's restoration.[226] During the reconstruction of the church, the Anglo-Saxon frieze was probably discovered and inserted, in an arbitrary fashion, into the tower north face.[227] The tower clock was erected to commemorate those parishioners who died in the First World War.[228] Two bells were added to the ring in 2000 to celebrate the millennium, taking the total to eight.[229] The tower was re-roofed in 2019, as part of that year's repair and development project.[230]

In 1893, a porch (in Arts and Crafts style, decorated by Alfred Hill Parker[231]) was erected in memory of Hampden.[232] This replaced a 'rather late' porch recorded in 1849 which was, like the surviving lychgate, of the 16th or 17th century.[233]

In 1907, the rector Thomas Ayscough commissioned the vestry.[234]

Village Hall

The timber-framed village hall, formerly the boys' school, straddles the churchyard boundary in its south-east corner, and is likely to have been built as a church house or ale house by a team of carpenters working for Charles Booth, bishop of Hereford 1516–35.[235] Its oak timbers were felled in 1530–1.[236] The two-storey building is of six bays, with a single-bay extension at the eastern end of the north side. It is possible that the original building was of only four bays, but later repairs and alterations, particularly at its east end, have obscured any firm evidence of its development.[237] The building is jettied along both sides and at the west end. It is strikingly similar to the church ale house in nearby Colwall, also an episcopal manor under Bishop Booth, whose timbers have also been tree-ring dated to 1530–1. The primary timbers of both buildings were trestle-sawn, as were the two frames in the church tower.[238]

226 HAS, AA51/1, cuttings from the *Builder*, 9 July 1870.
227 HAS, AH85/1, suggested by Canon Ayscough who noticed it in 1908.
228 HAS, AH73/40; HAS, BS37.
229 http://www.cradleychurch.org.uk/tour (accessed 17 Nov. 2022).
230 Inf. from local resident.
231 HAS, AH85/1; Brooks and Pevsner, *Worcs.*, 484; *Littlebury's Dir.: Worcester, Malvern, Droitwich, Pershore* (Worcester, 1905).
232 Above, 14th to 16th centuries; HAS, AH85/1–2, vol. 1.
233 RCHME, 61–2; *Herefordshire Churches through Victorian Eyes*, ed. John Leonard (Little Logaston, 2006), 53. Drawings of the previous porch were made in the following: Specification of Works 18 May 1869 – Nave; A Painting by Miss Hampden *c.*1870.
234 HAS, AH85/1; NHLE, no. 1082298 Ch. of St James (accessed 1 Aug. 2023).
235 D. James is the primary contributor to this paragraph. It may be significant that William Bothe was appointed to Cradley in Sept. 1526 and made rector in Mar. 1529: A.T. Bannister (ed.), *Registrum Caroli Bothe* (Hereford, 1921), 327, 339. See above, Religious Life.
236 *Centre for Archaeology report 10/2004 – Historic England*; HER, 937; *TWNFC* 63 (2015), 25.
237 HER, 937.
238 *Ancient Monuments Laboratory Report 106/91, Historic England.*

Storridge St John the Evangelist

Concerns during the 19th century about the long walk Storridge's population had to church led to Charles Scott Luxmoore's decision to commemorate his deceased only son by building a church in Storridge. He died before this could be done, but his sisters bought land on which to build Storridge church and vicarage as a memorial to both men.[239] In December 1856, the commissioners for building new churches agreed to assign a district to St John chapelry in Storridge,[240] and it was formed in 1857.[241] The living was a perpetual curacy, worth £120 annually with residence in 1867, and was in the gift of the rector of Cradley.[242]

Even in 1857, the seating capacity, 185, was considered large for the hamlet's population (212 in 1881),[243] and the 19th-century churchwardens 'had much difficulty in meeting the ordinary expenses of the Church', presumably because of its small and relatively poor congregation.[244] The Latin inscription on the pulpit, and the depiction in the east window of angels swinging censors, suggest high church leanings.[245] The 1895 'improvements' strengthen this hypothesis, since they insisted that congregants kneel in prayer on hassocks purchased to that end.[246]

The last vicar of Storridge (the Revd E.C. Moir) left in 1956. From 1956 to 1961, there were resident priests who served the church, but since 1961 Storridge has had no resident vicar. In 1982, the benefice was united with Cradley and Mathon, and since then has been served by a rector based in Cradley. The church stands beside the A4103 (the old Worcester to Hereford turnpike road).[247]

The church, built in 1856, is in Gothic revival style.[248] Both church and vicarage were designed by Frederick Preedy, and built by George McCann. All its windows are plain glass, except the east window, which was designed and produced by Preedy and features Christ crucified. The church has a bell tower, with recessed lancets and a broached spire, which is a significant landmark.[249] The brick, high-gabled vicarage, east of the church, was finished in 1856.[250]

Little has changed in terms of the church's architecture and furnishings since its foundation. The church was reseated and minor alterations were made in 1895.[251] The original small graveyard was extended in the 1930s. A war memorial, added to the church in 2017, commemorates those from Storridge who died in the two world wars.[252]

239 http://www.storridgechurch.org/uk/tour (accessed 25 June 2021).
240 HAS, BJ2/1.
241 HAS, AH85/1–2, vol. 1; http://www.storridgechurch.org.uk/tour (accessed 25 June 2021).
242 *Littlebury's Dir.* (1867).
243 HAS, AH73/71.
244 HAS, BL20/1.
245 http://www.storridgechurch.org.uk/tour (accessed 25 June 2021).
246 HAS, BO80/17.
247 http://www.storridgechurch.org.uk/tour (accessed 25 June 2021).
248 NHLE, no. 1082287, Ch. of St Jn the Evangelist (accessed 1 Aug. 2023).
249 *Berrow's Worcester Jnl* (*BWJ*) 13 Aug. 1856; NHLE, 1082287 (accessed 1 Aug. 2023).
250 http://www.storridgechurch.org.uk/tour; http://www.flicks.com/photos/tudorbarlowcollections (accessed 17 Nov. 2022).
251 HAS, BO80/17.
252 http://www.storridgechurch.org.uk/tour (accessed 17 Nov. 2022).

Figure 30 *Storridge, St John the Evangelist, 2020. (Photo by David Whitehead)*

Protestant Nonconformity[253]

In 1676, no Nonconformists were reported in Cradley, unlike in many neighbouring parishes.[254] This may be inaccurate, since the rector's figure of 300 attending the parish church is a suspiciously round number and probably estimated.[255] The rector, Edmund Skinner, although with family connections and property in the parish, was a pluralist who in 1674 employed a curate, and was probably non-resident, so whoever completed the return may have been unfamiliar with the details of Nonconformity in Cradley and the parish's population.[256]

Until 1815, no Nonconformists appear in Cradley's records. The 1716 Articles of Enquiry reported no Dissenters in the parish,[257] and no Nonconformist places of worship were certified in the bishops' registers between 1772 and 1815.[258] Between 1815 and 1840, however, ten were listed, all but two as houses. Two were affiliated to the Countess of Huntingdon's Connexion, another probably to the Plymouth Brethren and two (the house of James Birch or Jonathan Bird at Birchwood Common in 1834[259] and the house of James Hadley at Ridgeway Cross in 1835) to the United Brethren.

Countess of Huntingdon's Chapel[260]

The Countess of Huntingdon (Methodist) chapel community in Cradley began as a village station attached to the major chapel in Worcester, probably in 1815, in Elizabeth Bough's dwelling house, which was certified for public worship.[261] The Cradley chapel was built in 1823, at the south end of a narrow 1¼-a. parcel of land running back from what became Chapel Lane, which had at some period been enclosed from Westfield. To its front is a burial ground first used in 1828, which was extended before 1963,[262] and is still in use in 2023.[263]

The building, of two storeys, is of Cradley stone, with the chapel on the first floor, accessed by an external staircase, and a Sunday school room on the ground floor. The chapel seats 140.[264] The 1851 religious census recorded 59 adult attendees and 50 children in its Sunday schools.[265] In the late 1960s, the schoolroom was also used as the

253 Most of the research in this section was done by Dr J.E.C. Peters, and, in addition to archival research, is based on his viewings of the buildings and oral histories from Cradley residents.
254 Meaning here Protestants who never attended their parish church.
255 A. Whiteman (ed.), *The Compton Census of 1676: A critical edition* (Oxford, 1986), 260.
256 Above, Religious Life: 1560–2023.
257 HAS, HD5/14/107.
258 HAS, CA19/1.
259 HAS, HD8/11a.
260 J.E.C. Peters is the primary author of this section.
261 HAS, AS88/407; HAS, HD8/2/16.
262 As evidenced by the gravestones.
263 HAS, AS88/407.
264 HAS, AS88/407.
265 J.E.C. Peters, 'The Countess of Huntingdon chapel, Cradley, Herefordshire', *The Chapels Soc. Newsletter* 54 (2018), 10–14.

Figure 31 *Cradley chapel, 2023. (Photo by Charles Watkins)*

village library.[266] Ministers were almost always non-resident, although a small area of living accommodation in the chapel was occupied by caretakers.[267] A manse was built in 1927,[268] but only used for around a decade;[269] In 2023, it was being converted into a private dwelling.[270] After a period of closure, the chapel was reopened in 1980.[271] Services were still held in 2023, although most other Countess of Huntingdon's chapels in the vicinity had ceased; the minister was Sam Hart.[272]

Other Denominations[273]

The United Brethren, a local schism from Wesleyan Methodism, had been formed in 1832 by Thomas Kington, who registered a house in Birchwood in 1834. Another house, James Hadley's at Ridgeway Cross, registered the following year, seems to have been connected to the same group, and both appear still to have been functioning in early 1840.[274] Nearly all their members converted to Mormonism later that year.

Wilford Woodruff, a Mormon missionary from America, preached a number of times in Cradley in 1840, including at James Hadley's house, and some Cradley residents converted. Many of these converts emigrated to America.[275] There was a Mormon chapel

266 Peters, 'The Countess of Huntingdon Chapel', 10–14; inf. from Mrs Preston (local resident).
267 Censuses, 1841–1911.
268 Date on manse.
269 Peters, 'The Countess of Huntingdon Chapel', 10–14.
270 Inf. from resident.
271 CHC, Parish Council Minutes, II, 18 Mar. 1980.
272 Peters, 'The Countess of Huntingdon Chapel', 10–14; inf. from local resident.
273 J.E.C. Peters is the primary author of this section.
274 HAS, CA19/2-3; United Brethren Preacher's Plan, Apr. 1840, at Gadfield Elm Chapel.
275 Religious Census, 1851: TNA, HO 129/350/25; https://www.bosburyhistoryresource.org.uk/BosburyLDSEmigrants.html#start (accessed 9 Mar. 2025).

in Cradley in 1851, in Bridgeroay Road, the south end of the road from Ridgeway Cross to Bromyard. The chapel was held within a house on the road and seated 80.[276] In 1856, the rector noted that there were still a significant number of Mormons in the parish.[277]No later references have been found to them.

Plymouth Brethren meetings in Cradley began *c.*1839.[278] By 1840, they seem to have met in a room at Birchwood Common registered by William Yapp, a leading member of the Barton Street congregation, Hereford.[279] In the same year, Yapp also registered a house in Storridge, about which nothing further is known.[280] When the Brethren divided in 1848–9 at Plymouth, the Cradley meeting seems to have become Exclusive, and appeared as such on lists in the later 19th century.[281] The Cradley congregation at Birchwood Common probably continued until at least the 1940s.[282] Attached to the meeting house was Birchwood cemetery, which was used for burials by the Plymouth Brethren for *c.*46 years until 1912. The chapel (by then in ruins) and the ground around it were sold in 1959, and the remains demolished.[283]

Roman Catholicism

After John Parfey's deprivation in 1560, there is only scattered evidence of recusancy among a few of Cradley's elites, and none among ordinary people in the parish. John Scudamore, seneschal for Cradley manor between at least 1595 and 1596,[284] was from a family of recusants.[285] Robert Gower, lord of Cradley manor, had two thirds of his lands (including Cradley manor) sequestrated by Parliament during or after the English Civil Wars, because of his recusancy.[286] In 1676, no Papists were reported,[287] and the Revd Richard Chambers stated in his Recusants Return of 1767 that there 'is no Papist residing in the Parish of Cradley'.[288] There is no record of any Catholic community after Catholic emancipation in the early 19th century.[289]

276 HAS, AS88/407.
277 TNA, HO 129/350/25; HAS, AK 19/20; Hunt, *Cradley*, 18–20.
278 TNA, HO 129/350/27; HAS, AS88/407.
279 HAS, CA19/3.
280 HAS, CA19/3; H. Pickering (ed.), *Chief Men among the Brethren* (n.d.), 158; H.H. Rowden, *The Origins of the Brethren* (Glasgow, 1967), 164–5.
281 Lists of Meetings of the Exclusive Brethren, 1877, 1884/5, J.E.C. Peters' collection.
282 HAS, AS88/407.
283 HAS, AS88/407.
284 TNA, SC 2/176/54.
285 W. Skidmore, *The Skydmores/Scudamores of Holme Lacy, Herefordshire, and their Descendants, 1300–1915*, ed. by Linda Moffatt (published online, 2015), http://www.skidmorefamilyhistory.com/page27.html (accessed 17 Nov. 2022).
286 Mary Anne Everett Green (ed.), *Calendar of the Proceedings of the Cttee for Compounding* (1891), 1781, 1809.
287 Meaning recusant Catholics – i.e., those who never attended services at their Anglican parish church alongside secret Masses.
288 HAS, HD2/16/34.
289 Nathaniel Loftus Best is described as a 'Carthusian' in his 19th-century memorial in the parish church; this means that he attended Charterhouse School: HAS, BM81/1/19.

LOCAL GOVERNMENT

CRADLEY LAY WITHIN RADLOW HUNDRED. From 1836 to 1930, the parish was in Bromyard Poor Law Union and from 1894 to 1974 Bromyard Rural District. In 1897, small parts of Cradley were transferred to Worcestershire, Ledbury, Suckley and Martley poor law unions.[1] In 1898, part of the parish was transferred to Leigh and Martley Rural District.[2]

Manorial Government

Manor of Cradley

Besides rentals of *c*.1288 and 1533, a few court rolls before and after 1500 survive.[3] Apart from a rent roll of 1682,[4] and some copies of court rolls recording surrenders and admissions,[5] all 17th-century records of Cradley manor are lost, as are those of any other manors then existing in the parish. Surviving 19th-century records include an 1830 perambulation of Cradley manor bounds,[6] numerous documents relating to the mass enfranchisement of manorial land 1862–93,[7] and a detailed index and description of court rolls of the period.[8] But because the rolls themselves do not survive, the date of the last manor court is unknown.

Until the 12th century, and probably originating before 1066, a hereditary reeve, who in 1086 was a landholder, managed the bishop's demesne.[9] Before 1500, the manor was overseen by a reeve charged with rendering account of its various issues to the bishop's receiver. From at least 1496–7, he was sometimes drawn from among the bishop's

1 HAS, K42/19, pp. 462, 469. No details are given in the minutes of which parts these were.

2 HAS, BL20/1, pp. 54–5.

3 HAS, AA59/A/1, pp. 148–53; R13/10537; AM33/13–15; TNA, SC 6/HENVIII/1511; BL, Add. Roll 27311.

4 HAS, E21/1.

5 The most important sources are: a very faint 1721 rent roll (HAS, R13/10604); William Fifield's copy of his portions of the rentals 1721–91 (HAS, R13/10634); Hill House's copy of a 1724 presentment of manorial customs (HAS, R13/10606); copies of court roll relating to surrenders and admissions (HAS, W9/1, pp. 6–59; HAS, R/13, pp. 10546–626; HAS, BJ43/29/1–14; HAS, S82/42–53); T.A. Melville's Index to the Court Rolls, including notes on court business beyond simply surrender and admission from the 18th century onwards (HAS, BJ2/1).

6 HAS, K68/7–10.

7 TNA, MAF 9/112/1–46; TNA, MAF 20/52.

8 HAS, BJ2/1.

9 Above, Social Character for more on reeves; *Domesday*, 502.

Cradley tenants.[10] From the late 13th century, rent was rendered at the four customary quarter days: the feasts of St Andrew (30 November), the Annunciation (25 March), St John the Baptist (24 June) and St Michael (29 September).[11]

Cradley's medieval manor court's jurisdiction covered a range of legal proceedings, which included adjudicating in land disputes, frankpledge (presumably) and recording tenures. After 1241, when the bishop was granted free warren in Cradley and his other manors without the royal forest,[12] trespassers would have been tried in the bishop's court, in his capacity as lord of the warren.[13] In 1292, he asserted considerable rights in Cradley, including view of frankpledge, assizes of bread and ale, and the right to hear pleas of the Crown.[14] Cradley's manor court's perquisites were an important source of income, rising from 10*s.* in 1292 to 13*s.* 4*d.* in 1404,[15] 39*s.* 4*d.* by 1496–7 and 44*s.* 8*d.* in 1536.[16]

The chancellorship of Sir Thomas Audley (1533–44) saw a sudden spurt of pleas to the Court of Chancery from Cradley residents.[17] John Bromfeld alleged to the Court of Chancery that he had many times been denied a trial in the Cradley court on his claim to disputed lands because the customary tenants 'would *gesse* the said lands and other premises unto your said orator'. He accused his opponent, William Bullock, of making 'sinister labour to the steward of the said court' and had 'given unto them gifts and rewards' to prevent the case coming to trial.[18]

Insufficient source material survives from the 17th century onwards to assess what routine matters came before the manorial court. Surviving copies of court roll largely relate to surrender and admission to copyholds, but the court certainly dealt also with repairs to roads and footpaths, and appointed parish officials,[19] including, from at least 1679 onwards, constables. The earliest surviving reference to swearing a foreman of the jury, Richard Yapp, occurs in 1822.[20]

With no known manor house or principal messuage, the customary venue of Cradley's medieval courts is unknown. Only the customary tenants, *c.*1288, and one freeholder, Geoffrey of Cradley, attended Cradley, as the remaining freeholders owed suit of court at Bosbury.[21] In the late 16th century, courts leet (called view of frankpledge) were held bi-annually, conducted by the steward,[22] and may then have been combined

10 Christopher Wheeler in 1496–7, and Thomas Hill in 1506, both of parish families: HAS, AM33/13, rot. 21d.; BL, Add. Roll 27311, rot. 5d.; TNA, SC 6/HENVIII/1511. The same Thomas Hill may occur in the 1475 charter, HAS, R13/10535; and a Christopher Wheeler appears in a 1533 rental, HAS, R13/10537.

11 HAS, AA59/A/1, pp. 148–53.

12 *Cal. Chart.*, 1226–57, 261.

13 G.J. Turner (ed.), *Select Pleas of the Forest* (Selden Society) (1901), cxxvi.

14 *Plac. de Quo Warr.*, 270.

15 John Duncumb (ed.), *Collections towards the History and Antiquities of the County Hereford*, 1 (1804), 445; *Cal. Inq. Misc.* VII, 152.

16 HAS, AM33/13; TNA, SC 6/HENVIII/1511, rot. 16d.

17 The court was seen as faster and more impartial than manorial courts. For the context of the court's developing role at this period, see Harvey, *Manorial Records*, 56; For the other cases, see TNA, C 1/1031/53–55; TNA, C 1/866/83.

18 TNA, C 1/696/3.

19 HAS, BJ2/1.

20 HAS, BJ2/1.

21 HAS, AA59/A/1, p. 149. Presumably alongside the tenants of Storridge.

22 TNA, SC 2/176/54.

with courts baron, as they certainly were from the 17th century.[23] From the later 18th century, the court was usually held at Stifford's Bridge (probably the Red Lion).[24]

More than 634 a. of the manor's copyhold was enfranchised and sold between 1862 and 1891,[25] although it still retained customary estates in 1900. The copyholds were of inheritance, and fines arbitrary, but the lord was not entitled to heriots. Nor did he have a right to either timber or minerals (hence, perhaps, the proliferation of quarries in the parish), and tenants were free to demise their land.[26]

Other Manors

At least four other manorial courts had jurisdiction in the parish during the 14th to 16th centuries: Bosbury, The Barrow, The Hyde and the Hill family's sub-manor. No courts are known for Cowleigh or the rectory manors during this period. A 13th-century court was held for land in Hanley. From the 17th century, only two manorial courts are recorded sitting in the parish, for Cradley manor and the rectory.

As part of Bosbury lordship, tenants of Storridge attended the bishop of Hereford's manorial court covering Bosbury, Colwall and Coddington alongside the rest of its tenants.[27] By the late 16th century, the heriot for Storridge tenants was either an animal, such as a horse, or taken in money.[28]

Barrow, and later Overbarrow, possessed its own manorial court. Rolls survive from 1515, controlled by the prior and convent of Worcester, and 1542, under the dean and chapter. Both courts punished infringements of the lord's rights, such as illegal assarts or forest offences.[29]

As a discrete manor of St Katherine's hospital, Ledbury, The Hyde had its own court. Transcribed rolls from the early 14th century do not specify a venue, and suggest that sittings were held irregularly. With few landholders, the entries are brief and concerned primarily with tenure. In 1346, lands in The Hyde were subject by custom to a heriot of one cow and one horse,[30] and tenants owed no labour services, since the hospital held no land in demesne.[31] Court rolls and rentals of the 14th century do not specify who collected rent, but by the 16th century the manor was held at farm, first by Thomas Hyde for 8*s*., and then by Thomas Blou[.] in 1513–14.[32]

The sub-manor of the Hill family had a court in 1402–3, at which tenants paid a heriot.[33]

23 HAS, W9/1; HAS, R13/10546; HAS, R13/10553; HAS, R13/10555; HAS, R13/10556; HAS, R13/10558; HAS, R13/10564; HAS, R13/10576; HAS, R13/10588; HAS, R13/10592; HAS, R13/10595–6.

24 HAS, W9/21. See also HAS, W9/22–4; HAS, AH73/69; HAS, S82/31.

25 TNA, MAF 20/52/787; TNA, MAF 20/52/788; TNA, MAF 9/112.

26 *TWNFC* (1900–2), 5.

27 For more on the Bishop's manorial court, see *VCH Herefs. Bosbury*, 27–8; HAS, AA59/A/2, ff. 9v–25v.; HAS, AA59/A/1, pp. 157–8.

28 The sum appears variable, HAS, AA59/A/2, f. 11v.

29 WCM, E182 and E101.

30 While the contraction is for '*et*', this could be a copyist's error: HCA, 3295.

31 HCA, 7018/2, ff. 77–8; Hillaby, *St Katherine's*, 60.

32 The last letter of Thomas's surname is illegible. For 'at farm', see Glossary. HCA, 7018/2, f. 82.

33 The charter is not entirely clear, but it may have been held at Stifford; HAS, R13/10531.

Robert de Furches of The Seed held a court for lands in Hanley in the late 13th century, though it is unclear if it was for the manor or a sub-manor.[34] Tenants were liable for rent, heriot, wardship, relief, escheats, aids and tallages.[35]

The earliest reference to the rectory as a manor, with the privilege of holding courts baron, is the 1589 terrier.[36] A few copies of court roll from its courts survive from the 17th to 19th centuries. Courts baron for the rectory manor were held by Edmund Skinner in 1624 or 1667,[37] Thomas Bisse in 1718,[38] Henry Ford in 1811[39] and Charles Scott Luxmoore in 1823.[40] Luxmoore was described explicitly as rector of Cradley and lord of the manor.

Parish Government

Parish Officers

A constable of Cradley subject to instructions from the bishop is recorded in 1448–50.[41] Parish constables were appointed from at least 1679, and by 1718–19 there were two, responsible for 'Le Heath' and 'Childes';[42] from 1720 constables were simply appointed for the east and west of the parish.[43] In 1740–1, there was a rate of 2*d.* to fund two constables and 4*d.* to fund two overseers of the poor; in 1743, a rate of 2½*d.* was added to fund churchwardens.[44] In 1742, the parish reportedly was infested with robbers and disturbed by piracy, so the constables were permitted to search any house in the parish and charge proper assistance.[45] In 1897, the parish council decided that parish constables were no longer required.[46]

'Gallows Coppice' (unlocated) is recorded in the 18th century,[47] and in the 19th the parish had a pound at Stifford's Bridge, said to have been in use for 60 years, as well as stocks (unlocated).[48] In 1872, Cradley was in the petty sessional division of Bromyard, 13 miles away, although the parish was only 5 miles from the Worcester justices' building in Great Malvern. Memorials from the inhabitants of Cradley were presented to the Herefordshire justices alleging that offences in the parish frequently went unpunished, because of the distance from Bromyard police office, and requesting that Cradley offences might be dealt with at Great Malvern police office instead. It was

34 Above, Manors and Principal Estates: Hanley/Handley's End/Little Hanley.
35 TNA, C 146/9734.
36 HAS, HD2/1/30.
37 Regnal year dated 18 Charles (unspecified), i.e. 1624 or 1667; Skinner was rector in both years.
38 HAS, W9/1.
39 HAS, W9/6.
40 HAS, W9/1.
41 *Reg. Ricardi Beauchamp*, 10.
42 HAS, BJ2/1. 'Heath' was a farm and small estate in the east of the parish: Tithe Map (1839).
43 HAS, BJ2/1.
44 HAS, N37/32 5 May 1743.
45 HAS, N37/32 4 May 1742.
46 HAS, BL20/1, p. 39.
47 HCA, 6437/II/1.
48 HAS, N37/35 4 Dec. 1862.

agreed that the Herefordshire justices could use the petty session room and lock-up house at Great Malvern for hearing crimes committed in Cradley.[49]

The first recorded highways surveyor was the rector, Richard Chambers, in 1736–7.[50] The number appointed annually thereafter fluctuated between none and two (one for the east and one for the west).[51] In 1751, the parish owned tools for use on the highways,[52] and the following year the highway surveyors had liberty to dig stones for their use.[53] Cradley still had surveyors in 1778, though the toll roads may by then have assisted the surveyors in discharging their responsibilities.[54]

Cradley's churchwardens can be fairly well traced from 1597, since they usually signed off each page of the parish register.[55] Two churchwardens served at a time and were usually in post for a brief period, sometimes only a year.[56] Until 1896, when the parish council began appointing charity trustees,[57] churchwardens sometimes functioned as trustees for parish charities or helped to appoint such trustees.[58]

Poor Law Administration

The first recorded appointment of overseers of the poor was in 1724. For most of the 18th century, four were appointed annually, two serving the east of the parish and two the west.[59] After 1800, numbers fluctuated, but they continued to be distributed equally between east and west.[60] The overseers were sometimes entrusted with charitable bequests in early modern wills, though not so often as the churchwardens, and usually in conjunction with them.[61]

In 1737, Cradley arranged to send its paupers to Ledbury workhouse at an annual cost of £8.[62] But, in 1756, the overseers of the poor agreed to build a workhouse in Cradley for its paupers, of whom many were then in Bromyard workhouse. Its first location is unknown, but in 1777 Richard Racster agreed to rent Stifford's farm to the overseers, churchwardens and inhabitants of Cradley for 21 years, at £6 annually, for the poor of Cradley parish.[63] Some of Cradley's paupers, however, were sent to Hereford workhouse

49 HAS, AB86/2/X/1.
50 HAS, N37/32 27 Dec. 1742.
51 HAS, N37/32 various.
52 HAS, N37/32 6 Feb. 1751.
53 HAS, N37/32 7 May 1752.
54 HAS, N37/33 list at front.
55 The rector (Morgan Powell) *c.*1597 copied the parish register onto parchment, in obedience to the royal directive. Therefore, although the surviving register begins *c.*1560 (the first page is damaged), the signatures in all years before 1597 were those of Powell and the 1597 churchwardens, Rowland Hales and William Hall: HAS, AH73/1.
56 HAS, AH73/1.
57 HAS, BL20/1 1 Apr. 1896. It is unclear from the minutes to which charity this applied.
58 HAS, AH73/64.
59 HAS, N37/33 list at front.
60 HAS, N37/35 26 Mar. 1841.
61 E.g. see Appendices, Sample 2, 24.
62 *VCH Herefs. Ledbury: A market town*, 75–6.
63 HAS, N37/33 19 Feb. 1877. The source material suggests the workhouse was located elsewhere prior to 1777.

before *c.*1800,[64] and in 1771 it was decided that the overseers should contract with Hereford workhouse to maintain Cradley's poor.[65] In 1799, the parishioners agreed to pay all doctors' bills for the workhouse poor, and to pay for the removal of paupers, the cost of paupers' marriage licences and half the costs of illegitimate children.[66] By 1814, Cradley workhouse was situated at Taswolds on Barley hill, maintained by Richard Hill's charity.[67] At both the Barley hill workhouse and its Stifford's farm predecessor, the poor were put to work, and a master or mistress was appointed who managed the workhouse under the supervision of the overseers.[68] In 1836, following the 1834 Poor Law Amendment Act, Cradley workhouse was discontinued, and pauper parishioners were admitted instead to the new union workhouse at Bromyard Down.[69]

By 1779, the parish also owned land and houses for the poor; at least one of the houses was at the end of Malvern hill.[70] By 1844, there were houses for the poor at both Crumpsend hill and North hill.[71]

In 1836, Bromyard Poor Law Union appointed two elected representatives from Cradley and a resident relieving officer.[72] Two guardians were selected for Cradley,[73] which was the largest parish in the union by 1877, with about 130 paupers.[74] In 1890, for the first time, some children were boarded out from the Bromyard union to Cradley.[75]

In 1837, William Addison was appointed by the union as surgeon for Cradley; this was unusual, as all other parishes were in divisions.[76] Cradley still had its own surgeon in 1845.[77] In 1838, a medical officer was appointed solely for Cradley,[78] but from 1839 his responsibility included Acton Beauchamp and Evesbatch.[79] It was agreed in 1869 that Cradley should be separated from the union for medical relief,[80] and in 1872 a medical officer was appointed for Cradley alone; this arrangement continued until 1930 or later.[81]

64 HAS, N37/33 various.
65 HAS, N37/33 17 Mar. 1771.
66 HAS, N37/35 22 Jan. 1799.
67 HAS, AH73/65. Above, Social Welfare.
68 Hunt, *Cradley*, 24–6.
69 HAS, K42/1, 11; Hunt, *Cradley*, 26.
70 HAS, N37/33 17 Oct. 1779.
71 HAS, N37/35 1 Dec. 1843; 23 Feb. 1844.
72 HAS, K42/1 31 May 1836; 20 June 1836.
73 HAS, K42/12, p. 400.
74 HAS, K42/13, p. 175.
75 HAS, AH73/36.
76 HAS, K42/1, p. 208.
77 HAS, K42/3, p. 301.
78 HAS, K42/1, p. 320.
79 HAS, K42/2, p. 164.
80 HAS, K42/10, p. 353.
81 HAS, K42/11, p. 217; HAS, K42/28 13 Mar. 1930.

Post–1894 Arrangements

District Council

On the establishment of rural district councils (RDCs) in 1894, Cradley became part of Bromyard rural district, with three councillors representing it, but in 1898 part of Cradley was transferred to Leigh and Martley Union.[82] In 1889, the rector was elected to Herefordshire County Council, representing Cradley, Bishops Frome and Evesbatch,[83] and in 1894 three Bromyard RDC councillors were elected to represent Cradley.[84] During the first half of the 20th century, they were often drawn from the social elite of the parish.[85] In 1965, it was agreed to raise the number to four councillors on the district council, more than any other parish.[86] In 1974, when Herefordshire and Worcestershire amalgamated, Cradley became a constituent of Malvern Hills District Council, but this arrangement ceased in 1998 when Herefordshire was reconstituted as an independent county. In 2023, Cradley lay in the Bishops Frome and Cradley ward of Herefordshire Council.[87]

In the 1920s, Cradley, previously a Liberal stronghold, developed a thriving Women's Unionist Association.[88] In 1949, it was divided into two polling districts, with polling stations at Storridge parish hall and Cradley School.[89]

In the early 20th century, Cradley still had a parish pound at Stifford's Bridge, but by 1914 it seems to have become disused.[90] By 1902, there was a police station with a sergeant,[91] and by 1913 the Cradley sergeant had a constable to assist him during the hop-picking season.[92] In 1952 a new police station for Cradley was built on the B4220 close to Chapel Lane.[93] It was altered in 1973–4, but had shut by 2000.[94] Part of a field adjoining the east side of the road from Stony Cross to Bosbury was purchased for a police house in 1954; the house was built in 1960,[95] and sold in 1990 for £90,000.[96]

82 HAS, BL20/1, pp. 54–5.
83 HAS, AH73/36, Jan. 1889.
84 HAS, K42/18, p. 350.
85 HAS, BW15/1/4.
86 HAS, BW15/1/10, p. 1213.
87 The Hereford and Worcester (Structural, Boundary and Electoral Changes) Order 1996; https://www.herefordshire.gov.uk/directory-record/3166/cradley-and-storridge-parish-council (accessed 17 Nov. 2022).
88 Edwards, *Cradley*, 40.
89 HAS, BW15/1/8, p. 267.
90 HAS, BL20/1, p. 194.
91 *Jakeman & Carver's Dir.* (1902 edn).
92 Edwards, *Cradley*, 15
93 HAS, BW15/2/5, p. 408.
94 HAS, BW15/3/3 4 July 1973; CHC, Parish Council Minutes, II, 22 May 1973.
95 HAS, CJ10/42.
96 HAS, CJ10/41.

Parish Council

In December 1894, a meeting in the boys' school elected 15 councillors to the first parish council. Early meetings were repeatedly concerned with the state of roads and bridges, and with the parish charities. In 1895, the parish council appointed two overseers, but later that year their duties were taken on by a paid assistant.[97] In 1897, two additional councillors were appointed as parochial charity trustees, and in 1903 one councillor was elected as a manager for each school in the parish.[98]

From 1910, parish council meetings were held at the boys' school.[99] The council was responsible for parish housing for the poor, and noted in 1914 that 25 empty cottages needed repairs, and six additional cottages were required.[100] In the early 20th century, the council owned land at Pontick Pitch.[101] In 1926, the parish council wrote to the trustees of Turner's old school proposing a joint application to the Charity Commission to alter trust terms, enabling the parish council to raise money to improve the building for the parishioners' benefit.[102]

Although still concerned with roads, bridges and charities, meetings from 1950 were much more involved with planning permission and, in the 1950s and 1960s, with creating and administering the two village halls.[103] From 1955, meetings were held either at Cradley (village hall or school) or Storridge (village hall), and from 1967 they generally alternated between Cradley and Storridge.[104] In 1965, despite objection, Cradley's 15 councillors were reduced to nine, the second-largest number in the district after Bromyard.[105] In 1986, the council had planning, footpath, churchyard and playing fields committees, and also appointed representatives to the village hall management committees.[106]

97 HAS, BL20/1, p. 11. The assistant's salary, £40, was reduced by £6 in 1897, when part of the parish transferred to West Malvern: HAS, BL20/1, p. 42.
98 HAS, BL20/1, p. 48.
99 HAS, BL20/1, p. 171.
100 HAS, BL20/1, p. 195.
101 HAS, BL20/1, p. 127.
102 HAS, AH73/67.
103 CHC, Parish Council Minutes, various dates.
104 CHC, Parish Council Minutes, various dates.
105 HAS, BW15/1/10, pp. 1251, 1298.
106 CHC, Parish Council Minutes, II, April 1986.

APPENDICES

Sources Used in Data Sampling (Wills; Sales Particulars)

Sample 1: 100 Early Modern Wills (1550–1700)

Around 250 wills from Cradley parish survive for the period 1500 to 1700, although the vast majority date to post 1550, and there is a preponderance of late 17th-century material.

For the purpose of statistical analysis, 100 wills were selected from the period 1550–1700. The selection was deliberately balanced so as to have (as far as possible) a similar number of wills for each 50-year period within the overall time period 1550–1700, in order to create a viable and representative sample. This sample is the basis of detailed statistical analysis in Economic History (above).

Full details of these 100 wills are as follows:

1. HAS, 1/01/10, will of William Hill alias Perkins, 1559[1]
2. HAS, 31/4/20, will of Dauyd Nicolls, 1559
3. HAS, 39/1/19, will of John Strode, 1560
4. HAS, 40/1/43, will of Walter Taylor, 1561
5. HAS, 31/4/36, will of Isobell Nokes, 1562/3
6. HAS, 33/3/21, will of Richard Pemerton, 1562
7. HAS, 39/2/14, will of Anne Strode, 1563
8. HAS, 34/4/16, will of Richard Powell, 1563
9. HAS, 33/3/27, will of Hughe Peede, 1570
10. HAS, 7/3/27, will of James Benet, 1570
11. HAS, 24/4/33, will of John James, 1570/1
12. HAS, 31/4/44, will of William Nokes, 1570/1
13. HAS, 34/4/26, will of _ Shyryffe, 1572
14. HAS, 21/2/39, will of James Hall, 1574
15. HAS, 28/1/30, will of Rowland Long, 1574
16. HAS, 31/4/62, will of Margaret Nokes, 1575

1 The date given (as elsewhere in this volume) is the date of probate when known, or the date of the writing of the will when the date of probate is not known.

17. HAS, 31/4/70, will of John Nokes, 1579
18. HAS, 38/3/32, will of William Smythe, 1579
19. HAS, 39/2/55, will of William Stoakes, 1582/3
20. HAS, 12/4/8, will of Thomas Collings, 1587
21. HAS, 3/2/16, will of Unknown Yeoman, 1587
22. HAS, 37/5/34, will of William Sheparde, 1587
23. HAS, 22/1/33, will of Nathaniel Hill, 1591
24. HAS, 4/2/19, will of William Bullock, 1591
25. HAS, 6/3/42, will of Thomas Barrett, 1592
26. HAS, 2/3/32, will of Walter Rayneford, 1592
27. HAS, 35/3/29, will of Richard Reynolds, 1596
28. HAS, 33/3/64, will of John Peede, 1597
29. HAS, 39/1/60, will of Thomas Strowd, 1597
30. HAS, 6/4/20, will of William Barber alias Millard, 1597
31. HAS, 39/1/63, will of Richard Stokes, 1597
32. HAS, 35/5/40, will of Margaret Reynolds, 1598
33. HAS, 5/4/51, will of William Smith, 1600
34. HAS, 1/2/17, will of Elizabeth Rainford, 1600
35. HAS, 4/2/12, will of Elinora Stokes, 1601
36. HAS, 7/5/25, will of Anna Stroud, 1604
37. HAS, 64A/1/9, will of John Sklyser, 1604
38. HAS, 8/1/22, will of Richard Longe, 1605
39. HAS, 8/2/3, will of Elizabeth Turner, 1605
40. HAS, 8/2/9, will of Richard Woodiat, 1605
41. HAS, 8/3/17, will of Christopher Long the Elder, 1606
42. HAS, 9/2/36, will of Robert Cager, 1607
43. HAS, 9/3/67, will of William Sheere, 1607
44. HAS, 10/1/45, will of Richard Nokes, 1608
45. HAS, 10/2/39, will of Woodiatt, ?1608
46. HAS, 12/2/18, will of Elizabeth ?Turnerdyn, 1610
47. HAS, 15/3/31, will of Alice Collins, 1611/12
48. HAS, 16/3/14, will of Nicholas Young, 1611
49. HAS, 17/2/17, will of Leonard Hill, 1612/13
50. HAS, 18/1/11, will of Anne Bullock, 1613
51. HAS, 20/4/40, will of Richard Poughnell, 1615
52. TNA, PROB 11/125/78, will of George Pychard, 1615
53. HAS, 23/2/21, will of Alice Barrett, 1616
54. HAS, 24/3/4, will of Richard Mintrich, 1617

55. HAS, 29/2/53, will of Thomas Collins, 1620
56. HAS, 30/2/35, will of Blanche Bullock, 1621
57. HAS, 32/1/37, will of Margaret Smith, 1622
58. HAS, 32/2/6, will of Peter Nokes, 1622
59. HAS, 33/1/66, will of John Nokes, 1623
60. TNA, PROB 11/142/177, will of William Unett, 1623
61. HAS, 35/1/24, will of Edmund Lock, 1624
62. HAS, 45/1/16, will of Joyce Stokes, ?1634
63. HAS, 45/4/25, will of Christopher Long, 1634
64. HAS, 51/2/21, will of Richard Stokes, 1639
65. HAS, 52/1/7, will of Rowland Sheere, 1639
66. TNA, PROB, 11/200 /659, will of Stephen Skynner, 1647
67. TNA, PROB, 11/253/575, will of Edward Spencer, 1655/6
68. TNA, PROB, 11/269/113, will of George Wooddiatt, 1657
69. HAS, 20/4/87, will of Rowland Barrett, 1660
70. HAS, 6/2/22, will of John Barrett, 1664
71. HAS, 14/3/8, Richard Hales
    a. Will, 1667
    b. Inventory, 1667
72. HAS, 20/2/45, inventory – John Dipper, 1668
73. HAS, 24/4/17, Elizabeth Turner
    a. Will, 1670
    b. Inventory, 1669
74. HAS, 28/1/25, Anne Fifield
    a. Will, 1670/1
    b. Inventory, 1670/1
75. HAS, 29/1/11, inventory – John Crisp, 1671
76. HAS, 28/2/29, Thomas Stoakes
    a. Will, 1671
    b. Inventory, 1671
77. HAS, 29/1/47, inventory – Dorothea Pichard, 1671
78. HAS, 35/4/1, indenture between Elizabeth Webster and Elinor Hide, 1672
79. HAS, 36/2/10, will of William Comby, 1673
80. HAS, 39/1/18, John Hill
    a. Will, 1673/4
    b. Inventory, 1673
81. HAS, 40/2/15, inventory – John Collins, 1674
82. HAS, 40/2/35, inventory – Thomas Collins, 1674

83. HAS, 46/1/16, inventory – Sarah Pengriffe, 1675
84. HAS, 58/2/18, Anne Comby
    a. Will, 1678
    b. Inventory, 1678
85. HAS, 58/2/19, Rowland Hales
    a. Will, 1678
    b. Inventory, 1677
86. HAS, 65/2/42, Richard Griffiths
    a. Will, 1680
    b. Inventory, 1680
87. HAS, 71/1/7, Eleanor Stowers
    a. Will, 1681
    b. Inventory, 1681
88. HAS, 69/1/36, William Hall
    a. Will, 1681
    b. Inventory, 1681
89. HAS, 84/2/5, John Wooddiatt
    a. Will, 1684
    b. Inventory, 1683
90. HAS, 79/2/1, Richard Clarke
    a. Will, 1683
    b. Inventory, 1683
91. HAS, 78/2/53, will of Anne Barrett alias Fawkes, 1683
92. HAS, 80/1/25 and 79/1/7, inventory – John Racster, 1683
93. HAS, 87/2/1, Richard Bullock
    a. Will, 1684
    b. Inventory, 1684
94. HAS, 88/3/41, Richard Child
    a. Will, 1684/5
    b. Inventory, 1684
95. HAS, 101/1/25, William Hall
    a. Will, 1687/8
    b. Inventory, 1687
96. HAS, 101/1/26, inventory – John Fawkes, 1687
97. HAS, 102/2/2, Richard Woodiatt
    a. Will, 1688
    b. Inventory, 1688
98. HAS, 104/3/10, Elizabeth Bullock

a. Will, 1689
b. Inventory, 1689

99. HAS, 108/2/3, Thomas Stoakes
    a. Will, 1690
    b. Inventory, 1690
100. HAS, 110/4/4, Amy Faulke
    a. Will, 1691
    b. Inventory, 1690

Sample 2: Wills Indicating Testator's Social Status or Occupation, 1550–1700

Of the surviving wills from Cradley parish between 1559 and 1699, 117 indicate the testator's social status or occupation. These were analysed as a data set for the purpose of statistical analysis in Economic History and Social History (above).

Full details of these 117 wills are as follows:

1. HAS, 8/3/22, will of Richard Bothe, 1558 (rector of Cradley)
2. HAS, 31/4/20, will of David Nicolls, 1559 (yeoman)
3. HAS, 33/3/21, will of Richard Pemerton, 1562 (husbandman)
4. HAS, 33/3/27, will of Hugh Peede, 1570 (fuller)
5. HAS, 24/4/33, will of John James, 1570/1 (husbandman, ?blacksmith)
6. HAS, 7/3/27, will of James Benet, 1570 (yeoman)
7. HAS, 31/4/44, will of William Nokes, 1570/1 (husbandman)
8. HAS, 34/4/26, will of _ Shyryffe, 1572 (tinker)
9. HAS, 21/2/39, will of James Hall, 1574 (husbandman)
10. HAS, 31/4/70, will of John Nokes, 1579 (husbandman)
11. HAS, 38/3/32, will of William Smythe, 1579 (yeoman)
12. HAS, 39/2/55, will of William Stoakes, 1582/3 (yeoman)
13. HAS, 45/4/52, will of Thomas Woodiatt (miscatalogued as Thomas Woodall), 1584 (husbandman)
14. HAS, 12/4/8, will of Thomas Collings, 1587 (yeoman)
15. HAS, 3/2/16, will of Unknown Yeoman, 1587
16. HAS, 37/5/34, will of William Sheparde, 1587 (husbandman)
17. HAS, 22/1/33, will of Nathaniel Hill, 1591 (weaver)
18. HAS, 4/2/19, will of William Bullock, 1591 (husbandman)
19. HAS, 35/3/29, will of Richard Reynolds, 1596 (collier)
20. HAS, 6/4/20, will of William Barber alias Millard, 1597
21. HAS, 33/3/64, will of John Peede, 1597 (tinker)
22. HAS, 39/1/60, will of Thomas Strowd, 1597 (husbandman)

23. HAS, 5/4/51, will of William Smith, 1600 (yeoman)
24. HAS, 64A/1/9, will of John Sklyser, 1604 (yeoman)
25. HAS, 8/1/22, will of Richard Longe, 1605 (yeoman)
26. HAS, 8/2/9, will of Richard Woodiat, 1605 (yeoman)
27. HAS, 8/3/17, will of Christopher Long the Elder, 1606 (yeoman)
28. HAS, 9/2/36, will of Robert Cager, 1607 (yeoman)
29. HAS, 9/3/67, will of William Sheere, 1607 (husbandman)
30. HAS, 10/1/45, will of Richard Nokes, 1608 (yeoman)
31. HAS, 11/2/7, will of William Dipper, 1609 (husbandman)
32. TNA, PROB 11/115/421, will of Edward Frogmer, 1610 (yeoman)
33. TNA, PROB 11/118/222, will of William Harris, 1611 (yeoman)
34. HAS, 16/3/14, will of Nicholas Young, 1611 (shoe maker)
35. TNA, PROB 11/117/183, will of William Thomas, 1611 (labourer)
36. TNA, PROB 11/120/510, will of Rowland Halles, 1612 (yeoman)
37. HAS, 17/2/17, will of Leonard Hill, 1612/13 (tailor)
38. TNA, PROB 11/121/160, will of William Fawke, 1613 (yeoman)
39. HAS, 18/4/27, will of John Hales, 1614 (yeoman)
40. HAS, 19/1/31, will of Thomas Hill, 1614 (tailor)
41. TNA, PROB 11/126/320, will of Richard Harris, 1615 (yeoman)
42. TNA, PROB 11/125/78, will of George Pychard, 1615 (gentleman)
43. HAS, 20/4/40, will of Richard Poughnell, 1615 (husbandman)
44. HAS, 20/4/87, will of Rowland Barret, 1615 (yeoman)
45. HAS, 22/2/1, will of Thomas Drayton, 1615 (turner).
46. HAS, 21/2/12, will of Richard Jones, 1616 (victualler)
47. TNA, PROB 11/129/102, will of Richard Nokes, 1617 (yeoman)
48. HAS, 24/3/4, will of Richard Mintrich, 1617 (gentleman)
49. HAS, 29/2/53, will of Thomas Collins, 1620 (husbandman)
50. HAS, 31/4/9, will of Roger Need, 1622 (gentleman)
51. HAS, 32/2/6, will of Peter Nokes, 1622 (carpenter)
52. HAS, 33/1/66, will of John Nokes, 1623 (husbandman)
53. TNA, PROB 11/142/177, will of William Unett, 1623 (gentleman)
54. TNA, PROB 11/141/510, will of John Clarke alias Shewster, 1623 (yeoman)
55. HAS, 10/1/45, will of Richard Nokes, 1624 (yeoman)
56. HAS, 34/3/50, will of Thomas Hariots (tailor)
57. TNA, PROB 11/143/177, will of John Strowd, 1624 (yeoman)
58. TNA, PROB 11/156/413, will of Richard Strowd or Strowde, 1629 (yeoman)
59. TNA, PROB 11/158/586, will of Thomas Strowde, 1630 (yeoman)
60. HAS, 41/2/29, Francis Coomby, 1631 (yeoman)

61. HAS, 44/01/18, James Hall, 1633 (yeoman)
62. TNA, PROB 11/168/93, will of John James, 1635 (yeoman)
63. HAS, 49/01/66, William Hall, 1637 (yeoman)
64. HAS, 49/01/67, John Stowers, 1637 (yeoman)
65. HAS, 50/2/37, William Bullock, 1638 (yeoman)
66. HAS, 52/1/7, will of Rowland Sheere, 1639 (yeoman)
67. HAS, 57/1/35, will of Thomas Barrett, 1646 (husbandman)
68. TNA, PROB 11/200/659, will of Stephen Skinner, 1647 (gentleman)
69. TNA, PROB 11/224/311, will of Thomas Arundell, 1652 (yeoman)
70. TNA, PROB 11/229/173, will of Edmund Dunn, 1653 (yeoman)
71. TNA, PROB 11/253/575, will of Edward Spencer, 1655/6 (mason)
72. TNA, PROB 11/269/113, will of George Wooddiatt, 1657 (tanner)
73. TNA, PROB 11/279/417, will of John Abel alias Bullock, 1658 (yeoman)
74. HAS, 20/4/87, will of Rowland Barrett, 1660 (yeoman)
75. TNA, PROB 11/309/585, will of James Turner, 1662 (yeoman)
76. TNA, PROB 11/311/415, will of Richard Fawlke, 1663 (yeoman)
77. TNA, PROB 11/313/45, will of Leonard Turner ,1664 (yeoman)
78. TNA, PROB 11/313/380, will of William Herbert, 1664 (yeoman)
79. HAS, 20/2/45, inventory of John Dipper, 1668 (butcher)
80. HAS, 28/2/29, will and inventory of Thomas Stoakes, 1670 (yeoman)
81. TNA, PROB 11/333/493, will of William Fyfield or Fyfeild, 1670 (yeoman)
82. HAS, 29/1/11, inventory of John Crisp, 1671 (husbandman)
83. HAS, 36/2/10, will of William Comby, 1673 (yeoman)
84. HAS, 39/1/18, John Hill, 1673/4 (husbandman)
85. HAS, 40/2/17, will of John Racster, 1674 (Doctor of Law)
86. HAS, 40/2/15, inventory of John Collins, 1674 (yeoman)
87. HAS, 40/2/35, inventory of Thomas Collins, 1674 (yeoman)
88. HAS, 58/2/19, will and inventory of Rowland Hales, 1678 (yeoman)
89. HAS, 58/2/6, will of Edmund Skinner, 1678 (Rector of Cradley)
90. HAS, 58/2/18, will and inventory of George Cotton, 1678 (joiner)
91. HAS, 64/1/16, inventory of Edward Bosworth, 1679 (Rector of Cradley).
92. HAS, 68/2/40, will and inventory of Roger White, 1680 (yeoman)
93. HAS, 65/2/42, will and inventory of Richard Griffiths, 1680 (mason)
94. HAS, 69/1/18, will and inventory of Humphrey Suthall, 1681 (yeoman)
95. HAS, 74/1/15, will and inventory of John Longe, 1681 (yeoman)
96. HAS, 81/1/5, inventory of Thomas Shakle, 1683 (husbandman)
97. HAS, 80/1/25 and 79/1/7, inventory of John Racster, 1683 (gentleman)
98. HAS, 79/2/1, will and inventory of Richard Clarke, 1683 (yeoman)

99. HAS, 87/2/1, will and inventory of Richard Bullock, 1684 (yeoman)
100. HAS, 84/2/5, will and inventory of John Woodiatt, 1684 (yeoman)
101. HAS, 87/1/34, inventory of Percival Taylor, 1684 (husbandman)
102. HAS, 87/2/1, will and inventory of Richard Bullock, 1684 (yeoman)
103. HAS, 87/2/17, inventory of William Harvey, 1684 (yeoman)
104. HAS, 88/3/41, will and inventory of Richard Child, 1684/5 (yeoman)
105. HAS, 89/1/7, inventory of Rowland Barrett, 1685 (?carpenter)
106. HAS, 96/2/7, inventory of John Hay, 1686 (yeoman)
107. HAS, 101/1/25, will and inventory of William Hall, 1687/8 (yeoman/gentleman)
108. HAS, 102/2/2, will and inventory of Richard Woodiatt, 1688 (yeoman)
109. HAS, 108/2/3, will and inventory of Thomas Stokes, 1690 (glover)
110. HAS, 116/1/16, will and inventory of Francis Pengrief, 1693 (yeoman)
111. HAS, 118/3/33, will and inventory of Richard Turner, 1694 (yeoman)
112. HAS, 112/6/9, will and inventory of Richard Kent, 1695 (yeoman)
113. HAS, 122/1/23, inventory of Thomas James, 1695 (blacksmith)
114. HAS, 128/5/4, inventory of John Davies, 1698 (husbandman)
115. HAS, 130/3/11, will and inventory of Thomas Wood, 1699 (tanner)
116. HAS, 130/2/12, will and inventory of William Harrell, 1699 (yeoman)
117. HAS, 131/2/1, inventory of Henry Jones, 1699 (wheelwright)

Sample 3: 19th- and 20th-Century Sales Particulars

Numerous sales particulars survive from Cradley parish for the modern era (*c.*1800 to 2023), with a preponderance of sales particulars from the first half of the 20th century. For the purpose of statistical analysis, 50 were selected to form a sample, used as the basis of detailed statistical analysis in Economic History (above).

Full details of these 50 are to be found below:

	Date	Property	Reference
1	1842	Cradley Hall	HAS, K68/8
2	1842	The Hill Estate	HAS, K68/8
3	1842	Handley's End	HAS, K68/8
4	1861	The Hill Estate	HAS, K68/8
5	1909	The Hill Farm	HAS, M5/68/10
6	1909	Seed Farm	HAS, M5/68/10
7	1909	Tan House Farm	HAS, M5/68/10
8	1911	Lot 16 (unnamed)	HAS, M5/6A/9
9	1919	Cowleigh Park Farm	HAS, AH72/2
10	1919	Croft and Birches Farm	HAS, AH72/2
11	1919	Hill Farm	HAS, AH72/2
12	1919	Cowleigh Gate Farm	HAS, AH72/2
13	1919	Beanhouse Mill	HAS, M5/6A/5
14	1919	Yew Tree & Wold Mill Farm	HAS, M5/6A/5
15	1919	Byefields Storridge	HAS, M5/6A/5
16	1919	Barrow Mills	HAS, M5/6A/5
17	1919	Harp Farm	HAS, M5/6A/5
18	1919	Birch Farm	HAS, M5/6A/11
19	1919	Hill Farm	HAS, M5/6A/10
20	1919	Cradley Hall	HAS, M5/6A/10
21	1919	Seed Farm	HAS, M5/6A/10
22	1919	Tan House Farm	HAS, M5/6A/10
23	1920	Lower Vinesend	HAS, M5/6A/2
24	1920	Upper Vinesend	HAS, M5/6A/2
25	1920	Red House	HAS, M5/6A/2
26	1920	Mines & Yokes Farm	HAS, M5/6A/2
27	1920	Hope End Farm	HAS, M5/6A/7
28	1920	White House Farm	HAS, M5/6A/7
29	1920	Pullins Pit	HAS, M5/6A/12
30	1929	Hill House Estate	HAS, M5/6A/3

	Date	Property	Reference
31	1929	Upper Vinesend	HAS, M5/6A/3
32	1931	Beanhouse	HAS, M5/6A/4
33	1931	The Home End	HAS, M5/6A/4
34	1931	The Upper House	HAS, M5/6A/4
35	1931	Coombe Farm	HAS, M5/6A/4
36	1933	Pullins Pit	HAS, M5/6A/8
37	1933	The Sturts	HAS, M5/6A/8
38	1937	Pullins Pit	HAS, M5/6A/6
39	1991	Cradley Hall	HAS, CO7/3
40	1991	Woodend Farm	HAS, CO7/3
41	1991	Seed Farm	HAS, CO7/3
42	1991	Hill Farm Ridgeway Cross	HAS, CO7/3
43	1991	Hollingshill Farm	HAS, CO7/3
44	1991	Home House Farm	HAS, CO7/3
45	1991	Tan House Farm	HAS, CO7/3
46	1991	Sunnyside	HAS, CO7/3
47	1990s	Old Vinesend Farm	WAAS, 705:1087 BA12989 (xxxiv)
48	2005	Hope End Farm	Sales Particulars, Cradley Heritage Centre
49	2012	Seed Farm	Sales Particulars, Cradley Heritage Centre
50	2018	Hill House Estate	Sales Particulars, Cradley Heritage Centre

ABBREVIATIONS

Abbreviation	Full Title
Alumni Oxon.	*Alumni Oxonienses 1500–1714*, ed. J. Forster, 4 vols (Oxford, 1891–2).
BL	British Library
Brooks and Pevsner, *Herefs.*	A. Brooks and N. Pevsner, *Herefordshire: The Buildings of England* (2012).
Cal. Chart.	*Calendar of Charter Rolls preserved in the Public Record Office* (HMSO, 1903–27).
Cal. Close	*Calendar of Close Rolls preserved in the Public Record Office* (HMSO, 1892–1963).
Cal. Inq. Misc.	*Calendar of Inquisitions Miscellaneous (Chancery) preserved in the Public Record Office* (HMSO, 1911–62).
Cal. Inq. p.m.	*Calendar of Inquisitions Post Mortem preserved in the Public Record Office* (HMSO, 1904–2010).
Cal. Papal Pets.	*Calendar of Papal Registers: Petitions to the Pope* (HMSO and Irish MSS. Com., 1891–1960).
Cal. Papal Regs.	*Calendar of Papal Registers: Papal Letters* (HMSO and Irish MSS. Com., 1891–2005).
Cal. Pat.	*Calendar of Patent Rolls preserved in the Public Record Office* (HMSO, 1890–1986).
CCED	*The Clergy of the Church of England Database*, http://theclergydatabase.org.uk.
CHC	Cradley Heritage Centre, Cradley Village Hall
Close	*Close Rolls Henry III, 1227–72* (HMSO, 1902–).
Cur. Reg.	*Curia Regis Rolls preserved in the Public Record Office* (HMSO, 1922–79).
Domesday	A. Williams and G.H. Martin (eds), *Domesday Book: A Complete Translation* (2002).
Edwards, *Cradley*	E. Edwards and M. Edwards, *A Parishioner's Account of Cradley in 1913* (Cradley, 1994).
EHR	*English Historical Review*

Expenses of Swinfield	*A Roll of Household Expenses of Richard Swinfield Bishop of Hereford during Part of the Year 1289–90*, ed. Rev. J. Webb (Camden Soc., 1854).
Fasti Eccles. Ang.	*Fasti Ecclesiae Anglicanae*
Feud. Aids	*Inquisitions and Assessments Relating to Feudal Aids Preserved in the Public Record Office* (HMSO, 1899–1920).
HARC	Herefordshire Archive and Record Centre
HAS	Herefordshire Archives Service (formerly Herefordshire Record Office)
HCA	Hereford Cathedral Archives, Cathedral Library, Hereford
HER	*Historic Environment Record* (formerly SMR or Sites and Monuments Record) at Herefordshire Through Time, http://herefordshire.gov.uk.
Herefs. Taxes	*Herefordshire Taxes in the Reign of Henry VIII*, ed. M.A. Faraday (Hereford, 2005).
Hillaby, *St. Katherine's*	J. Hillaby, *St. Katherine's Hospital, Ledbury c.1230–1547* (Eardisley, 2003).
HJ	*Hereford Journal*
HMSO	His (Her) Majesty's Stationery Office
HT	*Hereford Times*
Hunt, *Cradley*	W.M. Hunt, *Cradley – A Village History* (Trowbridge, 2004).
L&P Hen. VIII	*Letters and Papers, Foreign and Domestic, of the Reign of Henry VIII* (HMSO, 1864–1932).
NHLE	National Heritage List for England, https://historicengland.org.uk/listing/the-list.
Nonarum Inquisitiones	*Nonarum Inquisitiones in Curia Scaccarii, Temp Regis Edwardi III*, ed. G. Vandersee (Rec. Comm., 1807).
ODNB	*Oxford Dictionary of National Biography*, http://www.oxforddnb.com.
OS	Ordnance Survey
Plac. de Quo Warr.	*Placita de Quo Warranto* (Record Commission, 1818).
Poll Taxes of 1377–81, ed. Fenwick	*The Poll Taxes of 1377, 1379, and 1381*, ed. C.C. Fenwick (Oxford, 1998).
RCHME	*Royal Commission on Historical Monuments, England, An inventory of the historical*

	monuments in Herefordshire. Vol. 2, East (HMSO, 1932).
Rec. Com.	Record Commission
Reg. Bothe	*Registrum Caroli Bothe, episcopi Herefordensis 1516–1535*, ed. A.T. Bannister (Canterbury & York Society, 28, 1921), 2 vols.
Reg. Cantilupe	*Registrum Thome de Cantilupe, episcopi Herefordensis 1275–1282*, ed. W.W. Capes (Canterbury & York Society, 28, 1921).
Reg. Gilbert	*Registrum Johannis Gilbert, episcopi Herefordensis 1375–1389*, ed. J.H. Parry (Canterbury & York Society, 18, 1915).
Reg. Mascall	*Registrum Roberti Mascall, episcopi Herefordensis 1404–1416*, ed. J.H. Parry (Canterbury & York Society, 21, 1917).
Reg. Mayhew	*Registrum Mayhew, episcopi Herefordensis 1504–1516*, ed. A.T. Bannister (Canterbury & York Society, 27, 1921).
Reg. Orleton	*Registrum Ade de Orleton, episcopi Herefordensis 1317–27*, ed. A.T. Bannister (Canterbury & York Society, 5, 1908).
Reg. Stanbury	*Registrum Johannis Stanbury, episcopi Herefordensis 1453–1474*, ed. J.H. Parry (Canterbury & York Society, 25, 1919).
Reg. Swinfield	*Registrum Ricardi Swinfield, episcopi Herefordensis 1283–1317*, ed. W.W. Capes, 2 vols (Canterbury & York Society, 6, 1909).
Reg. Thomas Charlton	*Registrum Thome de Charlton, episcopi Herefordensis 1327–1344*, ed. W.W. Capes (Canterbury & York Society, 9, 1913).
Reg. Trefnant	*Registrum Johannis Trefnant, episcopi Herefordensis 1389–1404*, ed. W.W. Capes (Canterbury & York Society, 20, 1916).
Reg. Trillek	*Registrum Johannis de Trillek, episcopi Herefordensis 1344–1361*, ed. J.H. Parry (Hereford, 1910).
Smith, *Malvern*	B. Smith, *A History of Malvern* (Leicester, 1964).
Tax. Eccl.	*Taxatio Ecclesiastica Angliae et Walliae auctoritate P. Nicholai IV circa AD 1291* (Rec. Com., 1802).
TNA	The National Archives

TWNFC	*Transactions of the Woolhope Naturalists' Field Club*
Valor Eccl.	*Valor Ecclesiasticus temp. Hen. VIII auctoritate regia Institutus*, ed. J. Caley and J. Hunter (Rec. Com., 1810–34).
VCH Herefs. Bosbury	J. Cooper, *The Victoria History of Herefordshire: Bosbury* (2016).
VCH Herefs. Colwall	J.P. Bowen and A. Craven with J. Comber, *The Victoria History of Herefordshire: Colwall* (2020).
VCH Worcs. IV.	*The Victoria County History of Worcestershire: A History of the County of Worcester: IV*, ed. William Page and J.W. Willis-Bund (1924).
WAAS	Worcester Archive and Archaeology Service
WCM	Worcester Cathedral Muniments, Worcester Cathedral Archives

GLOSSARY

THE FOLLOWING TECHNICAL TERMS MAY require explanation. Fuller information on local history topics is available in D. Hey, *The Oxford Companion to Local and Family History* (2nd edn, 2010), or online from the VCH website: http://www.victoriacountyhistory.ac.uk. The most convenient glossary of architectural terms is *Pevsner's Architectural Glossary* (2010), now available for smart phone and tablet.

assart: land cleared in forest or woodland for use in agriculture.

bay: in architecture, a unit of a building inside or out regularly divided from the next by features such as columns or windows. Can apply to a window projecting from a bay.

Black Death: outbreak of plague caused by the bacterium *Yersinia pestis*, which killed an estimated third of the population of England in 1348–9.

carucate: unit of taxation, originally the amount of land that a team of eight oxen could plough in a year. This varied according to the quality of the land, but was about 120 acres.

charivari: a noisy mock serenade, made by clattering household implements, used to express communal disapproval and to annoy and insult.

chiminage: a toll paid for passage through a forest.

common (open) fields: communal agrarian organisation under which an individual's farmland was held in strips scattered among two or more large fields, intermingled with strips of other tenants. Management of the fields and usually common meadows and pasture was regulated through the manor court or other communal assembly.

copyhold: form of land tenure granted in a manor court, so called because the tenant received a 'copy' of the grant as noted in court records. Often given for several lives (e.g. tenant, wife and eldest child).

court baron: manor court dealing with tenants' services, agricultural regulation and transfer of copyright land. Additional powers were sometimes exercised by the court leet.

court leet: local criminal court for punishment of minor offences.

cowlstaff: a pole on which a vessel is supported between two persons. Being forced to ride on a cowlstaff was an informal, communal punishment for someone who had transgressed social norms, especially a husband who had been physically or verbally abused by his wife.[1]

curate: a member of the clergy who served as the assistant priest in a parish.

1 *Oxford English Dictionary.*

customary tenure: unfree or copyhold tenure regulated by local manorial custom.

demesne: in the Middle Ages, land farmed directly by a lord of the manor, rather than granted to tenants. Though usually leased out from the later Middle Ages, demesne lands often remained distinct from the rest of a parish's land.

enclosure: the process whereby open fields were divided into fields, to be redistributed among the various tenants and landholders. From the 18th century usually by an Act of Parliament obtained by the dominant landholders; earlier, more commonly done by private agreement, or by a powerful lord acting on his own initiative.

estreat: an extract from a list of fines returned to the Exchequer.

farm (medieval): a leasehold rent where the lord of a manor leased out the demesne or a grange in return for a fixed rent to a tenant referred to as the farmer. From the Latin *firma*, meaning fixed. While its popularity varied during the 12th and 13th centuries, it became increasingly common around 1400.[2]

forlet land: originally those parts of the bishop of Hereford's demesne land which were let to tenants for the life of the bishop for the time being. By the late 16th century, the term was used more generally for a leasehold tenure.

eyass/eyesses: falconry term referring to any raptors taken into captivity as a nestling.

glebe: land assigned to the rector (q.v.) or vicar (q.v.) of a church for his support and the endowment of the church.

hatchel: a type of comb that was used to separate fibres of textile crops, such as flax and hemp.

hay or haia: a hedged enclosure, sometimes designed for the capture of wild animals, such as deer, during the hunt, but often denoting an area of woodland pasture.

hearth tax: royal tax, assessed based on the number of hearths or fireplaces in each taxpayer's house; first imposed in 1662, and continued until 1689.

heriot: customary payment to the lord of the manor on a tenant's succession to a family holding, often comprising the tenant's best beast. Free tenants paid a financial equivalent called a relief.

hide: unit of land measurement: in the early Anglo-Saxon period, the amount required for a family to subsist on; in the Domesday Book (1086), a taxation unit; and by the 13th century the sum of four yardlands (see below).

husbandman: terms for a free tenant farmer or a small landholder below the status of yeoman.

lent grain: oats or barley planted on a third of the cultivated farmland under the three-crop rotation system.[3]

lynchet: the green ridge between two strips of ploughed land.

manor: a piece of landed property with tenants regulated by a private (manor) court. Originally held by tenure, manors descended through a succession of heirs but could be given away or sold.

2 Dyer, *Making a Living*, pp. 120–1, 346.

3 https://bosburyhistoryresource.org.uk (accessed 1 Aug. 2023).

messuage: portion of land or a holding, generally with a house and outbuildings on it.

military service: land held on condition of the holder providing 40 days' military service to the chief-lord of the manor. Alternatively translated as knight service, though the holder did not have to be of knightly status. Later often commuted for money.

muncorn: mixed grains.

mustmill: a mill 'concerned with the pressing of fruit, in Herefordshire probably cider apples'.[4]

parish: the area attached to a parish church and owing tithes to it. From the Elizabethan period it had civil responsibilities, hence a 'civil' as opposed to an 'ecclesiastical' parish. At first the two were usually identical, but from the 19th century, when many parishes were reorganised, their boundaries sometimes diverged.

patron (of a church): the person having the right to nominate a candidate to the bishop for appointment as rector or vicar of a church. Often the lord of the manor, but the right could be bought and sold.

poppyhead: a carving on the top of the end of a church choir stall or bench.

prebend: land or other property (including tithes) owned by a cathedral and allocated in perpetuity to one of the cathedral's canons (or prebendaries).

quitclaim: legal term for giving up all claim to a piece of property.

radman: riding man, from Old English *rad*, road. A retainer who performed specific services including that of riding escort to his lord.

rectory: (a) a church living served by a rector, who generally received the church's whole income; (b) the church's property or endowment (the rectory estate), comprising tithes, offerings and usually some land or glebe.

recusancy: refusal to attend Church of England services.

sigilarius: medieval Latin; an individual entrusted with the protection and use of an official seal, such as the Great Seal of State. A prestigious position of trust. By the late medieval period referred to in English as the Keeper.

selions: narrow strips of land in an open field, usually owned or rented by small farmers.

socage: tenure of land on terms of paying rent or other non-military services.

stint: the number of animals a tenant was allowed to graze on the common pastures, dictated by local custom, and usually enforced through the manor court.

trumpery: attractive items of little value or use.

turner: a craftsman who made items from wood on a lathe (rotating machine tool).

voussoir: one of the stones forming an arch or vault.

vestry: (a) in a church where clerical vestments are stored; (b) assembly of leading parishioners and ratepayers, responsible for poor relief and other secular matters as well as church affairs.

vicar: until the 19th century, a clergyman appointed to act as priest of a parish, particularly as assistant to or substitute for the rector. He received a stipend or a proportion of the church's income.

4 https://bosburyhistoryresource.org.uk (accessed 1 Aug. 2023).

vicarage: the endowment (often of lands or tithes) from which the vicar's stipend was paid.

victualler: a person whose occupation involves selling cooked food, other provisions and drink; this included those who ran taverns, eating houses and inns.[5]

view of frankpledge: (a) term for a manorial court with jurisdiction over petty breaches of law and order, also known as a court leet; (b) more specifically, a special session of the court to ensure that all the adults belonged to a tithing.

yardland: a unit of land, the acreage of which could vary according to local custom and by period. It was 60 a. in Herefordshire in some manors by the late 13th century. A Herefordshire acre was described as worth 1.5 statutory acres in Butterfield's Survey in the 16th century, but the evidence for both figures in Cradley is inconclusive.

yeoman: from the 16th century, a term used for more prosperous farmers, many of them socially aspirational. The term husbandman usually denoted less well-off farmers.

5 *Oxford English Dictionary*.

NOTES ON SOURCES

THIS NOTE DISCUSSES THE PRINCIPAL manuscripts and printed sources used in writing the history of Cradley. It is not comprehensive and should be used in conjunction with the List of Abbreviations. Herefordshire Archive Service, the principal archive used, is listed first, followed by other archives in alphabetical order, and the published sources, primary and secondary.

Manuscript Sources

Herefordshire Archive Service, at Herefordshire Archive and Records Centre (HARC), Hereford, holds the records of county government (including inclosure awards and 18th- and 19th-century land tax assessments), the Hereford diocesan and archidiaconal records (including bishops' registers, documents relating to the administration of the bishop's estates and church terriers), estate and family papers and Nonconformist records. It also has a large collection of private records including charters and accounts. The principal documents used in this history are:

AA59/A/1	Rental of the bishop's manor *c*.1288 included in the Bishop's Red Book
AA59/A/2	Butterfield's Survey of the Hereford Bishopric Estates
AL19/1–23	Bishops' Registers
AH73	Parish records (large collection)
AM33	Bailiff's accounts and court records for the bishop's manors 1497–1592
BJ2/1	Transcripts of courts rolls and manorial documents by T.A. Melville that are mainly lost. There are four volumes but volume 1 contains information from the lost documents. Each is arranged chronologically by source
BP20/1–5	School log books
BW15/1–3	Bromyard RDC minutes, including those relating to Cradley
C96	Deeds 1393–1826, mainly for Cradley and Mathon

CF54/1	Pilley Collection – *Chartae Antiquae Hereford*, *c*.1237–1602
F78/5/131–2	Bridge Family Indentures, 1540–1
N37	Parish records (further large collection)
P46/7393	Chirograph of Fine 1537–8
P66	L.C. Deeds 1306–16 (Hill Family)
R13	East Herefordshire documents

Sources also include local wills proved in the diocesan court in the 16th and 17th century; these are numbered in the form 1/2/33, with no preliminary letters.

British Library, London, holds a complete bailiff's account roll for the bishop of Hereford's manors:

BL Add. Roll 27311

Cradley Heritage Centre holds a range of records relating to the parish's history, most importantly the parish council minutes from 1955 onwards, modern sales particulars, a collection of photos and a few paintings.

Herefordshire Historic Environment Record, Herefordshire Archives and Records Centre, Hereford (formerly the Sites and Monuments Record), holds notes on archaeological sites and features and of listed buildings. It is accessible at Herefordshire Through Time: https://htt.herefordshire.gov.uk.

Hereford Cathedral Library holds the cathedral archives, including early charters and transcripts of Chapter Act Books. In particular, they also hold the records of St Katherine's Hospital, Ledbury (including 7018/1/3), including details of its landholdings in Cradley.

The National Archives at Kew, London, holds the records of national government from the late 12th century onwards. Calendars or transcripts of some medieval administrative records which have been used in this history, such as the Patent and Close Rolls, have been published. The classes of documents used in this history include:

C 1:	Chancery, Pleadings, Richard II to Phillip and Mary
C 3:	Court of Chancery: Six Clerks Office: Pleadings, Series II, Elizabeth I to Interregnum
C 241:	Chancery: Certificates of Statute Merchant and Statute Staple
CP 25:	Feet of Fines (notes of agreements reached in, often fictitious, land disputes)

SC 6/HENVIII/1511:	Special Collections, Ministers' and Receivers Accounts: including Cradley

Worcestershire Archive and Archaeology Service at The Hive, Worcester, holds material relating to the areas formerly in Cradley now transferred to Worcestershire, as well as other material relating to land ownership and local governance in Cradley, including the Calendar of Deeds at Madresfield (BA892 970.5.99).

Worcester Cathedral Library and Archive contains a large collection of medieval documents relating to the holdings of the cathedral, including a large group of:

B230–244, 609:	Charters concerning the manor of The Barrow and Overbarrow
E101 and 182:	Court rolls, 16th century, including those for Overbarrow

Printed Sources

Primary Sources

The most important printed primary sources, including calendars of major classes in the National Archives, are included in the List of Abbreviations.

The registers of Bishops Cantilupe, Swinfield, Orleton, Thomas and Lewis Charlton, Trillek, Courtenay, Gilbert, Trefnant, Mascall, Lacy, Polton, Spofford, Beauchamp, Boulers, Stanbury, Milling, Mayew and Booth, which were printed by the Cantilupe Society between 1906 and 1921, contain information about Cradley manor and the rectors of the church.

Other published primary sources used in this history are:

English Episcopal Acta, 7: Hereford 1079–1234, ed. J. Barrow (1993)

English Episcopal Acta 35: Hereford 1234–75, ed. J. Barrow (2009)

Calendar of Probate and Administrative Acts 1407–1550 in the Consistory Court of the Bishops of Hereford, ed. M.A. Faraday (Logaston, 2008)

Herefordshire Militia Assessments of 1663, ed. M.A. Faraday, Camden 4th sers, X (1972)

Herefordshire Taxes in the Reign of Henry VIII, M.A. Faraday (Hereford, 2005)

Roll of the Household Expenses of Richard de Swinfield bishop of Hereford during part of the year 1289 and 1290, ed. J. Webb, Camden Society, old sers, LIX, LXII (1854–5)

Thomas Cave and Rowland A. Wilson (eds), *The Parliamentary Survey of the Lands and Possessions of the Dean and Chapter of Worcester Made In or About the Year 1649* (London, 1924)

E. Edwards and M. Edwards, *A Parishioners Account of Cradley in 1913* (Cradley, 1994)

The tithe maps for all Herefordshire parishes, including Cradley, have been privately published by Geoff Gwatkin. Copies of the maps, which incorporate place names and other information concerning land use from tithe awards, are available in Herefordshire libraries and at HARC.

The main trade or commercial directories consulted are: *Lascelles* (1851), *Littlebury's* (1876–7), *Kelly's* and *Jakeman's*. Many are available online at: http://specialcollections.le.ac.uk/cdm/landingpage/collection/p16445coll4; others are to be found in the Herefordshire Archive Services' Library and the Herefordshire Libraries collections.

The Woolhope Naturalists' Field Club (Archaeological Research Section) Herefordshire Field-Name Survey based on the tithe maps provides a published list of field names by parish. The field number and name are given.

Secondary Sources

The only secondary work on Cradley to date is Wynnell M. Hunt, *Cradley – A Village History* (Cradley, 2004). Brian S. Smith's *A History of Malvern* (Leicester, 1964) also includes material relating to Cradley.

The main sources for architectural history, in addition to the original research by Duncan James, Keith Ray and Edward Peters, are A. Brooks and N. Pevsner, *Herefordshire* (2012) and the Royal Commission on Historical Monuments of England, *An Inventory of the Historical Monuments in Herefordshire, II: East Herefordshire* (1932).

For place names in Herefordshire, see Bruce Coplestone-Crow, *Herefordshire Place-names* (Little Logaston, 2009).

Websites

The Herefordshire Field-Name and Landowners Database provides the Herefordshire Field-Name Survey information online with the addition of landowner names extracted from the apportionments by Geoff Gwatkin: https://htt.herefordshire.gov.uk/her-search/field-names-and-landowners.

British History Online: http://www.british-history.ac.uk

Clergy of the Church of England database: http://theclergydatabase.org.uk

England's Immigrants 1330–1550: https://www.englandsimmigrants.com

Henry III Fine Rolls Project: https://finerollshenry3.org.uk/home.html

Historic England's Red Box Collection: https://historicengland.org.uk/images-books/photos/englands-places

A Vision of Britain through Time: http://www.visionofbritain.org.uk

INDEX

A4103, 4, 5, 78, 126
Acton Beauchamp, Herefordshire, 119, 136
Acton Mill Farm, 3
Addison, William, 136
Adelelm, 41
advowson, 102–104
Agnes (wife of John the Priest), 109 n.89
agriculture, 1, 40, 50–62, 95
Albard, John, 72
ale house, church, *see* church house
Alfrick, Worcestershire, 41
Alfward, 41
Alice ap Powell, 41
Allen, John, 45
Apperley, Thomas, 75
Archer
  E.B., 69
  John, 73
  Thomas, 68
  Thomas William, 68
  William, 73
architecture, church, *see under* Church of St James, Cradley
Arden, John, 31
Arundell
  John, 82 n.17
  Thomas, 82 n.16
Ashton, Samuel, 107
Ashvale, 76, 78
assarts, 5, 30, 34, 43, 52, 54, 81, 133
Audley, Thomas, 132
Ayscough, Thomas, 86, 106, 113, 123, 125

Baconhill Farm, 49 n.287
Badham, Frank, 73
Badlesmere, Giles de, 37
Bailey, George Yapp, 32
Ballard
  family, 38 n.128
  John, 85
baptisms, 10–11, 113
bark, 66, 73
Barkeley family, 1
barley, 56
Barley Hill, 18, 66, 97, 136
barns, 1, 23, 24, 25, 26, 36, 46, 55, 56, 62, 75, 86, 104, 105, 116
Barrett, Rowland, 72
barrow, round, 12
Barrow
  family, 33, 37, 109
  John of the (I) (fl. 1275), 37
  John of the (II) (fl. 1329), 109 n.89
  Robert de, 109
  Robert of the (junior), 37, 52
  Robert of the (senior), 37
Barrow, the (manor), 1, 7, 10, 14, 15, 28, 29, 36–7, 38, 51–2, 133
  chapel, 39, 101, 108, 109, 110
  Old White House, 38
Barrow Coppice, 66
Barrow Hill, 66
Barrow Mills (manor), 8, 22, 39, 40, 66, 67, 98
  Barrow Mill farmhouse, 24 n.197, 40, 68
Batchcombe Brook, 29, 41
Beacon Hill Wood, 4, 41
Beanhouse (Behennes) (manor), 28, 39–40, 56, 57, 62, 83
  mill, 68, 68–9
beans, 56, 57
Bearswood Farm, 3
beehives, 59

Benson
  George, 106
  John, 106, 113
Berkeley
  Rowland, 31, 44
  William, 31, 44
Berton, Herefordshire, 30
Best, Nathaniel Loftus, 130 n.289
Birch, James, 128
Birches Farm, 16, 44, 46
Birchwood Lodge, 75, 84
Bird, Jonathan, 128
Birmingham, Thomas, 106, 121
Birtsmorton, Worcestershire, 44 n.208
Bishop's Frome, Herefordshire, 5, 80 n.2, 137
Bisse, Thomas, 106, **112**, 113, 134
Biyendenhe, John, 69
Black Death, 5, 10, 54–5, 81
Black Sabbath (band), 84
Blackhouse Coppice, 66
Blackhouse Rough Wood, 67
blacksmiths, 66, 72–3, 75, 77, 83
Bliss, Arthur, 84
Blou[.], Thomas, 133
Blount
  James, 38
  Roger, 38
books, 83
Booth
  Charles, bishop of Hereford, 30, 110, 125
  William, 107, 110
Bosbury (manor), 10, 15, 28, 29, 32, 41, 43, 49, 54, 63, 74, 78, 81, 82, 100, 101, 102, 132, 133, 137
  church, 124
Bosworth, Edward, 106
Bough, Elizabeth, 128
Bough Fell, 67
boundaries, 2–4
Bourne Villa, 60
Bowen, F.D., 68
bowling green, 86
Braces Leigh, Worcestershire, 97
Braose, Giles de, bishop of Hereford, 33 n.65
Breinton, Herefordshire, 115
brewing, 50, 62
brick, use of, 22, 23, 24, 26, 46, 56, 69, 104, 105, 126
bricklayers, 75
Bridge, Henry, 42
Bridgeroay Road, 130
bridges, 4, 8, 138
Bromald, Thomas, 111
Bromfeld, John, 132
Bromyard, Herefordshire, 1, 6, 7, 9, 44, 80 n.2, 91, 99, 115, 130, 134, 138
  workhouse, 135–6
Bromyard Rural District Council (RDC), 16, 18, 131, 137
Bronze Age, 1, 4, 12
Brookhouse Farm, 62
Bullock
  Anne, 61
  Catherine, 56 n.67
  Thomas, 59, 56 n.67
  William, 47, 59 n.97, 70, 92, 132
Bullshead, the (pub, later cottage), 20, 22, 23, 75, 78, 90, 91
bungalows, 26
Burghill, William, 107
burials, 10–11, 72, 113, 128, 130
buses, 9
butchers, 75, 76–8

Caldwell
  family, 34
  Susannah, 34
  Tracey, 34
Campagne, Bernard of, 108
Canon Frome, Herefordshire, 31, 85, 99
Cantilupe, Henry, 44
Cantilupe, Thomas, bishop of Hereford, 48, 60 n.120
Carles, Walter, 106
Carpenter, Thomas, 110 n.105, 111 n.109
carpenters, 72, 98, 122, 125
carriers, 9
Castle Frome, Herefordshire, 98

cattle, 50, 52, 59–60
Chambers, Richard, 99, 106, 113, 130
  highways surveyor, 135
Chapel Lane, 88, 128, 137
chapelries, 96, 113, 102, 126
chapels, see Barrow, the; Countess of Huntingdon's Chapel; Hill family; North Hill
Chapmon, William, 106
charcoal, 63, 72
Charles I, king of England, 48, 53
Charnes
  Alan, 42 n.190, 68
  Isabella, 42 n.190
chiminage, 63
chimney stacks, 20, 22, 23, 24, 40, 46, 92
Chockbury Lane, 6, 8, 16
Church of St James, Cradley, 50, 101, 103
  altar, 123
  architecture, 86, 117–25
  bells, 113, 115, 123
  chest, 121, 122
  choir stalls, 111
  churchyard, 75, 115, 116–17, 119, 120, 123, 125, 138
  domus of Blessed Mary, 103, 109 n.94
  endowment, 102–4
  font, 113
  Lady Chapel, 124
  origins, 101–2
  Pre-Conquest fabric in, 14, 117–20
  pulpit, 111
  restoration, Victorian 115–16, 123–5
  screens, 121–3
  stained glass, 123
  tower, 125
  west gallery, 113
church house (ale house), 125
churches, *see* Church of St James, Cradley; Mathon; Storridge
churchwardens, 49, 92, 93, 99, 116, 126, 134, 135
Cider Barn, 104
cider making, 25, 50, 56, 61, 62, 76–7, 79, 116
Civil Wars, English, 85, 111, 130
clearance, woodland, 5
clergy houses, 104–5
Clare, Gilbert de, earl of Gloucester, 48
Clarke, Richard, 59
Cliffe
  Allen Robert, 45, 115
  Elizabeth, 45
  Robert, 45
  William, 45
  William Bateson, 45
cloth, 56, 75
clover, 79, 95
Clubmen, Malvern Hills, 85
clubs, 99
coal, 1, 71–2, 73, 77, 99
Coddington, Herefordshire, 41, 81, 92, 133
  Coddington Cross, 85
coins, 13, 14
Colwall, Herefordshire, 1, 34 n.76, 41, 43, 46, 54, 57, 81, 82, 86, 109, 125, 133
Combwell Hill, 59
Comby, Anne, 59
common land, 5, 14, 18, 50–3, 63, 103
  Bearswood Common, 53, 63, 74
  Birchwood Common, 3, 53, 128, 53, 57, 58, 74, 128, 129, 130
  Merryhill Common, 53
  Poors Land, 49, 99
communal life, 85–9
communications, 5–9
constables, 132, 134, 137
Constance, Arthur, 123
Conveyant Hill, 53
Copley Farm, 13, 36
Coppice End House, 3
Corbet
  Roger, 43, 81
  Thomas (I) (fl. 1279), 43
  Thomas (II) (fl. 1455–6), 43
  Walter, 43
corn, *see* wheat
Cornwall, Duchy of, 28, 33, 49
Cottam, Ronald, 32, 48
Cotton
  Alethea, 31
  family, 31 n.33

John, 31
Michael, 31
Robert, 31, 85
Walter, 31
Cottrell, Charles T., 105 n.43, 107
Countess of Huntingdon's Chapel, 78, 88, 128–9, 129
Courteen, Anne, 44
courts baron, 35, 133, 134
courts, manorial, 1, 31, 33, 38, 42, 52, 55, 132–3
Covid-19, 50
Cowell, William, 92
Cowen, Dr, 100
Cowleigh
family, 37, 42, 68
Henry of, 42, 43, 65
Juliana of, 42
Margery of, 42
William of, 34, 42, 43
Cowleigh (manor), 1, 4, 28, 43–5, 52, 62, 133
Cowleigh Bridge, 8
Cowleigh Gate Farm, 22, 23, 44, 46, 48, 58, 69
Cowleigh Park Farm, 4, 44, 46, 59, 79
Cowleigh Road, 7, 23, 53
Cradley
Geoffrey of, 67, 132
John of, 73
Maurice of, 30
Robert de, 30 n.18
Roger de, 30 n.18
Cradley, manor of, 1, 15, 28, 29–33, 81, 131–3
demesne land of, 29–30
lordship of, 32–3, 37, 39, 42, 48
Cradley Brook, 1, 4, 5, 7, 8, 12, 14, 37, 40, 50, 59, 64, 65, 69, 95
Domesday mill on, 14
Cradley, etymology of, 5
Cradley Hall, 32–3, 60, 99
Cradley stone, 70–71
crafts, 71–76
craftsmen, 55, 122
Credenleigh Street, 26
cricket, 86
Crisp, John, 59
Croft and Birches Farm, 44
crops, *see* barley; beans; clover; hops; kale; Lent grain; mangolds; muncorn; oats; peas; potatoes; rye; sugar beet; swedes; wheat (corn)
Crown, the (pub), 84
Crumpal (Grumpal), Herefordshire, 4, 15
Crumpal Hall Farm, 32
Crumpsend Hill, 18, 136
Crumpton Hill Green, 46, 53
farm shop, 78
Crumpton Oaks Farm, 22, 23, 65, 78
Cuddon, James, 32

Dagger, Thomas, 109
dairy production, 59–60
Daniel, Amice, 82
Darowen, Montgomeryshire, 115
Davies, John Humphrey, 115
Deerhurst, Gloucestershire, 118
developers, 16
Devereux
Essex, 44
family, 44
Walter, 44
William, 44
Dixon, Henry, 72, 72 n.247
doctors, 100, 136
Domesday, 5, 10, 14, 54
donkeys, 60
dovecotes, 35, 60, 103, 104
Drake, Dr, 100
Drayton, Thomas, 72
Drew, Dr, 100
Drogo Fitzpons, 41
Druett, William, 109
Druy, Maurice, 106, 108, 121
Dyke, William, 115

earthworks, 4, 12, 14, 43, 49
East Cradley, 84, 88, 91
Eastbury Hill, 53
Eaton Bishop, Herefordshire, 115
Ebrington Road, 53

Ecclesiastical Commissioners, 49
economy, 50–79
Ede, A.G., 100
Edith de la Heath, 108
education, *see* school
Education Act (1870), 92
Edward I, king of England, 30
Edward II, king of England, 102, 106 n.53
Edward III, king of England, 33
Edwards, Nurse, 100
electricity, 18
Elgar, Edward, 84
Elizabeth I, queen of England, 29, 109, 111
Elizabeth II, queen of the UK, 88
Emily Julia Purser Charity, 99
enclosure, 5, 12–13, 44, 48, 52–3, 128
  illegal, 53
End Hill, 49
Enderby, Samuel Herbert, 32, 48
endowment, ecclesiastical, 102–4
Evesbatch, Herefordshire, 12 n.105, 41, 49, 136, 137
Exchange, Act of (1559), 28, 29

fairs, 79
falconry, 64
Falke
  Elisabeta, 82 n.17
  Richard, 45
Farley, Thomas, 26 n.207
farming, arable, 22, 55–8, 81, 95
farmsteads, prehistoric, 12–13
Faulkes, James, 68
Fawkes
  Amy, 69
  Richard, 62, 69
Fell, William, 31
Featherstone, S.A., 38
field names, early
  Addeslond (plot of land), 50
  Arundell (plot of land), 50
  Bargeyne (customary land), 55
  Barrow field, 51
  Bason Croft (Jubilee Fields), 69, 104
  Batchcombe (tenement of land), 14, 29, 32, 50, 56, 57, 58, 60, 62, 82
  Big Run, 69
  Blackhouse, the, 29, 37
  Brookholm, 22
  Buriend (tenement of land), 15, 34, 60
  Buryfield, 7, 14, 16–17, 26, 33, 50, 88
  Butchers Field, 85
  Calcoumbe (tenement of land), 15
  Churchfield, 14, 16, 33, 50, 51, 52, 57, 104
  Colwrecroft (selion of land), 51, 52
  Combe, The, 60
  Cradley Ingrounds, 53
  Deep Leasow, 67
  Dingle, the, 69
  Edcroft Field, 93, 94, 104
  Hales (tenement of land), 14
  Herdingestockynge (messuage of land), 52
  Hethe (tenement of land), 14–15
  Hetheplace (tenement of land), 15, 63
  Holmede (parcel of land), 58
  Homeland (tenement of land), 14, 41
  Hopend (tenement of land), 15
  Horseland, 59
  Howeyland, 100
  Hulcroft, 65
  Lamb Bank, 53
  Lewesacre (plot of land), 50
  Leye, the, 42
  Lideyard (tenement of land), 15
  Little Halesend, 12
  Little Hanley, 109
  Little Meadow, 70
  Messengerland 42
  Middlefield (selion), 51
  Mill Meadow, 69
  Millclose 70
  Morfeld (selion of land), 51, 52
  New Meadow, 86
  Nupend, 12, 15, 60, 62, 78
  Oaklands, 26
  Old Hollow, 53, 79
  Overbocke, 42
  Pixiefields, 17, **27**
  Poors Meadow, 98 n.224, 99
  Rastheall, 52

Raynoldes (tenement of land), 63
Reabridge, 8
Ruggeley (selion of land), 51
Ryefield, 67
Seedwood, 85
Stonyforlong (selion of land), 51
Sullithurne (selion of land), 51
Tanhouse Field, 73
Taswolds, 57, 95, 97–8, 136
Tatwelle Meadow, 59
Tickley, 38
Titbath (parcel of land), 58
Tyckeleinsfeld (selion of land), 51
Tyrell (plot of land), 50
Vicaresland (pasture), 109
Vineyard, The, 61
Westfield, 6, 14, 16–17, 50, 58, 128
Weteland (selion of land), 51
Winthill, 14, 37, 51, 58, 60, 62
Wodefield (selion of land), 51
Woodcroft (selion of land), 51
Woodhouse, 64
Woodward (messuage of land), 64
field systems, 12
First World War, 100, 124
fishponds, 33, 34, 103
flints, worked, 24
Foliot
Hugh, bishop of Hereford, 36, 43
Ralph, 106, 108
Robert, bishop of Hereford, 102
football, 86
Ford
D.H., 83 n.27
Henry, 106, 134
foresters, 64
forestry, 50
forlet land, 15 n.127, 54, 71
freeholders, 52, 81, 132
Fromes Hill, 6
fruit-growing, *see* orchards
Furches, Robert de, 15 n.129, 42, 134

Gallenters, Robert, 107
Gallows Coppice, 134
gamekeepers, 85
gentry, 28, 31, 48, 80, 83, 84, 113
geology, 4–5
Gibbs, H.F., 40
Glastonbury Thorn tradition, 116
glebe land, 52, 59, 94, 102, 103–4, 105, 115
glebe terriers, 52
glovemaking, 73, 74, 84
goats, 60
Godwin, 41
Godwyn, Thomas, 107, 111
government, local (post-1894), 137–8
government, manorial, 131–4
government, parochial, 134–6
Gower
Abel, 31
John, 31
Robert, 31, 101, 130
granaries, 25, 56
grazing, 57–8
Great Malvern, Worcestershire, 1, 9, 102, 134–5
Abbey, 102
Great Vineyard Wood, 60
Green Hill, 97
Greenwiche, Thomas, 107, 113
Griffiths
Richard, 59, 62
W.J., 36
Grittlesend, 7, 12, 13, 60
Guarlford, Worcestershire, 70
guesthouses, 50, 78

Hadley, James, 128, 129
Haket, Alice, 103
Halcuit, Walter, 30
Hales
family, 14, 34, 39
Frances Caldwell, 34, 39
George, 39
Richard, 62, 76
Rowland, 135 n.55
Halesend (estate), 14, 15, 32–33, 40, 47–8, 69, 71, 89
Halesend Hamlet, 48
Halesend Wood, 12, 65, 66, 67

Hall
family, 42
Peter, 64
Sybil, 42
William, 42, 59, 135 n.55
Hallis, Rychard, 76
Hampden, Edward Renn, 99, 105, 106, 113, 114, 115–16, 123
Handy, William, 32
Hanley (manor), 1, 10, 14, 15, 28, 29, 41–2, 51, 52, 54, 59, 133, 134
Hanley's End, 61
Hanley Castle, Worcestershire, 44 n.218
Happy Jack (Lamb) (pub), 91
Harewell
Edward, 44
Thomas, 44
Harford, Richard, 111
Harley, John, bishop of Hereford, 111
Elizabeth, wife of, 111
Harrinton, John George, 106
Harris, N.L., 45
Harrison, R., 40
Hart, Sam, 129
Hawkhurst Cottage, 21, 22, 65
Haywards Barn, 116
hearth tax, 15, 82–3
Heath
family, 30
Robert de la, 108
Heath Mill, 68, 77
Heganbothen, Christopher, 109, 110
Henlegh, Henry of, 42
Henry II, king of England, 108
Henry III, king of England, 48
Henry VIII, king of England, 38
Hereford, bishops of, 1, 5, 9, 10, 15, 28, 29–30, 33, 36, 37, 39, 41, 43, 48, 54, 55, 60, 67, 80, 81, 82, 85, 89, 101, 102, 103, 108, 109–10, 113, 115, 116, 121, 128, 132, 134
Hereford Cathedral, 101, 108, 110, 111, 115, 120
dean and chapter of, 83
vicars choral of, 28 n.2, 42
Herefordshire County Council, 137
Herefordshire Rifle Volunteer Battalion, 92
Hickman, R.W., 40
Hidelow Farm, 3, 36, 57
Higgins
Bernard Arthur, 32, 48, 69
Thomas, 85
High Grove Wood, 4, 104
High Wood, 4, 67
Hill
Adam, 52
Adam of the (de Hulle), 33, 34 n.75
Agnes, 34
Alice, 33, 34, 67
Elizabeth, 34 n.80
family, 28, 30, 34, 37, 58, 63, 64, 67, 110, 132
chapel belonging to, 34, 110
John (I) (fl. 1379), 31, 81
John (II) (fl. 1401), 33, 34, 67, 82
John (III) (fl. 1475), 33, 34
John (IV) (fl. 1523), 33
John (fl. 1673), 59
Leonard, 34
Nathaniel, 74
Peter of the (junior), 33, 34, 109 n.89
Peter of the (senior), 33
Richard, 33, 66, 72 n.247, 97, 110, 121
Thomas (I) (fl. 1393), 33, 34
Thomas (II) (fl. 1458), 33, 34
seal of, 64
Hill estate (manor), 33–5
Hill Farm, 13, 42, 44, 46, 49, 60
Hill House, 34, 56
Hill's Charity, *see* Richard Hill Charity
Hills Cottage (Goodyears), 99
Hilsey, John, bishop of Rochester, 110
holiday homes, 50, 78
Hollings Hill Farm, 49, 60
Holme Lacy, Herefordshire, 80 n.2
Holmes, John, 39
Holywell Cottages, 6
Home (surname), 14
Home End Farm, 78
Homehouse Farm, 41, 49
hop pickers, 63, 84, 137

hops, 50, 59, 62–3, 84, 137, *see also* hopkilns; hopyards
Hope, Ernaldo of, 15 n.130
Hope family, 15
hopkilns, 1, 57, 24, 96
Hopkinson, William, 70
Hopton
  family, 1
  James, 31, 69
  Richard, 31
hopyards, 41, 56, 62, 85
horses, 32 n.55, 43, 56, 58, 59, 133
Howe, Dr, 100
Howell, Geoffrey P., 107
Hugh Jonesservant *Le Glovere*, 73
Hugh le Despenser, 37
hunting rights, 63, 65, 85
Huntingdon (estate), 26
Hurden, Edmund, 39
Hyde, the (manor), 1, 10, 14, 15, 28, 30, 36, 37, 38, 51, 55, 66, 83, 133

illegitimacy, 74, 84, 136
industry, 75–6
inns, 89–91, *see also* pubs
internet access, 9

jam-making, 62
James
  A.M., 40
  Maxwell, 40
  Thomas, 69, 72 n.248
  William, 62, 66, 69, 72 n.248
James Turner's Charity, 93, 98, 138
Janvrin, William Langston Benest, 107, 113
Janyn 'Frenschman', 82
John the Priest, 109
Johnson, Luke, 48
Jones
  Frank, 57
  John, 32
  Joseph, 53
  William, 92
  William (mapmaker), 103

kale, 57
Kent, Sarah, 84
Kilner, Celia, 116
Kilpeck, Herefordshire, 120
King's Bridge, 6, 7, 8
King's Third, 48–9, 53
Kingswood, Robert de, 106
knight service, *see* military service

Lacy, Roger de, 43 n.199
Lamb Inn, 49
landholdings, medieval, 54–5
landownership, patterns of, 28–49
landscape, 4–5
  agricultural, 50–3
Larchgrove (house), 78
Leadon, river, 4, 5, 41
leather working, 73, 75
Lechmere
  Anthony, 44
  Edward, 44
  family, 44, 46
Ledbury Borough, Herefordshire, 1, 6, 9, 24, 36, 74, 81, 82, 91, 116, 117, 131
  Grammar School, 97
  market hall, 46
  Minster, 101
  St Katherine's Hospital, 28 n.2, 36, 133
  workhouse, 135
Ledbury Foreign, Herefordshire, 54, 82, 102
Leigh, Worcestershire, 4, 48
Leigh Sinton, Worcestershire, 6, 85
Lent grain, 56
Leofing, 41
Leominster, Herefordshire, 10 n.94
  Priory, 120
Lewis, John Wilfrid, 107
libraries, 88, 95, 99, 129
life expectancy, 84
Lim, Sue, 97
Limekiln Coppice, 67
limekilns, 71
Little Malvern Priory, 33 n.65
Little
  family, 95 n.196

Mary, 41
Thomas Henry, 41
Little Vineyard Coppice, 60
livestock, 55, 56, 58–60
local government, *see* government, local; government, manorial; government, parochial
Loggin, John, 69
London, Gervase of, 106, 108, 109
Long
Christopher, 98
family, 47
John, 98
Richard, 40 n.162, 47
Longe, Rowland, 82 n.16, 110, 111
Lower Nupend Farm, 22–3, 26, 99
Lower Vinesend Farm, 22, 23, 60–61, 71, 76
Lumbridge Hill, 16, 33, 66 n.158
Luxmoore, Charles Scott, 96, 105, 106, 113, 115, 126, 134
Lygon
family, 28
Frederick, 6th earl Beauchamp, 95
Henry Beauchamp, 4th Earl Beauchamp, 45
John Reginald, 3rd earl Beauchamp, 44, 46
William, 7th earl Beauchamp, 96
lynchets, 12, 14

McCann, George, 70, 126
McCausland, Mark Thompson, 107
Maclean family, 89
Madresfield estate, 28, 44, 45, 46
Mallins Coppice, 67
Mallins Wood, 67
malthouses, 76
Malvern, Worcestershire, 4, 9, 70, 76, 78, 79, 85, 100, 116
Malvern Chase, 5, 9, 48–9, 53
Malvern Council, 18, 49, 137
Malvern Hill, 53, 136
Malvern Hills, 1, 4, 12, 13, 17, 50, 71, 85, 101
Malvern Hills Conservators, 49
Malvern Link, 9, 70
mangolds, 57
manorial courts, *see* courts, manorial
manors, *see* Barrow, the; Barrow Mills; Beanhouse; Bosbury; Cowleigh, Cradley, manor of; Hanley; Hill estate; Hyde, the; Netherbarrow; Overbarrow; rectory manor
markets, 57, 79
Martley Poor Law Union, 131, 137
Martley Rural Sanitary Authority, 18
Martyn, Henry, 107
Mary I, queen of England, 110
Mascall, Robert, bishop of Hereford, 108
Mathon, Herefordshire, 1, 7, 9, 12, 42, 43 n.199, 53, 68, 85, 86, 92, 96, 101 n.2, 102, 117, 126
Mathon Urban (West Malvern), 4
National School, 96
St James' Church, 96
transferred to Herefordshire (1897), 3 n.1
Mathon, Odo of, 43, n.199
Matthews, M., 36
meadows, 5, 14, 16, 18, 34, 44, 50, 58–9
medical services, 100
Meikle, Dr, 100
Mesolithic settlement, 12
midwives, 100
Mildfrith, king of the *Magonsaete*, 101
military service, 30, 33, 41, 81
Mill Bank, 67, 77
garage, 78
Mill Coppice, 4
Mill, Croft, 69
millennium celebrations, 89
Miller, Edward, 69
mills, 67–70
Mills, the (estate), 98
mining, 1, 72
moats, 24, 25
Moir, E.C., 126
Monkhall ('The Quiet Woman') (pub), 90–1
Montagu, Elizabeth, 37
Morgan, Peter H.C., 116

Mormons, 129–30
Morrell's Wood, 4
Morton, Richard, 52
muncorn, 56
must mills, 76
Myntrigge, John, 31, 82

Nans, John, 107, 108 n.83
Neolithic settlement, 12
Netherbarrow (manor), 22 n.184, 39
Nethergreen Farm, 75
New Inn, 90
Nonconformity, Protestant, 10 n.92, 128–30
Norden, William, 45
Norrest Wood, 3, 62
North Hill, 1, 16, 18, 80, 71, 80, 84, 101 n.2, 136
    Chapel of St James, 101, 102
North Malvern, 18, 91, 99, 104
North Malvern Road, 91
Nott, George, 89
nucleation, 14, 16
nurses, 100

Oaken Coppice, 67
Oaken Grove, 67
oats, 32 n.55, 56
Oddfellows, Order of, 87, 88, 89
Old Rectory, 1, 69, 78, 84, 86, 88, 89, 96–7, 101, 104–5, 105, 115, *see also* rectory manor
Old Upper House Farm, 22, 23, 24, 60
Old Vinesend Farm, 8, 15, 60, 91, 113
Old White House, 24, 26, 38
Oldcastle, Richard, 44
Ome Lane, 7
open-field systems, 51
orchards, 41, 55, 56, 61–2, 99, 103
origins, 2–4
Osbert (son of Reginald of Hame), 14 n.122
Overbarrow (manor), 28, 38–9, 52, 59, 64, 65, 85, 133

Palmer, Robert, 67
Parfey, John, 107, 111, 130
parish council, 8, 18, 86, 88–9, 93, 98, 99, 134–5, 138
parish hall, 86, 88, 96
Park Barrow Coppice, 66
Parker
    Alfred Hill, 125
    Roger, 38
parish officers, 134–5
parochial organisation, 101–102
pasture, 5, 30, 41, 50, 52–3, 55, 58–60, 63, 109
Pattrick, Charles Thomas, 115
peas, 56
Pengrifte, Francis, 76
Penson, William, 107
Perkins, A.E., 123
Peter de Aigueblanche, bishop of Hereford, 30
Philpotts, Mary, 97
Pichard
    Dorothea, 59, 61, 83
    family, 40
    John (I) (d. 1521), 38, 39, 52, 67, 73
    John (II), 67
    John (III), 67
    Lucy, 39
    Richard, 38, 39
    Thomas, 39, 67, 73
    William, 39
pig farming, 59–60
Pilling
    Eveline, 124
    John Lawrence, 124
Pitlick Farm, 49
Plymouth Brethren, 128, 130
Polayn, Robert, 63
police station, 137
politics, 92, 137
poll tax, 10, 33, 43, 81
ponds, 24, 69, 104
Pontic Bridge, 6
Pontick Pitch, 138
Poor Law Administration, 135–6
Poors Bridge, 99
Poors Coppice, 98

population, 9–12
post office, 8–9
potatoes, 56–7
pottery, 13, 23
poultry, 57, 59, 60, 92
pound, the, 134, 137
Pound Bridge, 8, 69
poverty, 80
Powell, Morgan, 107, 113
Preedy, Frederick, 102, 125
Price
  Daniel, 106, 113
  Thomas, 32
Provident Dispensary, 99
pubs, 50, 75, 77, 84, 89–91
public services, 18
Pullens Farm, 75
Purser, Charles, 39–40
Pyne, Frances Caldwell, 39

quarrying, 12, 46, 50, 70–1, 75, 133
Queenswood (house), 78
quoits, 86, 87

Racster
  Mary, 47
  Richard Long, 47, 83 n.27, 135
  Thomas, 83 n.27
Radlow Hundred, 82, 102, 131
railways, 1, 9, 57, 70, 76
Ralph de Hulla, 33 n.65
rape (crop), 56
rectors, 106–117
rectory manor, 28, 35, 102–4, 133, 134
Rectory Mill, 69
recusancy, 10 n.92, 31, 101, 130 *see also* Roman Catholicism
Red Lion Inn, 27, 78, 89, 91, 133
Redan Inn (Redan Bend), 71, 91
reeve of Cradley, 80, 131–2
refugee welfare, 99
religious life, 101–30
rents, 10, 15, 30, 36, 54–5, 97, 102
retail, 76–8
Reynolds
  Mary, 84
  Richard, 72
Richard son of Mariot, 41
Richard ap Powell (Rhisiart ap Hywel), 41
Richard de Hale, 102, 106
Richard Hill Charity (Hill's Charity), 92, 97, 136
Richards, H.U., 105
Ridgeway, 6, 8, 13, 26, 41, 50, 70, 116
Ridgeway Cross, 6, 8, 56, 60, 70, 75, 78, 90, 91, 128, 129, 130
Ridgeway Farm, 12 n.105, 60
Ridgeway House, 18, 90
Ridgeway Oak, 6
Riley Hill, 67
roads, 5–8
Roman Catholicism, 130
Romano-British period, 13
Rose Garth, 8
Ross-on-Wye, Herefordshire, 109
Rough Hill Wood, 67
Rudhall, Abraham, 115
Ruyhale
  Elizabeth, 44
  Richard, 44
rye, 55, 56

St Guthlac's Priory, Hereford, 102
St Katherine's Hospital, *see under* Ledbury
St Mary Aldermary, London, 110
St Thomas's Day Charity, 99
Salisbury Cathedral, 108
Saxon period, 14
school, 45, 46, 91–5
  Boys' School, 45, 80, 88, 91–3, 94, 95, 99, 101, 125, 138
  Buryfield Church of England voluntary-aided primary school (founded 2004), 95
  Girls' School, 94–5
  open-air school (Old Hollow), **96**, 97
  Storridge School, 46, 91, 95–6, 99

Scory, John, bishop of Hereford, 29
Scott, George Gilbert, 101, 123
Second World War, 87, 93, 99

Seed Farm (The Seed), 24–5, 25, 29, 32, 41–2, 44, 49, 58, 60, 61, 63, 66, 76, 134
Seedwood (hopyard), 85
selions, 50–1, 52
services, 76
settlement, 12–18
  18th to 21st centuries, 16–17
  before 1000, 12–14
  medieval and early modern, 14–16
servants, 35, 43, 76, 82, 84, 111
Seven Stars Inn, 66, 72, 89, 90
Severn Valley Ware, 13
sewage, 18
Shapland
  B.C. Hood, 34
  family, 34, 45
  John, 45
  Joseph, 34
  Susannah, 34
sheep, 50, 55, 59, 60, 102
Sheldon, Rafe, 30
Shepherd, Robert, 55
Shire Ditch, 4, 12
shoemakers, 73, 75, 91, 92
shopkeepers, 77
shops, 8, 24, 50, 58, 75, 77–8, 89, 90
Six Acre Wood, 67
Skinner
  Edmund, 107, 111, 113, 128, 134
  Frances, 31
  Stephen, 113
slaughterhouses, 60
Smith
  John, 72
  Samuel, 68
  William, 67, 72
socage, 14, 30
social character, 80–4
social history, 80–100
social housing, 17–18
social welfare, 97–9
sorcery, 82
squatting, 53
stables, 25, 75, 104, 105 n.37
Stanford
  family, 37
  John of, 36, 37
Staunton, Robert of, 37
Steens Brook, 41
Sterre, Richard, 103, 109
Stifford, 15, 33–4, 63
  mill, 15, 34 n.75, 67
Stifford's Bridge, 4, 34, 75, 78–9, 87, 89, 91, 100, 133, 134, 137
Stoney Villa, 100
Stony Cross, 6, 7, 14, 16–17, 26, 73, 78, 91, 137
Stores Cottage, 22, 77
Storridge, Herefordshire, 1, 4, 5, 6, 7, 10, 12, 13, 15, 28, 29, 50, 59, 61, 63, 64, 71, 81, 84, 116, 117, 130, 133
  Appletree Cottage, 22
  Bosbury, *see* Bosbury (manor)
  chapelry of, 102
  Church of St John the Evangelist, 70, 102, 115, 126, 127
  ecclesiastical parish, 101, 102
  football club, 86
  general stores, 78
  Hill Farm (Crumpton Oaks Farm), 22, 65, 78
  library, 88
  New Inn, 62, 90
  post office, 8
  school, 46, 91, 95–6, 99
  Tanners Cottage, 73
  village hall, 89, 137, 138
  Women's Institute, 87
Storridge Birchwood, 52
Storridge Farm, 6
Storridge Hill, 52
Stowers, Eleanor, 98
Sturts, The (farm), 60
Suckley, Worcestershire, 8, 36, 41, 59 n.104, 131
  railway station, 76
Suckley Road, 7
Suckley Stream, 14, 36
sugar beet, 57
Summerville House, 58, 84
surnames, 14–15, 29, 71, 82
swedes, 57

Swinfield, Richard, bishop of Hereford, 32 n.55, 79, 106 n.53

Tailor, Henry, 73
tailors, 73, 77
Tanhouse Coppice, 4
Tanhouse Farm, 73
Tanhouse Lane, 4, 73
Tanner, Henry, 109
tanners, 71, 73, 83
Taylor
  Isaac, 39
  Richard, 33 n.72, 59, 110, 111 n.109
telegraph office, 9
telephones, 9
Teme Valley, 4
tenants, 10, 14–15, 28, 30, 33, 36, 38, 41, 42, 43, 50, 51, 52, 53, 54–5, 58, 59, 60, 67, 69, 71, 80–1, 85, 97, 99, 132, 133, 134
tenements, 14, 30, 39, 43, 109
tennis, 83, 86
Thomas the Clerk, 42 n.189
Three Choirs Festival, 113
threshing machines, 56
Thruxton, Herefordshire, 92
timber-framed buildings, 1, 16, 20, 22–6, 34, 38, 40, 45, 46, 69, 71, 90, 104, 120 n.179, 122, 125
tithe barns, 105
tithe maps, 13, 37, 103
tithes, 59, 62, 66, 67, 102, 104, 108, 109
tollhouses, 6, 7
Tolly, Susannah, 45
tomatoes, 57
Tomes, Margery, 109 n.95
tourism and hospitality, 78–9
tractors, 58, 73
Trefnant
  John, bishop of Hereford, 30
  Maurice, 106
Trewlove, Adam, 106
Trillek, John, bishop of Hereford, 32 n.55, 43
Turner
  Anthony (fl. 1662), 98
  Anthony (fl. 1836), 98
  James, 45, 91, 113
  John, 68
  Richard, 92
  Robert, 71
turnips, 56–7
turnpikes, 6, 7, 126
Tytherington, Gloucestershire, 43

United Brethren, 128
Upcote, Herefordshire, 37
Upper Barrow Farm, 3, 12
Upper House Farm Greenhill, 76
Upper Vinesend Farm, 22, 43, 45–6, 47, 50, 60–1

Vallett Wood, 63
village hall (former Boys' School), 8, 23, 88–9, 93, 101, 123, 125, 138
Vineges, Philip of, 60, 65
Vinesend, *see* Lower Vinesend Farm; Old Vinesend; Upper Vinesend Farm
vineyards, 60–1, 81

Wall
  family, 1
  John Binns, 32
  Samuel (senior), 32
  Samuel (junior), 32
  William, 32
  William Ellis, 32, 42, 49
Wallewayn
  Ellen, 34, 67
  William, 34, 67
Walter (vicar of Cradley), 109
Walter de Cradley, 30 n.18
Walter de Intebawe, 109
Walter le Webbe, 50
war memorial, 89
Ward
  Bill, 84
  Robert, 107, 117
Warner, Charles Edward, 107
water, mains, 18
water meadows, 5
Watkins
  Emma, 98

John, 98
Webb, Thomas, 123
Webster, W.J.A., 100
Werthur
Agnes, 38
Robert, 38
West Cradley, 26, 78, 134
West Malvern, 4, 8, 16, 70, 78, 84, 86, 87, 88, 91, 96, 102
Elim Cottage, 70
wheat (corn), 55–6
Wheelwright, Robert, 71
wheelwrights, 72–3, 75
Whippets Brook, 4, 7, 8, 46, 69
Whippiats Farm, 32, 46
White, Roger, 76
Whitman's Hill, 12
coppice, 67
quarry, 46, 71
Whitmonds Farm, 32
Whitting, Tychias, 92
Wilkinson, Tom Anstruther, 107
William (chaplain), 109
William de la Gare, 106
William de la Morendo, 67
William de Vere, bishop of Hereford, 109
Wold House, 60
Wold Mill, 49 n.287, 69
Wood, Thomas, 83
Woodend Farm, 49, 60
Woodiat, Richard, 24 n.195
woodland, 5, 49, 50, 52, 53, 63–67, 71, 73
Woodruff, Wilford, 129
Worcester, Worcestershire, 4, 5–6, 9, 12, 13, 41, 74, 75, 85, 91, 99, 123, 126, 128
porcelain works, 75
St Nicholas' parish, 49
Worcester Cathedral, dean and chapter of, 28 n.2, 38, 83, 133
Worcester, prior and convent of, 37, 38, 64, 109, 133
Worcestershire, 1, 3, 5, 28, 43, 85, 131, 137
workhouses, 18, 97, 136
Wroxeter, Shropshire, 117
Wyneward, Robert, 60
Wythe, Thomas, 82 n.16

Yapp
family, 1
George Bailey, 48
Richard (I) (fl. 1708), 72 n.248
Richard (II) (fl. 1838), 32, 40, 47, 132
Richard (III), 47
William, 130
yardlands, 14–15, 30, 33, 34, 35, 36, 41, 42, 43, 45, 52, 54, 55, 72, 81, 102
yeomen, 28, 80, 82, 83

www.ingramcontent.com/pod-product-compliance
Lightning Source LLC
LaVergne TN
LVRC092139300826
846742LV00009B/20

9781908590886